ANEW Creation

Praise for ANEW Creation
and Brad and Beth Thorp

I have had the honor of watching Brad and Beth Thorp take the pain from the loss of their precious son Mitchell and turn it into a new purpose in life. Only God can redeem a story as tragic as this and make something beautiful come from it. Every one of us can find not only inspiration from this story, but healing and help for whatever hardships we are facing. My hope is that you will follow their example and believe that God can transform your tragedies into triumphs as well!

—JASON GRAVES
Lead pastor, Daybreak Church

This story leapt off the pages as I relived it with tears and joy. My friends Brad and Beth have done a superb job of retelling the story that changed so many of our lives. Truly, Mitchell Thorp's story will change your life as well.

—MARK FOREMAN
Lead pastor, North Coast Calvary Chapel

Few organizations see the "big picture" of charitable giving. But thanks to Brad and Beth Thorp, the Mitchell Thorp Foundation does. Through their own life tragedy in losing their son Mitchell in 2008, Brad and Beth Thorp have embraced their sorrow and have turned it into the most beautiful way of honoring his legacy, by helping those most vulnerable patients and their families.

—JOHN CRAWFORD, MD
Director of pediatric neuro-oncology, San Diego Rady Children's Hospital;
director of child neurology and professor of clinical neurosciences,
University of California San Diego

This incredible true story is how God can take what was meant for evil and turn it into something beautiful for his glory. This story will touch the hearts of many who need to know how to hear the voice of God, and how God intervenes in our lives in many amazing ways.

—MATT HALL
Mayor, City of Carlsbad

Brad and Beth Thorp are a couple of the finest people I have met who continually inspire others with their absolute selflessness. I cannot express my gratitude enough for the work their foundation does to help critically ill children and families with resources that the medical team could not provide.

—SCOTT McCARTY, DO
Department of pediatrics, hematology/oncology,
Kaiser Permanente-Southern California

ANEW
Creation

FINDING
MEANING
IN THE MIDST
OF TRAGEDY

BETH THORP

NASHVILLE

NEW YORK • LONDON • MELBOURNE • VANCOUVER

ANEW Creation

Finding Meaning in the Midst of Tragedy

© 2022 Beth Thorp

Published in New York, New York, by Morgan James Publishing. Morgan James is a trademark of Morgan James, LLC. www.MorganJamesPublishing.com

Proudly distributed by Ingram Publisher Services.

All Scripture quotations, unless otherwise indicated, are taken from the Holy Bible, New International Version®, NIV®. Copyright © 1973, 1978, 1984, 2011 by Biblica, Inc.™ Used by permission of Zondervan. All rights reserved worldwide. www.zondervan.com. The "NIV" and "New International Version" are trademarks registered in the United States Patent and Trademark Office by Biblica, Inc.™ Scripture quotations marked ASV are taken from the American Standard Version, public domain. Scripture quotations marked (ESV) are from the ESV® Bible (The Holy Bible, English Standard Version®), copyright © 2001 by Crossway, a publishing ministry of Good News Publishers. Used by permission. All rights reserved. Scripture quotations marked (HBFV) are taken from the Holy Bible Faithful Version, copyright © 2017. All rights reserved. Afaithfulversion.org. Scripture quotations marked (MEV) are from The Holy Bible, Modern English Version. Copyright © 2014 by Military Bible Association. Published and distributed by Charisma House.

Some names and details of some stories have been changed to protect the privacy of individuals.

Morgan James BOGO™

A **FREE** ebook edition is available for you or a friend with the purchase of this print book.

CLEARLY SIGN YOUR NAME ABOVE

Instructions to claim your free ebook edition:
1. Visit MorganJamesBOGO.com
2. Sign your name CLEARLY in the space above
3. Complete the form and submit a photo of this entire page
4. You or your friend can download the ebook to your preferred device

ISBN 9781631957529 paperback
ISBN 9781631957536 ebook
Library of Congress Control Number:
2021945636

Cover & Interior Design by:
Christopher Kirk
www.GFSstudio.com

Morgan James PUBLISHING Builds *with...* **Habitat for Humanity® Peninsula and Greater Williamsburg**

Morgan James is a proud partner of Habitat for Humanity Peninsula and Greater Williamsburg. Partners in building since 2006.

Get involved today! Visit MorganJamesPublishing.com/giving-back

Dedication

To Mitchell

Our precious son, Mom told you when you were ill, and we were struggling to find a diagnosis that God would heal you and set you free as the butterflies flying around us that day. I thought for sure in my heart that God would heal you here on earth. The ending did not turn out exactly as we all had in mind. Instead, God called you home to heal you. No one on this planet could figure out what was wrong or how to make you well. I know you fought as hard as your human strength allowed you to.

I know there was so much you wanted to say to me and your family, but you could not speak. I know you are well now in heaven and are ANEW in Christ.

I look back and can see how God worked through us to help you and so many others. God guided us every step of the way. He has never left our side. We hope and pray that our story will touch the hearts of many who need to know that eternity in heaven is a real place, and that God is alive and well. He does intervene in our lives in awe-inspiring ways.

We cannot wait to see you again soon, as this is not our home—heaven is. If anyone is in Christ, he is a new creation, the old is gone, the new has come.

We love you forever,

Mom, Dad, and Matthew

Contents

Acknowledgments

From the bottom of our hearts, Brad and I would like to thank several people who helped us birth this book, as it has been a labor of love. First and foremost, we want to thank God for directing our steps to the right people at the right time. Lynn Vincent connected me to Terry Whalin, acquisitions editor for Morgan James Publishing, who placed my book proposal in front of David Hancock, founder of Morgan James Publishing, who decided this story was worthy of publication.

There are not enough words to say how much we appreciate and thank our editor, Ginger Kolbaba, who read through our tear-stained words, our thoughts, our prayers, and Scriptures, and helped craft this true story about the power of one life—and that life was Mitchell—and how the ripple effect phenomenon is the direct result of people activating the biblically based principles of "loving in action and in truth."

Most importantly, I want to thank my husband, Brad, for reading what I wrote and contributing his part. Thanks to our son Matthew for being a great brother to Mitchell, and to my sister Cheryl, who helped craft the outline early on, as she knew that one day this story would be told. We're also thankful for the rest of my extended family who lived this life journey with us and were there every step of the way.

I even need to thank my two dogs, Teddy and Bear, who laid at my feet under my desk for hours on end, sacrificing the attention I could not always give as I wrote—at least until Teddy would nudge my arm when it was time to take a break and a walk.

Our prayer is that this book will touch the hearts of many throughout the world. We hope it will help renew faith, bring hope to the hopeless who are persevering through trials, and bring healing and restoration to your soul.

Introduction

All Because of Our Warrior Son

This inspirational true story is about a boy's legacy that has touched the hearts of so many, how the ripple effect keeps expanding to touch so many more, and how we encountered the mystery of God speaking to us through His Word and His promises.

We were just a happy couple with two beautiful children, living a glorious and happy life. Our family was grounded in faith, and it was the furthest thing from our minds that something bad could ever happen.

How does one young boy's life touch the lives of so many? Especially a young boy who had so much heart, so much love, and so much joy that radiated out of him like sunshine—only to be tragically stricken with an undiagnosed mysterious illness for five years, an illness that left all the doctors mystified.

Trying to save our child, 24/7 care, and hardship became "normal" for us, but certainly not welcomed. This unknown illness ravaged his body and took his life at the age of eighteen. Too often, afterward, we looked toward the heavens with tears in our eyes and asked, *Why? What is the meaning of all this?*

One day while reading my Bible, I came across a passage that comforted me more than anything I could have imagined: "Blessed is the one who preserves under trial because, having stood the test, that person will receive the crown of life that the Lord has promised to those who love him" (James 1:12).

We called him our warrior son because he was the bravest young man we had ever met. He made us and others who knew him stronger in our walk with God. Not only has he earned that crown of life in the next life, he is *ANEW* creation in Christ. My soul sighed with relief knowing, Mitchell, our warrior son, has received that crown—and he has many jewels in it.

Pain and suffering are part of this world; we cannot escape it. Jesus even spoke about it in the Bible: "I have told you these things, so that in me you may have peace. In this world you will have trouble. But take heart! I have overcome the world" (John 16:33). But somehow, we had deceived ourselves into believing that we would be immune to it. When the rug was suddenly pulled out from under us, we found ourselves in a season of life that we thought would never end.

God is able to bring good out of evil and can turn tragedy into something positive that will draw people toward him. "We know that in all things God works for the good of those who love him, who have been called according to his purpose" (Romans 8:28). Our purpose is to be a living witness for Christ to share with others who are suffering, to help heal broken hearts, and to bring hope and light into the darkness. As the apostle Peter tells us, "To this you were called, because Christ suffered for you, leaving you an example, that you should follow in his steps" (1 Peter 2:21).

Losing our son was the deepest pain my family and I had ever experienced, and yet God used that pain and suffering to fuel our fire to help others. We would not allow Mitchell's death to be in vain! The devil messed with the wrong mama and papa bear if he thought we were just going to insulate ourselves and not follow in Christ's steps.

So often people asked us, "How do we move forward after losing a child or loved one? Where do we find the strength to go on? Will we ever be happy again? Where was God in all this?"

All good questions—and all questions and emotions that need to be processed.

God spoke to both of our spirits, a day apart from each other. He revealed to me in my pain and sorrow, *This is not the end, but only the beginning.* Brad received a similar message. At the time, I did not know what God meant. But we have learned to trust in his Word and wait on him to reveal it in his time, and oh, how He did!

We would carry God's name, his strength, his courage, and the love we had for each other to share this love with others. We stepped out in faith, embracing a profound "knowing" that God was going to direct our steps. I told my husband that I do not want to do anything else on this earth unless it has eternal significance.

All because of our warrior son, I thought. What difference can one life make? Plenty. That one life can have the ripple effect to help so many others. And we've seen it with our own eyes. We stepped out in faith. We started this new endeavor and never looked back.

That's what we want for you. That's why this book is written. To help move you forward to find your new purpose or your new normal. We want to help you find confidence and strength by turning to the light of God within. The answers we need emerge from a feeling of peaceful trust. We are guided into right decisions. Any uncertainty and doubt we may feel melts away as the light of God brings us the guidance we seek and the energy to carry it out.

God's light shines through every problem and circumstance, dissolving any obstacles and comforting our hearts. Without a doubt, today Brad and I give thanks for the radiant light of God that has guided our way to be the light in the dark, so we, in turn, can bless and strengthen people's faith around us.

Part 1

The Power of One Life

Chapter 1

Forever in Love

One Friday night in January 1980, my girlfriends and I decided to take a break from our college studies and head to a local pub, Catballou's, in our hometown of Crystal Lake, Illinois. We had just ordered our drinks and sandwiches when my eye caught something familiar but very out of place.

"Scott?" I blinked and took another look. Sure enough, my older brother, who should have been downstate at Southern Illinois University, was walking toward me with an entourage of his friends.

"Hey, Sis!" he said, his smile as wide as could be. "We decided to come up surprise everybody for the weekend, since OJ is back in town." OJ, our older brother, had been living in Portland, Oregon.

Standing next to him was a tall, attractive, sandy-blonde-headed young man who looked vaguely familiar.

"You remember Brad Thorp?" my brother asked by way of introducing us.

He smiled. "We played sports together while we were growing up. You probably don't remember."

I had my own life going on when I was growing up, so I had never been that interested in my brother or his friends, so he was right—I didn't remember. But he certainly had my interest now.

3

Our eyes connected, intense electricity passed between us, and I was done for. My brother was still speaking, but I no longer heard a word he was saying.

Finally, he laughed. "Okay, I am leaving you two." He stepped away and began to talk with his friends, leaving Brad and me by ourselves.

Brad gently extended his hand for me to grab, which I took immediately. He led us to a small, quiet table in a corner, where we ordered a drink and began talking. He was easy to talk with. Neither of us could stop talking and smiling and laughing.

I told him I was a freshman at Illinois Institute of Art, studying fashion merchandising. When I wasn't studying, I was focusing on trying out for the Miss Illinois pageant, as I had already won the local pageants to move to the next level.

I learned he was a senior at Campbell University in North Carolina, playing on a baseball scholarship. But he was leaving school, because during his junior year he signed to play with the Los Angeles Dodgers organization. It was his dream come true. He was a talented, right-handed pitcher who threw a mean 95-mile-per-hour fastball, and had a terrific change up, followed by a mean curveball. He was intensely competitive, and wanted to make his mark in the world of baseball.

"So what are you doing back here?"

He laughed. "Well, that's a story!" He explained that since it was baseball's off-season, he decided to drive from Baton Rouge, Louisiana, where his parents lived, up to Crystal Lake to meet with friends and surprise my brother. "But when I got here this morning, your mom told me he was in southern Illinois at school. So I figured I'd drive down to see him. When I got there, I noticed he had his bags packed. I asked him where he was going, and he said, 'We're driving up to Crystal Lake,' so I tagged along."

"Wait," I interrupted. "That's a six-hour drive one way. You drove twelve hours?"

"Yep," he said, and we both laughed.

"You must have had a lot of free time for that kind of adventure."

He shrugged. "I just finished my first semester of my senior year and just finished all my baseball training. And I have time before spring training starts, so I figured, 'Why not?'"

We laughed again. I was glad he'd made the extra trip back to Crystal Lake. If he hadn't decided to come back, I never would have met him. *God's divine plan?* I wondered.

"How long are you in town?" I asked.

"Three days."

I groaned inwardly. *I've just met a really great guy, and he's only in town for three days.*

By the end of the evening, he offered to take me home. "Are you doing anything tomorrow?"

"No," I said. Even if I were, I was cancelling every plan to make room in my schedule for Brad.

We made the most of each day and night together. I couldn't believe how quickly I had fallen for this guy. He was so different from anyone I'd ever met before.

After three of the best days of my life, I stood and watched him load his car for the trip back to Baton Rouge. I wanted to appear strong, but I couldn't keep the tears from betraying me. And when I looked into his eyes, I could see tears welling up and betraying him too. He drew me into his arms.

"I wish you didn't have to go," I whispered into his ear. I breathed in the clean scent of his skin.

"Me too. But we will make this work somehow. It will be long distance for a while until we figure this all out. But we will figure it out. I promise. Okay?"

I gave him my weak smile and nodded.

He kissed me one last time, got into his car, and drove away.

He drove off in the mid-winter snow and left his tire tracks behind. And I let the tears I'd tried so hard to control flow down my cheeks.

Time went by, and we did our best to stay in contact through phone calls and letters. He often sent me flowers and cards, professing his love for me.

Though I dated a bit while he was gone, my heart was not in it. I wanted Brad. I was falling in love with him.

Spring finally appeared, the beginning of Brad's first spring training season. He traveled to camp in Vero Beach, Florida, where he trained with the big-league club and pitched in several games. The manager and pitching coach noticed his performances, as he was striking out so many batters. They called him into the office after one of his games and informed him that they were so impressed, they were going to assign him to the Los Angeles Dodgers' AA team in San Antonio, Texas.

He was so excited that he called me right away to tell me all about it.

"That's wonderful news, Brad!"

"Come to Texas and live with me."

I had just turned nineteen years old, and my family members were strict Catholics. "I can't. My parents will never allow that. But maybe I can come visit."

Though his voice sounded sad, he agreed.

"They're really strict. I'm not even sure that they'll let me go down to see you, but I'll ask. I'm so proud of you."

After we hung up, I tried to think how I could break this news to my parents and convince them, somehow, to let me go see him. I waited for the right time to bring it up. *While Mom is making dinner.*

That night I explained it all to my mother as she made stew. She stopped stirring the pot and looked at me intently. She must have been able to see how much I cared for Brad. She smiled and nodded. She promised to talk with my father, who also agreed.

I was surprised they said yes.

Brad bought my airline ticket, and off I went to Texas. I was so excited when I got on that plane! I just couldn't wait to see his face and get wrapped up in his arms again.

He met me at the airport. He was just as handsome as the last time I'd seen him that cold, wintry day several months earlier.

I threw myself into his arms and kissed him. I felt like I was coming home.

He drove us to his place to get settled. But when I walked in, I was surprised to see two other ball players hanging out in his living room. "These are my roommates."

I was so glad just to see him and for us to be together, I didn't care that we'd be sharing our space with two other guys!

It was such a special time as we got acquainted again. He was a perfect gentleman, and we connected even more and developed a deeper bond with each other. Every morning and early afternoon we had fun sightseeing, swimming, eating out at different restaurants, and learning how to dance the two-step to country music. Later in the day, he needed to rest for his evening games, and then he took me with him to the ballpark.

The Texas ballpark in San Antonio was unique. It had a real southern charm and served some great Mexican food and margaritas. Though I did not know much about baseball or the rules of the game, I enjoyed the atmosphere at the park. And now that I knew one of the players, it was even more of a thrill.

Brad pitched every five days, so I got the opportunity while I was there to watch him perform on the mound. This was my first time seeing him in pitching action. I was so nervous for him! I wanted him to succeed and get the win.

"Strike him out, Brad!" I yelled with the rest of the fans when each new batter from the opposing team walked up to home plate.

He pitched amazinly that night and got the win.

After the game, many of the wives, girlfriends, and groupies waited for the ballplayers to come out of the locker room and join them. I could understand the wives and girlfriends, but I thought it strange to see groupies vie for the ballplayers' attention.

This world was all so new to me that I stood toward the back, unsure of what to do. As the players slowly emerged from the locker room, I watched as they made their way, greeting people until they connected with their special person. Finally, Brad came out and looked for me. I waved and watched his eyes light up. He hurried to me and gave me a big hug.

"Good game! Congratulations. You were great out there," I told him.

"You're my good luck charm," he said.

We spent our remaining few days together growing more deeply in love. And just as had happened before, when we first parted, I dreaded having to leave him and catch my flight home. He promised again that we would make our relationship work.

For two years we continued our long-distance relationship. While we were apart, I tried to distract myself through my studies and pageant competitions. And he continued to do well with the Dodgers. Our separate ambitions and lives were going well—but could we make our relationship work?

By now we both knew that we either needed to get married or go our separate ways. Both of us were just stubborn enough to hold on. "I'm not giving up on us," Brad told me whenever we discussed the struggles of having a long-distance relationship.

Throughout each summer, I would travel to his games whenever I could, even following the bus to the next city to be near him. I would be escorted to the wives' and girlfriends' section and watch him pitch. I noticed that his eyes always scanned the stands to see if I was there. He lit up every time he saw me. And I tried to learn as much about the game as I could so I could be his biggest fan. I now understood the game he loved so much.

He definitely played for the love the game, because baseball in the minors was no picnic. Pay was low, and many ballplayers had to share apartments to make ends meet. Brad played with some all-time greats, such as Fernando Valenzuela, Oral Hershiser, Steve Sax, and Mike Marshall. He had great experiences playing—and he was really good. But like all athletes, he also struggled with some bad experiences. He threw out his rotator cuff during one game, which put him on the disabled list. This was a very hard time for him as he struggled mentally and physically to go through rehab and get back into the game.

Since he had more time on his hands while on the disabled list, he wrote me several letters each week.

We courted long distance for three years. By the end of the third season, he moved home to Atlanta, Georgia, where his parents lived. After I graduated, I also moved to Atlanta. I found an apartment and a job, hoping that being closer in proximity, we could see each other more often, and would make our relationship easier and stronger.

One night in December 1982, I invited him to my place, where I'd planned to cook a meal and enjoy a quiet, romantic evening. I even bought champagne! During dinner, he offered to refill our champagne goblets, picking them up and disappearing into the kitchen.

Within moments he returned. "Let's toast to our love," he said and handed me my glass.

We clinked our glasses together. As I took a sip, I saw a ring, tied loosely to the bottom of my goblet, like a wine charm, slide toward the top. My eyes grew wide.

Brad got down on one knee. "Will you marry me?"

My heart nearly burst, and I nodded. "I will marry you! You're my endless love Brad, and I will love you forever."

We set the date for February 12, 1983. All our plans seemed to be going smoothly—until a week before the wedding. Brad received a certified letter informing him that he was being released from the Dodgers.

He was devastated.

My heart broke for him—not because I cared about baseball as much as I cared about him.

"You'll find another team to play for, honey," I told him, hoping that would lift his spirits. I looked into his eyes. "I am marrying you for you, not what you do. I will stand by your side no matter what. Things will work out."

We both agreed not to share this news with anyone, as he did not want to have to spoil our wedding with having to answer people's *What's next?* questions.

The wedding was beautiful. We set it for Valentine's weekend—not just because of the romance of the holiday, but also because that was right before spring training would have begun.

It was a sunny yet cold day with snow on the ground—our winter wonderland wedding. The Catholic church was filled with guests. We had a full mass service. And we had a special treat, as my neighbor, an opera singer, sang

"Ava Maria." We also picked our own special songs—"Endless Love" by Lionel Richie and Diana Ross was particularly beautiful. We said our vows to each other before the Lord. The priest blessed us and said those famous words to my new husband, "You may now kiss the bride."

We kissed and began our lives together, through sickness and in health, for richer or poorer, to death do us part. We said those words and believed them—though at the time we had no idea what they really meant.

Brad at his college graduation.

Brad drafted to the Los Angeles Dodgers' AA team.

Miss Crystal Lake pageant.

Crowned Miss Crystal Lake 1980.

Our wedding,
February 12, 1983.

Happily married! Mr. and Mrs. Brad Thorp.

Posing with our parents, Dick and Carol Thorp
and Beth and Orv Bobek.

Bridesmaids and flower girls.

Groomsmen and ring bearer.

Chapter 2

Our Gift from God

We came back from our honeymoon and settled into married life. The first year we were married was rough. Brad tried out for different baseball clubs trying to get picked up. And I tried to find my place in it all—with pageants, fashion merchandising, and now, as a baseball bride.

Eventually, Brad decided to finish college and enter the business world. As difficult and frustrating as it was, I believe he made the painful realization that his baseball days were over and that it was time to do something different. Amid the loss and grief of that process, we believed God would somehow birth something new for him and that we would make it work. Somehow life would become good again.

We wanted to remain in Atlanta, so he focused on finding a job. Fortunately, I was teaching fashion merchandising, which helped cover the bills. But I was definitely glad he'd finished getting his business degree. That would make an ex-baseball player more hirable.

But with each week that passed without him landing a job, the financial stress began to affect us. Finances are one of the top conflicts in a marriage, and we began to understand that. Though we loved each other deeply, love wasn't keeping the mortgage paid or the electricity on.

Eight months into our marriage, we attended a networking event, hoping Brad would make some connections there. We met an older couple who were everything we wanted to be. They treated each other with honor and respect, they were successful in their endeavors, and they took a genuine interest in us when they learned we were newlyweds.

They seemed open to mentoring us—and we jumped at the opportunity. So when they invited us to attend their church with them that Sunday, we accepted. Though faith was important to us, we hadn't yet found a church "home" to get involved with.

That Sunday, Brad and I sat with our new friends and experienced church in a brand new way. The worship music was vibrant, so different from the traditional songs I had been accustomed to as a Catholic and Brad as a Lutheran. The sermon felt relevant, and the people were all so welcoming. We left that day more fulfilled and filled with joy than we ever had felt attending any other church.

We shared our feelings with the couple and then asked, "What makes this church so different?"

They smiled. "The filling of the Holy Spirit is what you are experiencing," she said. They began to explain the church's mission—to help people grow up in their relationship to Jesus and to know the Word of God; to grow together by building lasting friendships and true fellowship as the people of God and a community of faith; and to grow by serving others—in the church and the community—showing love in action.

Brad and I looked at each other. This was exactly what we wanted. We decided this would be our church home and we would be sponges soaking in all the learning we could.

Once we became serious about our faith and following Jesus, we soon reaped the benefits. Our marriage became much stronger. And Brad even found a great job with Xerox Corporation. He did so well that he became one of their top salespeople and was awarded a trip to Italy. It was like a second honeymoon for us! What an amazing time we had visiting Rome, Florence, Pisa, Milan, and Lake Como.

Two years later, Brad's talents caught the attention of other companies, and he accepted a management position with National Cash Register (NCR), where he quickly climbed the management ladder that transferred us out to California.

We were both thrilled for this new adventure, living out in sunny, beautiful California, and couldn't wait to see what God had in store for us here. The excitement crashed into reality pretty quickly when we tried to find a home we could afford and faced sticker shock. We had no idea how expensive living was in California—especially on one income, since I now had no job.

Brad spent most of his time with his new position, while I searched for employment, hoping I could continue in my field. Life there, without any family or friends, was quite an adjustment. So we searched for a church where we could connect with the people. We heard about a new church called Saddleback, which met in the school gymnasium at the time, and was pastored by Rick Warren, an exciting pastor to listen to. We looked forward to each week's service, where we learned more about God and volunteered to help wherever the church needed us.

We had now been married seven years. We'd traveled the world and were ready to start our family. I assumed I would get pregnant right away. But as the months passed with no baby, I started to grow frustrated. I couldn't understand why I could not get pregnant—it wasn't for lack of trying. Instead of us enjoying our intimacy, our lovemaking became almost mechanical. Every day I took my temperature to see when I was ovulating. If that was our "lucky" day, we'd drop everything and head to the bedroom, certain that *this* time would give us what we wanted. And yet each month, the pregnancy test came back negative.

And each month—and then each year—that passed, I felt more depressed and helpless. My mother had given birth to six children. All my sisters got pregnant easily and gave birth. What was wrong with me?

My mind began to taunt me. *You should just give up. You'll never have children.*

I began to pray desperately to God for answers and a breakthrough. As I prayed, I felt God speak to my heart. *Oh, you of little faith, do not worry. Live by faith, not by sight.*[1]

One day while I was having lunch with a friend, the topic of my pregnancy struggles came up. "You should see a fertility doctor," my friend suggested.

Could this be our breakthrough?

Brad and I decided to give it one last effort with hope in our hearts. The doctor was compassionate and straightforward as he explained the different tests he would need to perform. The first was to check Brad to see if the issue was with him. His test came back fine. We now knew the issue was me, so the doctor ran tests. They found nothing abnormal, so he suggested we try artificial insemination.

"Don't get your hopes up on the first try," he warned. "It might take several attempts."

Brad and I looked at each other and nodded. We both wanted children, and if this was the way, then so be it.

The doctor would inseminate me with Brad's sperm when I was ovulating. So we went home and waited, checking my temperature daily.

The day finally came. I was ready and called Brad and the doctor's office to schedule the procedure. Brad had to leave work to meet me. They checked us in and separated us. I waited in another room while Brad took care of what he needed to do. Afterward, the doctor began artificially inseminating me.

Lord, please let this take, I silently prayed.

"Okay, now we wait and see," the doctor said. "Don't forget, the first try doesn't often succeed, so if it doesn't, don't feel too bad. We'll try again."

As soon as I could use an early pregnancy test, I took it.

"I'm pregnant!" I shouted, holding the positive test and running to find him.

His eyes grew as wide as saucers, and his smile lit up the room.

I jumped into his arms, and he twirled me around.

After seven years of marriage, and fourteen hours of labor, our precious miracle baby came into the world and into our hearts on September 12, 1990. A healthy boy, who weighed eight pounds, eight ounces. We named him Mitchell. When I heard his first cry and got to hold him in my arms, my heart melted. And when Brad spoke, I watched his little head turn toward his daddy as he recognized his voice. This was the closest to heaven and God that we had ever felt. We were over the moon with gratitude.

My motherly instinct kicked in, and I wanted him close to me. When the nurse wheeled Mitchell out of the room to circumcise him, my heart ached, as I did not want him to feel pain. But that was a momentary pain, and it would soon be forgotten.

When we were finally released from the hospital, Brad and I couldn't wait to get home. We were officially a family, and we were ready to start our lives together. We had the nursery set up with everything a baby could need. The only thing missing was an instruction manual. The hospital hadn't provided one for us. Here we were with this new baby and no idea how to raise him. The one thing we did know was that we would provide him with lots of love and compassion.

Of course, everyone wanted to come see the baby. My parents came first, my mother stayed with me for a couple weeks to help me get my strength back and to help me navigate being a new mom. Then my sisters and in-laws came. The household was busy, but with so much joy and excitement. We loved every minute of it.

Two months later, we traveled two hours to Palm Desert, California, where my sister Cheryl lived. She invited us to have Mitchell baptized there. We felt that a destination baptism for those who could come for the celebration and some vacation time together with family would be nice.

On November 18, Mitchell was baptized in the Catholic church in Palm Desert. We asked Cheryl and Dave, my sister Linda's husband, to be Mitchell's godparents. They accepted the roles with honor. On Brad's side of the family, his grandma Violet Jacobson, and his mom and dad, joined us from Florida to witness the special day.

Mitchell cooed and smiled when the priest poured the holy water over his head, baptizing him in the name of the Father, Son, and Holy Spirit.

I had so much fun being a mom, and I loved dressing him up. For his first Christmas, when he was three months old, I put him in a cute little Santa sleeper and hat. Everybody loved Mitchell, who was such an easygoing baby.

Even our golden retriever, Justin, was patient with him. He never seemed to mind when Mitchell laid on him or pulled on his ears. They were two best friends, and Justin took it upon himself to watch over Mitchell.

As Mitchell grew, and we took him for his doctor visits, he was always in the upper ninetieth percentile in growth and development. And in no time, he pulled himself up to stand on his feet and try to take those first steps on his own.

One day while we were visiting my parents in Arizona, my father took us to the townhome they'd just moved out of and had for sale. As we walked into the empty living room, twelve-month-old Mitchell spotted an oversized teddy bear my dad had placed there for his grandson to discover.

As soon as Mitchell saw it, he wiggled and pushed against Brad, who was holding him. Brad put him down. We figured Mitchell would crawl to the bear. Instead, he stood and walked straight toward it without falling.

We were shocked! But immediately we cheered as he walked on his own for the first time. From that day on, he was on the go, and Brad and I felt as though we needed to wear running shoes to keep up with him.

Mitchell discovered that walking definitely had its rewards. A whole new world opened for him to explore. He especially loved when I took him to the park that had swings, slides, and sand to play in. But even better was the bonding with Brad. As soon as Mitchell could walk, Brad gave him a foam baseball bat and a miniature tee to hit a ball from. Mitchell laughed with delight as he hit the ball and then chased after it over and over again.

By the time Mitchell was twenty-two months old, I was surprised to find I was pregnant again. Brad and I were so thrilled to bring another child into the world.

"You're going to be a big brother," I told Mitchell, preparing him for this new journey. Brad and I did our best to prepare him for the changes to come. And he accepted them all like a little trooper.

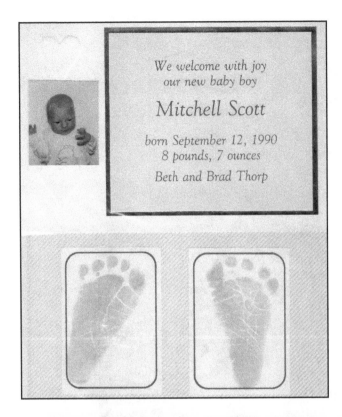

We welcome with joy
our new baby boy

Mitchell Scott

born September 12, 1990
8 pounds, 7 ounces

Beth and Brad Thorp

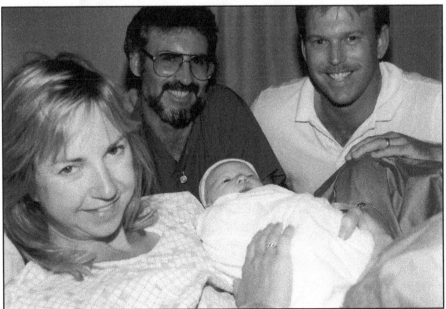

So happy bringing our baby into the world!

My sisters celebrating my joy as I hold Mitchell.
Cheryl Porter (L) and Linda Nelson (R)

L to R: My mother, Beth Bobek, my mother-in-law,
Carole Thorp, holding Mitchell, me, and Brad's
grandma and Mitchell's great grandma, Violet Jacobson.

Mitch's first Christmas, 1990.

Mitch at one year old,
already holding a bat and ball.

Ready to play.

Chapter 3

A Love of Mud and Laughter

Have you ever tried to answer a child's question and been bombarded with the classic "But why?" after you've given what you thought was a reasonable answer? After he or she has pushed all your buttons, your frustration grows to the point that you finally respond with an emphatic, "Because I said so!"

Toddler years are all about the "But why?" Children's little minds become curious about the world they live in. Mitchell was no exception. And being a new parent, I didn't always have the answers to his questions—or, for that matter, to many of my own.

Brad and I were learning how to parent before the Internet, so we couldn't Google our questions to find information about raising children or normal childhood development. We had to resort to early childhood books or get the information from our son's pediatrician.

Of course, we wanted Mitchell to be healthy and happy. But his physical and mental development weren't the only issues we focused on. Love was the center of our household and we wanted to raise him to know his Lord Jesus Christ at a very early age. We purchased a children's Bible, and I read him Bible stories as he followed along with the pictures. We also taught him to pray, to talk to Jesus who was his friend and who cared about him. We felt a strong urge to set this firm foundation early. We took seriously the scriptures that clearly directed us on how to share our faith with our son. We put into practice such passages as:

* Fix these words of mine in your hearts and minds; tie them as symbols on your hands and bind them on your foreheads. Teach them to your children, talking about them when you sit at home and when you walk along the road, when you lie down and when you get up." (Deuteronomy 11:18–19)
* Let all that you do be done in love. (1 Corinthians 16:14, ASV)
* Love one another. As I have loved you, so you must love one another. (John 13:34)

My heart overflowed with joy to see Mitchell try to apply spiritual lessons—he was so much better at sharing his toys with his playmates and learned to be a hugger to those he got to know and love.

His little mind worked in overdrive as he was always in a hurry to finish first in all he did, as though everything were a race. I often had to remind him to slow down. He found that difficult, except during prayer time before he went to bed, when he would slow down enough to quiet his mind.

"God wants to hear from you and me," I told him. "He loves it when you talk to Him in heaven. You can talk to Him anytime, anywhere you want, about anything! God hears every one of your prayers. Prayer is one of the most powerful weapons God has given us. Think of it like your superpowers!"

He smiled brightly. "I like that, Mommy."

"Okay, sweetheart, let's start with your bedtime prayer. I want you to repeat after me, all right?"

"Okay," he said, and faithfully repeated, "Now I lay me down to sleep, I pray the Lord my soul to keep. Angels watch me through the night and wake me with the morning light. Amen."

After prayers, he loved to nestle into his bed while I tucked all the angels in around him. I would lift the covers and shake them as I called all the angels to come and fill his bed. Then I would bring them down around him while I tickled him. He always giggled at that, as it gave him a nice happy memory to go to sleep.

He was just an all-around great little boy, and everybody loved him. He had beautiful blonde hair that people often noted. But even more than his appearance that drew people to him, he had an easy-going and fun-loving personality that made people love him even more.

Each year he developed something new in his personality that amazed us or made us laugh. He began to mimic movies he'd watched—the characters' body language and sounds of their voices, along with one-liners he thought were funny.

One day he mimicked one of the munchkins, whom we called the Lollipop Guy, from *The Wizard of Oz*. He put his hands in his pockets and danced the little jig as he said, "I'm the lollipop man, I'm the lollipop man." He loved to laugh and would do anything to make us laugh, too. He was pure joy and entertainment for us.

Mitchell had long fingers, which allowed him to pick up a ball at a very early age. Throwing the ball well came naturally to him. Brad often took him outside to teach him how to throw and catch. "Look here, Mitchell, watch the ball all the way in as you catch it; don't take your eye off the ball."

"Okay, Dad," he'd say and try his best to follow his father's instructions.

"We're going to learn to hit the ball off the tee," Brad would tell him.

Mitchell hit the stick several times but couldn't quite hit the ball.

Brad was so patient with him. "It's okay. Let's try again. This time, let's aim for the ball."

Finally, Mitchell would hit the ball and watch as it sailed into the yard. He looked so happy as he quickly ran to get it and try again.

"Great job, Mitchell! Let's do it again; only this time, I'll go out in the yard, and you try and hit it all the way to me."

That gave Mitchell something to aim toward, and his excitement grew as he said, "Okay, Dad!"

He would hit it, and Brad would catch it and shout out "Good job!"

Mitchell loved to hear that, and it kept him going. It was like when he played with his miniature basketball hoop. Every time he dunked the ball, the toy lit up and played loud applause.

Mitchell and Brad practiced over and over until Mitchell grew tired and moved on to something else—usually getting dirty. Like many boys, Mitchell seemed never to be satisfied unless he was filthy. One day, after a night of rain, I walked by a window that looked onto our backyard and stopped abruptly. Mitchell was outside, playing in one of our flowerpots. He was sticking his hands into the mud squishing it between his fingers. He was making a major mess, and I had no doubt he was going to track it into the house—and I would have to clean it up. But he was having so much fun that I didn't have the heart to make him stop.

At least he isn't naked, I thought and laughed, remembering when two-year-old Mitchell had had enough of wearing his diaper, so he took it off and sat naked outside, playing in the dirt and muddy water.

Beside playing in the dirt or playing sports with his dad, he was never happier than when he was playing with Justin, our Golden Retriever. Justin was always good for a game of tug-of-war with a towel. Mitchell laughed and laughed whenever they played, as Justin pulled the towel and him around the backyard.

I continually told Mitchell, "Think first about what you're doing before you do it. I don't want you to get hurt."

He tried to comply, but he was just unafraid and daring. At bath time, I often found bumps and bruises. At least he was having fun getting those bumps and bruises. It was part of being a boy growing up.

At eighteen months old, he loved dressing up and pretending to be a cowboy or superhero or super athlete. If he could have lived in a costume, he would have been happy. It was as though every day was Halloween for him!

I loved watching his imagination at work and looking through his child-eyes as he discovered new things from the world.

And I had my own imagination going: at nine months pregnant and due any day, I daydreamed about Mitchell and his brother playing in their new backyard at the house we were building. Brad and I wanted our children to have space to run and play. As our family grew, we needed to find a bigger place. We called it the castle house since it was so big compared to the house we rented.

With Brad doing well in business, we saved enough money to purchase a modest piece of land. My father was a professional home builder. He graciously offered to move in with us to help us with our first home, which took a little more than a year to build. And when I say help us build, I mean that we were going to do as much of the work as we could!

We prepared a budget and got financing from the bank. I secured bids from different contractors for the jobs we could not handle. My father taught me a lot, even though I had no experience. I knew how to talk to people, and I was a good shopper. I knew how to negotiate the best prices. I loved design, whether in fashion or interior. You could say I had an eye for everything beautiful.

We had researched different house plans and settled on a two-story, five-thousand-square-foot home. It had five bedrooms, four baths, and a large marble foyer. The focal point was the sweeping staircase that split up the middle at the landing. Huge arching pillars graced the foyer that led into the formal living room and the formal dining room. The large kitchen flowed into the family room at the back of the house, where we'd spend most of our time. Above the garage we wanted a suite with a mini kitchen for guests. Most important, though, was the large backyard for the children to play in.

With blueprints in hand, I packed up Mitchell, and headed to the city development office to get our house plans approved. I'm sure they gave me grace, looking at my *very* pregnant condition, and did not press me too hard on every little detail. I was thrilled to show my father that they approved the plans and that we could break ground.

Brad wanted to help but was so busy working and traveling with his job that he had to leave the building to my father and me. Of course, we included him on major decisions, but he empowered me when he said, "I trust you to do this. I know you'll build something wonderful."

This was the first time we built something from scratch and watched it come to fruition. It was much like giving birth. I took Mitchell to the construction site at times and loved watching him mimic his grandpa. He had his own set of play tools, so he'd grab a hammer and pretend to hammer nails. Or he'd move dirt around with his dump trucks—and, of course, get dirty.

It was a busy time, and I was more than ready to deliver this baby. On August 1, 1992, my water broke, and I yelled to Brad that it was time to go. He dropped everything, grabbed my packed bag, and helped me to the car. While my dad stayed with Mitchell, Brad and I headed to the hospital, timing contractions on our way. We didn't wait long. At the hospital, a staff member helped me into a wheelchair, checked me in, and wheeled me to my birthing room. I assumed my labor for this child would be the same as it was with Mitchell. But it was much quicker.

Matthew was a healthy big boy, weighing eight pounds, eight ounces. We were all excited finally to bring home a brother for Mitchell to play with.

Christmas soon arrived, and Mitchell began to understand what the holiday was all about. He made out a list of what he wanted—a truck, movies, a baseball, a football, and candy. And as he clutched his list, we headed to visit Santa.

I saw Mitchell's excitement building as we waited to see Santa. He pulled out his Christmas list from his pocket, and as soon as Santa looked at him and exclaimed, "Ho ho ho. Come up here little boy," Mitchell ran and jumped onto the bearded man's lap.

"What is your name?"

"Mitchell," he replied as he stared into Santa's jolly old face and long, white beard.

"Have you been a good boy this year?"

"Yes, Santa."

"What do you want for Christmas?"

Mitchell held out his list and recited from it.

"That sounds great, Mitchell," Santa said kindly. "Let me have your list and I will give it to the elves to hold for me. Does that sound good?"

Mitchell handed, oh so gently, the list to Santa and hugged him.

Santa's helpers snapped some photos and off we went, with Mitchell chattering about the experience and how the elves had his list and what he would do with his toys when he got them on Christmas.

"You know, Mitchell, all those toys and seeing Santa is great, but those aren't the real meaning of Christmas," I told him. I wanted him to understand that Jesus was what really mattered. So as we decorated our tree and home and got ready for the holiday, we also read books to him about the birth of Jesus and had him help us set up the manger.

On Christmas Eve, we finalized our Christmas preparations, and celebrated Brad's birthday. We sang happy birthday to Brad and to Jesus and opened some presents.

As Mitchell's bedtime neared, I announced. "Let's get some milk, cookies, and set them out for Santa. He can enjoy them when he comes down the chimney with your presents."

His eyes grew with excitement. He sprang from the floor and followed me into the kitchen. After we placed everything by the tree, Brad and I tucked him into bed and then Brad read *The Night Before Christmas*.

Early the next morning Mitchell jumped on our bed to wake us up. "Get up, get up, Santa came!"

There was nothing better than to see Mitchell's joy and excitement. It was so priceless, I never wanted it to end. And I honestly never thought it would.

Playing in the mud.

Our little man.

Mitchell at his second birthday. My dad is holding Matthew.

First Halloween party at school.

Our new home—our castle house—is finally finished.

Move in day. L-R Beth, Mitchell, Brad holding Matthew,
and my parents, Beth and Orv Bobek.

Mitchell loved Santa. Christmas was his favorite holiday.

Mitchell and his new baby brother, Matthew.

Chapter 4

His Love of Baseball Grows

When Mitchell was four years old, I discovered the local YMCA had sign-ups for T-ball. I knew he'd be thrilled to play on a team.

"Honey, what do you think about signing Mitchell up?" I asked Brad.

He looked pleased. "Yes, let's do it. He's ready, and mostly it's for him to have fun and meet some new friends."

When I asked Mitchell if he wanted to play, I thought he might pass out from excitement. It was as though Christmas had come early. "Yes!" he yelled.

On the day of the sign-ups, Brad, Mitchell, and I checked in at the Y. The staffers gathered everyone around the bleachers to talk about the T-ball program and their need for coaches.

"If any of you parents would like to volunteer, that would be great," the leader said.

All the dads looked at one another, but not one raised his hand.

I tapped Brad on the leg. "Why don't you volunteer?"

He shook his head. "I'm traveling too much to commit to it." Then he smiled. "Why don't you do it?"

Funny that no dad will come forward to coach the team. I don't think they have enough patience to handle young kids. So I raised my hand. "I'll volunteer to coach the team."

I saw a lot of jaws drop. But somebody needed to do it. And why *not* me?

Since the kids were so young, I think the men thought it was more about babysitting than playing real baseball. I understood that it takes lots of patience and love to coach these little ones about anything, much less baseball.

On the drive home, I asked Mitchell what he thought about Mom coaching his team.

He did not look disappointed but did ask, "Why not Daddy?" That made more sense to him since Brad had been the one playing catch and teaching him to bat.

Brad jumped in. "Son, Dad will take over when you get a little older. But your mom will be great. She is one of the best teachers I know."

Mitchell smiled.

"I'll make it lots of fun, don't you worry," I told him.

Our first practice came, and I looked at my team of twelve excited children. "Come along, kids, and gather around me," I told them, and had them sit in a circle.

Mitchell sat next to me. He sat up proudly, as if he was meant to be a leader like his mom.

"I'm Mrs. Thorp," I said and encouraged each child to say his or her name as we went around the circle. Then I explained some of the rules of the game, how to throw, how to stay in their positions, how to get ready when the ball is hit, and what to do with the ball when they get it. Now that we'd gotten the lecture out of the way, it was time to put everything into practice.

"Okay, kids," I exclaimed. "Let's get out there and have some fun. Are you ready?"

"Yeah! Let's go," the kids shouted.

My heart melted as I looked at all these darling little faces staring up at me, enthusiastic just to be out there playing something new. I'm not sure who was having more fun—them or me!

Brad had given me some guidance, which I put into practice. I began to implement drills and basic things. We started by stretching, and then we practiced throwing the ball properly. I taught them to keep their eyes on the ball and their gloves down and in the ready position when the ball was hit to them.

When we completed our drills, I blew my whistle. "Okay, let's bring it in. I'm going to divide you up and rotate some of you in to hit the ball. As we do this, we will rotate positions, starting at home plate with the catcher and batter, and then moving to pitcher, first base, second base, shortstop, and third base—like a big circle. This way each of you will get to play at each position." We didn't bother with any positions beyond the infield, since none of these little guys could hit that far.

I assigned Mitchell to first base and watched him happily run to his position.

I looked at the batters lined up. Each swung the bat as though he or she were in the big leagues. The first player came to the plate.

I placed the ball on the tee and reminded him to swing hard.

He did and headed toward first base.

Unfortunately, the team in the field immediately forgot what they had learned. They all left their positions to chase the ball.

I placed my hands on my head and sighed. "Oh no!"

Eventually everyone had a position and stayed there. I reminded them that only if the ball came in their direction, they should go after it and throw it to first base to try and get the player out.

We practiced hard and, finally, we were ready for our first game. Each team received a different colored T-shirt and baseball cap. We were the blue team playing against the red team. The kids were giddy to play "for real."

Mitchell was so excited, as he was the first person up to the tee. He took practice swings like the big-league players do and then stepped to the batter's box and swung. He smacked the ball toward third base and ran like the wind to first base.

The boy nearest the ball scrambled to get it in his glove. He threw it with all his might, but did not quite make it there. The pitcher picked it up and threw it to first.

"Safe!" the umpire called. Mitchell glowed with pride. His teammates cheered.

When our next player hit the ball, Mitchell ran to second. Our hitter did not make it to first base fast enough, though, and was called out. We had one out, as the next couple of hitters went to the plate, not only with the intention of getting on base but also helping Mitchell make it home to score.

When Mitchell finally got his chance, he slid in feet first. Of course. He loved getting dirty, and what a way to make his dramatic score, just like he watched the big leaguers do it on television.

The blue team won that day, eight to six. I felt proud of my team!

While obviously I wanted the children to learn the game, my goal as a team mom was to make sure they all had fun and had a good experience. After the game, the fun continued as I brought out snacks. They'd worked hard—and though they hadn't quite mastered the game yet, they deserved some rewards. They were all learning what it meant to be part of a team sport.

"Did you have fun?" I asked Mitchell on our way home.

"Yes, Mommy, I really liked hitting. I liked to run too."

"Good, I'm glad. You did a great job listening to Mom, your coach, and doing everything I told you to do. I can't wait until you tell Dad how you did today."

"Me too!"

That evening, after dinner and when Mitchell was in bed, I looked at my husband. "Now I know why you didn't want to volunteer to help with this age."

He laughed. "I'm sure you did great, honey. I will coach when he gets a little older."

All too soon, school was getting ready to start again. Earlier that summer, Brad had received an opportunity to be a partner in a health-and-wellness startup company. He loved the idea of running his own company. With much thought and prayers, we put our dream home up for sale and were stunned when it sold in less than thirty days. Though I was sad to leave this home we'd put so much hard work and money into, I learned the important lesson of never getting too attached to material possessions, as they will come and go.

By August we packed everything and moved an hour south into a new home in Carlsbad, which was closer to Brad's work. Since we were in a new area and Mitchell had been the youngest in his previous class, we decided he should repeat kindergarten. We felt it would be better for him to be on the older side of his classmates. Plus, it would give him that extra development in growth.

September arrived and we turned our focus to Mitchell's first day in his new school. We had seen how smart Mitchell was and how quickly he caught on to things. He had a head start in the alphabet and learning to count early, so we knew he would feel very confident going into this year's class. He was able to learn and grow so much that year.

Many of the parents volunteered to watch the kids on the playground, so I volunteered to be a playground mom for one week. During that time, I talked with Mitchell's teacher about his progress.

"He's such a special boy," she told me. "He's such a little perfectionist. He wants so much to do everything right and does not want to let anyone down or himself." She told me that one day he'd had a meltdown when something did not go right on one of his tests. "I told him it was okay that it wasn't perfect, and that sometimes we all make mistakes. We learn from it and go on."

I knew Mitchell's personality. He wanted to please everyone. As I listened to her story, I was struck by such an important lesson she had taught him—that we're all human, we make mistakes, and it's okay.

While Mitchell enjoyed school, he couldn't wait for summer vacation to start—because that meant baseball. We enrolled him in the La Costa Youth Baseball League in the five- and six-year-olds' division for T-ball. This time Brad took over the coaching, along with Kim Healy. Kim's son, Brandon, quickly became the best of friends with Mitchell.

That July 1995, we had a special treat for Mitchell. We took him and Matthew to Jack Murphy Stadium in San Diego, where the Padres played. Though he loved watching the Padres on television with his dad, he'd never been to a game. And this was kids' day at the ballpark! When we arrived, we saw thousands of kids lined up on the outfield warning track. It was all fenced in, so we scrambled to find our place by the fence to watch and wait for some of the professional players to come and sign autographs before the game.

I said a silent prayer that God would give Mitchell and Matthew a special surprise. The Lord was shining on us, as Tony Gwynn came over. Nicknamed Mr. Padre, this right fielder had hit eight batting titles in his career, tying him for the most in National League history. He spotted our boys and greeted them warmly. Then he lifted them over the fence so we could take a picture of him with the boys. That was a God-appointed moment, because we could never have pulled that off on our own if we'd tried.

As the school year progressed, we noticed how much Mitchell liked to draw. He could capture shapes and colors in his imagination and put them to paper. Every time he came home from school with an art project, he said, "Here, Mom, I have something special for you."

He always placed the treasure in my hands for me to evaluate—I thought all were magnificent—and then we hung it on the refrigerator so his dad could enjoy seeing it after work.

I chuckled one day as we got to the kitchen, and he held out his hand to take the art back from me. "I can reach the magnet and do it myself," he said. "I'm a big boy now."

Each time we hung a new drawing or art piece, I took the old one down and tucked it away. Soon the pile grew, but I didn't care. Each was special, and I cherished each as being from a part of his soul.

My mother always told my siblings and me growing up: "Live each day as if it's your last." She instilled in me an understanding that our days are numbered, so we must cherish each moment. That lesson would come to mean more to me than I ever could have imagined.

Matthew and Mitchell.

Age four, playing YMCA T-ball.

Age five, with Tony "Mr. Padre" Gwynn and Matthew.

Age six, in kindergarten.

Proudly displaying the handprint art he gave me for Christmas.

Chapter 5

Lessons Learned from Baseball and Life

After that first major-league experience on Kids' Day, Brad always took the boys to games so they could develop a love of the game. He got to the ballpark during warm-ups so the boys could see how hard the players practiced before a game.

This also was the only time to get autographs from favorite players. The boys would scramble toward the players and try to get their attention by holding out their baseballs or yelling their names. To see their faces light up when they succeeded was often the best part of the game-day experience.

Since my parents lived in Arizona, every spring, we took a road trip to visit Grandma and Grandpa Bobek. And how could we go to Arizona and *not* attend the big-league spring training games? All my boys loved it.

"We're going to see the Padres play today," Brad would tell Mitchell and Matthew, "so let's wear your Padre gear and grab your mitts and balls so you can get some autographs."

"Yeah!" the boys shouted, as they ran to get ready.

As we entered the ballpark, the boys followed their dad down front to watch the players warm up.

"Look, Dad, there's Tony Gwynn, Trevor Hoffman, and Steve Finley," Mitchell said, his eyes as wide as saucers.

Baseball was in Mitchell's DNA. Each year he got better and better in skills, as he had excellent hand-eye coordination. We soon discovered he had mixed dexterity. He threw right-handed but hit left-handed. We chose not to correct that, since mixed dexterity ran in Brad's family.

"I can teach him to be a switch hitter down the road," Brad told me.

Brad continued to coach Mitchell's teams, which they both loved, as it was a wonderful way for their relationship to grow and create good memories.

Mitchell was now old enough to graduate from T-ball and hit from a pitcher. Many days throughout the summer the team went to the batting cages to get their reps in, hitting from a pitching machine. The boys loved it as Coach Brad gave the players hitting instruction.

"Okay, listen up," he'd say. "Today we'll work on your hitting. I will demonstrate three basic things: it starts with good balance, quick hands to the ball, and keeping your head still and not pulling out." He assigned them to cages and watched each hitter, offering pointers. Brad's goal wasn't just to make them better players, but also to instill confidence within each of them.

Their first game day finally came, and all the parents and their children arrived at the park. Something about going to a ballpark is so special; it stimulates all the senses—the smell of fresh-cut grass, the leather of the baseball mitts, and the hot dogs from the snack bar. The music began playing, and the crowd sang the national anthem. The home-plate umpire shouted, "Play ball."

I'm not sure who was more excited—the kids or the parents.

"Remember all the practice we've put in," Brad said as he gave the players a pep talk. "Now is the time to make it work for us. If you feel what I call butterflies in your stomach, that's okay. That is called adrenaline, and it will give you superpowers when you get up to the plate. I want you all to go out and have fun—even if you strike out or miss catching the ball. I want all of you to encourage each other. This is a team sport, so we play as a team. Okay, on three. One, two, three—"

And they all yelled, "Bandits!"—their team's name.

As we watched each player go to bat, we cheered. I admit that I cheered loudest for Mitchell. I wanted him to do well. But I also wanted the whole team to do well. As Brad told them, baseball is a team sport. They all must do well to win.

Baseball, however, is a game of frustration and failure, as the boys soon learned when they lost their game by one run. The boys wore sad faces as they sat on the dugout bench afterward.

Brad called them to the outfield for their after-game review. "No long faces," he told them. "Carry your head high. You played hard, and that is what counts. It takes a lot of practice and a lot of work. It doesn't happen just by snapping your fingers. Did you know that most hitters fail seven out of ten times? So you must figure out how to deal with failure—that's one of the keys to having longer term success."

I was so impressed as I watched Brad teach those kids important life lessons about building character, perseverance, and strength.

As we drove home, Mitchell was still sad. He loved winning and contributing to the team's success. He would hit homeruns over the fence as early as he began hitting off the pitching machine at seven years old. So, this loss hit him hard.

"Baseball is like any sport, Son," Brad told him. "It's about winning and losing, learning to pick yourself back up and never give up, and going out and giving it your best every time you step out on the field. But most of all, you have to have fun and love the game."

I turned and looked at him in the back seat to see if he accepted his dad's words of wisdom.

He looked at me, and slowly his sweet smile returned.

"Okay, let's go out for ice cream," I said.

Oh, how quickly ice cream can get one to forget the loss!

As the season continued, the boys succeeded and made it to the play offs. They won their championship game and were noted as that season's standout team. The All-Star game soon followed, with Brad picked to be the head coach, aided by three other coaches. They picked the top players from all the teams to make up the All-Star team. This selected group of boys that would compete against other top All-Star teams in the region. This was a big honor, and the names of the boys who made the team would be announced on championship day, when they were to receive their trophies from the season.

When Mitchell heard his name announced, he jumped up and down with excitement. On the way home, Mitchell asked, "What's next, Dad? When do we start playing in the All-Star game?"

"Hang on, Son, we have two weeks to practice with your new teammates, so we are all in sync with one another. The tournament will follow after that."

The day finally came for the team to have their first practice. The coaches had the players do some warmup drills and then watched a practice scrimmage game to access the players' strengths and weaknesses. They then placed the players in the right lineup and best fielding positions. The coaches handed the players their new jerseys and hats for the tournament.

"What's are our team's name?" Mitchell asked.

"You will be competing as the La Costa All Stars," Coach Brad announced.

The boys looked at each other, smiled, and high-fived.

Eight different teams from the North San Diego region competed to move to the next level. Each team would play three games. The winners of each bracket would move on to the final two teams to determine the champions.

We had a lot of baseball ahead of us.

As nighttime fell, we tucked the boys to bed.

"Can we ask God to help our team and give us all the strength we need to play each day and hopefully win?"

I smiled. "Of course, sweetheart. That is a really good prayer. Why don't you start by talking to God about it? I know this is a big deal, and God wants to be part of it with you, so invite him in to join you."

After we prayed and said good night, I realized, *I know he will be up thinking and dreaming about all of this.*

Game day arrived, and we all made it to the field with plenty of time to warm up before the first game. All the boys had their game faces on and were ready to play. Mitchell hit third in the batting lineup. In the field he played at first and the outfield for his speed and great arm.

The brackets were in; the boys had to win three games to reach the championship game. Mitchell was eager and nervous going into the first game as he bounced around. His first at bat was a ground out to the first baseman as he was a little too quick to jump at the ball.

His second at bat, Coach Brad pulled him aside for instruction. "You have to calm down and take some deep breaths. This time I want you to wait for the perfect pitch. Don't jump at the first pitch you see unless it's perfect for you. I want you to stay back on the ball."

"Got it" he said. As he stood in the batter's box, he watched the first pitch come in.

"Ball one," the umpire shouted. The next pitch came in and hit the dirt. "Ball two."

As the ball came out of the pitcher's hand, he watched it all the way in. He roped the ball to the right center fence for a double.

As his third at bat came around and the team was leading by five to three, he was back to his old self, driving a single up the middle to finish the game.

Mitchell would live all-baseball-all-the-time if he could. But Brad and I wanted to raise the boys to have a balanced life outside of baseball. That included going to church. We all enjoyed Sunday school and church each week. That time fueled our souls to conquer daily life. At the end of his message, our pastor often said, "Folks, this is the locker room. Out there in the world is the playing field. Go take what you have learned and be the salt and light of the earth."

I joyously affirmed; *I delight in the illuminating power of God in me.* It was a good reminder that we must live not just for ourselves but for others, and that started in the home. Everything kept coming back to how we cared for our family.

One way we did that was to take a family vacation every year. One year we flew to Fort Myers, Florida, where we spent time with Brad's side of the family. Then we drove to Walt Disney World to spend three days at one of the happiest places on earth. Mitchell and Matthew loved it. We got up early each morning and stayed at the park until dark, until the boys could not take another step. We carried them back to the hotel for the night, rested, and repeated the same thing the next day.

We also made sure we celebrated birthdays, holidays, and even casual times.

Family life could not have been better. We felt so blessed to have two amazing boys in our lives and the support and love from our extended families.

Fortunately, each year baseball season ends, giving way to school. Mitchell was as good in school as he was on the field. Each semester his report card reflected all As, and his teachers wrote wonderful comments about his character, such as, "Mitchell always lights up the room" and "Mitchell listens well, and is willing to help other students."

That's my boy, I thought with a smile, pride filling my spirit.

When Mitchell was eight years old, he came home from school one day and presented a Happy Mother's Day drawing and message he'd written:

> This is to certify that my mom is the greatest! Here's why. She can bake the best cookies. Also, she is good at baking the best pizza and she does the best work. She is special because she takes me everywhere. She lets me ride my bike. I like it when my mom takes me to Burger King and the store. My mom can do many things! I think she's best at driving good on the road and cooking well. My mom has a pretty smile! I like to make her smile by telling jokes and doing something funny. My mom is as pretty as a diamond. I'd like to tell my mom,
>
> You are the best mom in the world.
>
> Love, Mitchell

I stopped reading and looked into his beautiful blue eyes. As tears rolled down my face, I knelt and hugged him tightly. "Thank you, sweet Mitchell. Mom loves you *soooo* much!"

He pulled away. "Mom, look at the back page, at what I made."

I turned it over and saw his handprint and another note: "I give my hand to you this day! Remember me now, as I grow and play." I laid my hand on top of his handprint and felt warmth flowing through my fingers.

Be salt and light, our pastor had reminded us. Brad and I had worked to be those things to our children—to teach them good life lessons, not just through baseball but through all of life. My spirit picked up that Mitchell understood those lessons. I believe he wanted to tell me to always remember him in those joyous moments. I promised him in my heart that I would.

Mitchell's 6th birthday.

Mitchell's 8th birthday.

Mitchell, age 8, with Matthew and their dogs.

Mitchell and Matthew
watching the game.

Mitchell and Brad after All-Star win!

Part 2

A Life Celebrated

Chapter 6

His God-Given Talents

When we are kids, sometimes we are not aware of all our giftings, we just want to play until someone points out what we do really well. We are all created in God's image, and we are all unique. Our uniqueness is a great contribution to the world.

Mitchell stood out among his peers, whether he understood it at the time or not. But we began to recognize his God-given talents and his tender heart and determined to nurture those.

He was so naturally talented in many sports with his great hand-eye coordination. We had to raise the bar for him to be challenged, and he always rose to the occasion, wanting to be challenged more. For example, in baseball he liked to play against the older division. He wanted to test himself and his talent against them to see if he was that good.

One day Brad asked Mitchell, "Would you like to play in a competitive travel baseball league?"

"Yeah!" Mitchell said immediately.

"You understand that means more practice, playing more games, traveling to different states, and playing against better competition," Brad explained.

"I'm ready," he assured Brad. "But can I still play with Brandon?" Brandon was his best friend. "Brandon told me that he played last season with the travel team called the Stars, and he really liked it."

"Let me check with his dad to see what their plans are and to see if that will work for next spring. Sound good?" Brad said.

It was another challenge, and Mitchell was all in.

We wanted him to be a well-rounded athlete. He was young and still developing, and we wanted him to be exposed to other sports to let him choose the one he really liked and excelled at best, even though he shined the most at baseball. But still, we encouraged him to keep an open mind. So besides playing baseball, he was in karate, basketball, flag football, and golf.

He also loved being in the water, whether swimming in the backyard pool or boogie boarding in the ocean. He loved to catch the waves and ride them into the shoreline. Being tossed around by the power of the waves exhilarated him. He would laugh his way in from the waves to run out and catch some more.

Learning from all these other sports and using different muscle groups, he was developing into an amazing athlete. When he was twelve, high school coaches were already scouting him to enroll at their schools when he became a freshman. Our area had two public high schools, plus private schools. Many coaches spoke about how talented he was. Though Brad always knew our son was good, now others recognized it.

Mitchell was usually the cleanup hitter and hit in the fourth spot in the lineup. He also liked to pitch and was becoming very good. He was developing into a five-tool player: he had a high batting average, his hitting was powerful, he had speed to run the bases well, he possessed a strong arm to throw well, and he could field the ball well.

Before one game, I stood behind the fence and watched my boy who was in the on-deck circle taking his warm-up swings. Though I wanted him to do well, I also wanted him to stay safe, so I continually prayed for his protection. As I stood there, I happened to overhear some of the other dads and coaches chatting.

"Boy, I love to see this kid swing," they said, referring to Mitchell.

Wow, I thought. How wonderful to see that others also saw his God-given talent. While my heart burst with pride, I knew that this talent needed to be balanced with humility and kindness. I'd seen too many athletes ruin their reputations by being "too big for their britches" or losing the joy of the game. I was going to make sure this didn't happen to Mitchell.

Fortunately, he seemed to already understand this truth. He seemed content to share the spotlight with others. His character was developing into him being a loving, servant-leader. He taught other ballplayers how to improve where they were struggling by playing catch or hitting ground balls to them. And the bonus of that work was that they could win the next game—and he loved winning!

Some players were so competitive that they forgot to enjoy the sport, but Mitchell never did. His sense of humor was spontaneous and silly. He loved to make himself laugh and bring others along for the ride. He really liked his teammates and joked with them on and off the field. If he was not having fun, it wasn't worth doing. For instance, he would get the boys to see who could spit their sunflower seed shells into a cup that was set up at a distance for points. Whoever got five shells in the cup got the bragging rights.

He was the same at home. One day I told him to bring the dirty laundry downstairs so the boys could learn to wash clothes. As he dragged the hamper down the stairs, he thought how much fun it would be to dump the pile of clothes on top of himself and his brother. They both laughed as I turned and looked at what had just happened. I laughed too. He captured a good idea—if you have to do the boring stuff, like chores, you might as well have fun doing it.

He was so gifted, yet he had no ego. He was compassionate and tender hearted for those who were challenged, and he would go out of his way to be a friend. He would even stand up and protect others who were bullied at school. My neighbor once told me that she never had to worry about her son when Mitchell was on the street with the other kids. Her son had Asperger's syndrome, a form of autism, and she knew Mitchell would protect him from any bullies.

Many people were naturally drawn to the light and joy of his spirit. As a mother, I couldn't have been prouder—not about his abilities as an athlete, but about how his character was being developed into a Christ-like spirit. He learned early on the power of the Golden Rule—to treat others the way you want them to treat you (Matthew 7:12). I loved seeing how God was growing Mitchell's character into something truly beautiful. I could see the light of God shining brightly within him—his soul radiating like a beacon; a reminder of the sacred nature of this human journey and his place in it.

Mitchell, age nine.

Age ten; showing off his basketball trophy with Coach Healy.

Age eleven, playing on the Cardinals team.

Mitchell's homerun ball as coaches and teammates look on.

Mitchell's 11th birthday.

Being funny throwing the laundry on top of themselves.

Playing catch on the beach with his brother, Matthew.

Mitchell loved the ocean.

Mitchell boogie boarding and riding the waves into the shoreline.

Chapter 7

Much to Celebrate

By 2003, Mitchell, now twelve years old, had really hit his stride, and we had so many wonderful things to celebrate in his life.

The first celebration as a family was to travel to different places. Because both boys were getting older, they were easier to travel with, so we took advantage of family time together. We traveled to Cabo San Lucas, Mexico, over Easter break with my parents. We filled our days playing beach volleyball and poolside bingo games at the resort, where we were also learning Spanish, as they called out everything in that language. We delighted swimming in the beautiful zero-edge pools that looked out to the ocean, and we loved the arts-and-crafts table where we painted ceramic sculptures while being serenaded by a trio of strolling mariachi musicians.

When school ended in June, we traveled to Sedona, Arizona, to visit my sister Cheryl and her husband, Bob. We were in awe as we marveled at the majestic red rock mountains. There, we were introduced to hiking trails and learned about the history of the Native Americans who first inhabited this land. Sedona is one of the most scenic areas of Arizona and one of the best destinations for casual hikers, like us, looking to spend a few hours walking along the red rocks and scenic canyons.

Cheryl, Mitchell's godmother surprised Mitchell with an early birthday present—his very own walking stick to take on his hikes. He loved it! We also enjoyed visiting western shops and craft stores. Mitchell and Matthew caught the shopping bug as they threw on some cowboy hats to fit in with the crowd. We felt such a sense of peace in this sacred land.

One day, we wanted to visit The Chapel of the Holy Cross, which sits high atop the red rocks. We climbed the mountain from the parking lot to get to the entrance of the chapel and then took a self-guided tour to learn about it.

The church was commissioned in 1932 by local rancher and sculptor, Marguerite Brunswig Staude, who was inspired by the construction of the Empire State building. The Chapel of the Holy Cross has long declared the glory of God through art.

Many people from around the world visit this place to light a candle for their loved ones or to kneel and pray in the chapel. Below the church was a gift shop to support the chapel and their mission work. My senses were on overload when I stepped into the shop, marveling at all the beautiful artifacts and gifts.

I told the boys they could find something to take home with them. So they left to browse.

As I turned a corner, I was drawn to a display of cards showing individual names and their meanings. I began to read all of our names and what they meant.

"What are you looking at?" Mitchell said, now standing next to me.

"Name cards. Do you want to know what your name means?"

His face lit up. "Sure."

"Well, they shortened it to Mitch. But that's the same. It has a Hebrew origin, and it means *like God*. Then below, the card says, 'Delight yourself in the Lord; and He will give you the desires of your heart' (Psalm 37:4)."

"I like that! Can we buy it, Mom? I want to put it in my back pocket of my baseball pants for protection and good luck when I play my games."

"Absolutely! This is a good purchase."

As we stood in the check-out line, I couldn't help but think, *I can see how Mitchell's personality is like God, as we are all made in his image, and I know his character is Christ like in his joy, his love, and his compassion for others.*

After our ten-day visit, we traveled back to San Diego. The next day, our neighbors invited us to go sailing on their boat. Brad had sailed a lot growing up and he was happy to share this experience with the boys. The boys loved to watch Brad pull the lines and tie them down, tacking back and forth to catch the wind. Our neighbor let Brad take over the wheel.

"Want to try it?" our neighbor then said, looking straight at Mitchell. "Want to steer?"

"Yeah!" Mitchell said and jumped up. With Brad close by, they switched places as we all watched him take this challenge like a grown up. He focused with such intensity! We could tell he was in his element just like his dad, feeling strong and free.

Our other travels included going with Mitchell's baseball team. He was becoming such an impressive player. Mitchell was growing like a weed. When I hugged him, he was now looking at me eye to eye. His muscles were getting bigger, and he was getting stronger. He was now training and working out with some ex-pro-ball players who helped coach him. This was a family commitment to his travel baseball as it took us all over the United States where he competed with other great teams. It sharpened his skills and made him a better ball player. We traveled to Las Vegas in July to play in a tournament. This was a big deal as teams competed there from all around the United States.

The team arrived a day early so they could practice at the Big League Dreams stadium. To get to the championship game, Mitchell's team, the Reds, needed to win three games in their pool play to move on to the championship round. In the championship round, the team needed to win two games to win the tournament.

For game two, Mitchell was the starting pitcher and ended up throwing a perfect game. During the championship playoff round in the bottom of the first inning, Mitchell came up to bat with runners on first and second. He worked the count to two balls, no strikes. He anticipated that the pitcher would throw him a fastball. When the pitcher released the ball, Mitchell's eyes got big as quarters, his bat made a thundering crack, and the ball soared over the right-centerfield fence for a three-run homer. The next two times he was at the plate, the pitcher walked him so he wouldn't have the chance to hit again! The team went on to win five-to-three and received the opportunity to play in the championship game.

The following day the players geared up for the championship game. The boys were putting their game faces on to go on to compete against another strong team. So much excitement filled the air. The boys felt like major leaguers as the big game moved to the best field in the Big League Dreams Park, named Fenway Park, a replica of the real stadium. Mitchell would bat third and pitch second in relief, if needed. The game was a close contest, with neither team scoring until the Reds opened the bottom of the fourth with two runs. Mitchell doubled to drive in one run, and the next hitter drove Mitchell in to make two-to-zero. With two more innings to close out the game, Mitchell relieved the starting pitcher. He made quick work of the next two innings, with the final score two-to-zero.

Mitchell jumped off the mound and ran to the catcher as they both jumped up to hug each other, all the other ballplayers running to celebrate with them. Coach Brad called them in to lineup to shake the other team's hands. After the trophy ceremony the boys all threw their gloves into the air and celebrated their win!

When we returned home, Michell and Matthew wanted to create their own field of dreams in our backyard, which they named Thorp Field. They got busy making their own score board out of wood and painting it to look like the real thing.

They gathered all their team hats from all the major league teams. They created their own World Series by dividing up the American and National league hats. Mitchell chose the National league and Matthew accepted the American league.

Mitchell took a coin from his pocket. "Heads or tails?" he asked Matthew. "Heads," Matthew replied.

Mitchell tossed the coin, which landed on heads. Matthew won the toss and became the home team. They challenged each other and had the best time, playing whiffle ball until the sun went down.

With the new school year starting, we ended our travels. I couldn't believe our little guy was already graduating into middle school, which was a big deal, as he had to learn how to change classes and get used to a different teacher for all his subjects.

Where had the time gone? It felt as though I blinked, and my baby was already in middle school and almost a teenager!

"Are you nervous about starting middle school?" I asked.

"Yeah, a little bit," he admitted, though I could tell he was trying to put on a brave face.

"Let's sit down here, and Mom will pray with you, that you have nothing to fear, okay?" I said. "Starting something new and not knowing what to expect can get anyone a bit nervous. Think of it like this: You know how you get a little anxious before a big game? When that happens, what do we do?"

"We pray," Mitchell said.

"Yes, that's right! We turn whatever you are worried about over to the Lord. We can do that about school, too. God wants you to go out and walk in peace. I want you to repeat after me, okay?"

He nodded, expectantly.

"I can do all things through Christ who strengthens me."[2]

Mitchell repeated.

"Good, now say, 'The joy of the Lord is my strength.'"[3]

He repeated that too.

"Those are two Bible verses you can always pray. Whenever you are walking into a stressful situation, repeat these verses in your head. And God will help you."

His first day of school arrived, and I wasn't sure who was more nervous—him or me! I reminded him to pray those verses, and I prayed for him throughout the day.

When he got home that afternoon, he smiled ear to ear.

"So how was it?" I asked.

"I really liked changing classes and meeting new teachers. I did get confused trying to find my science class. The bell rang, and I walked in late, but the teacher said I was excused for today."

"Well, that is good to know, sweetheart. Middle school is prepping all the students for what high school will feel like."

"I know, Mom," he said.

What a jump in his learning, especially in English, which was one of his more difficult classes. He had become a much better writer, he excelled in math, history, and science, and of course he aced physical education. Academically, he was a straight-A student with a 4.0 grade point average. He took pride in his schoolwork. And I was impressed with his many short stories. He was especially proud that the teacher gave him an A+ on one. The teacher wanted the students to write about something special that happened over summer break. Mitchell chose to write about his perfect game that he pitched. "Here, Mom, read what I wrote!" he said, handing me the paper.

I took it and began to read:

Exhaling deeply and digging my foot into the soft dirt, I was getting ready to throw what I hoped to be the final pitch of the fifth inning. Focusing on this one pitch, I was determined to blow the ball by the batter. I blocked out all distractions and sounds and stared at my leather target, the catcher's glove.

The burley umpire called, "Strike!"

The count was one ball and two strikes. The catcher gave me the sign. I shook it off and I thought, *Forget the curveball! Throw him the heater!*

I wound up and let the ball fly. The umpire wrung him up for a strike three. The inning was over, and the game was now in the very last inning. During our time at bat, we were quickly retired.

We returned to the field for the final three outs. These outs were the most important of the game. We needed them to win. I was determined to pitch a perfect game.

The first batter came to the plate, and he grounded out softy to second base for the first out. The next batter was a pretty good contact hitter, but with three heater fastballs, I sat him down for my fourth strikeout. They were down to their last out and this out was a big one. I thought, *I'm going to get it.*

I got ahead in the count with one ball and two strikes, and it all came down to the next pitch. I rocked and loaded and swished the ball past the hitter and into the catcher's glove with a loud pop. "Strike three!" the game was over. I was so elated that I jumped off the mound and gave my teammates and coaches congratulation high fives.

Afterward, I walked over and gave my dad and mom big hugs. I got the ball for my hard work getting my perfect game, and my dad wrote the stats on the ball. They were zero walks, zero errors, five strikeouts, and fifty-one pitches in five innings of play. That was my first perfect game, and there are many more to come.

"This is really well done, Mitchell," I told him, and he beamed with joy. "I'm so proud of you."

The following week, Mitchell wrote another short story, which he titled, "Changing the Movie Industry." Again, he handed me his paper to read:

Change—do you ever feel uncomfortable when things change all around you? Change brings about opportunities, growth, conflict, and history. When you walk into a movie store, looking for a movie to watch at home, many movies you see on the shelves are violent, disturbing, and aggressive.

I would like to see the movie industry change their scripts by writing the movie and casting of the characters by using less violence and making more enjoyable family movies. If Hollywood could show less violence in the making of their movies, then there would be less violence, crime, and hatred in our world.

Getting the movie industry to change won't be easy. It should require some government laws to be put in place. The movie industry should look to the younger generation for good story telling. There are many talented writers out there that can submit their stories to Hollywood.

They need to make more movies for kids and adults to enjoy. The kind of movies I would like to see are more, laughter and comedy movies. Great action stories about people's lives with lighthearted endings are excellent movies. Some great inspirational stories, like "The Rookie." Autobiographies are really decent to watch, too. Entertainment movies that make people laugh so that you get a kick out of it. You can't stop laughing because it's so humorous. When one laughs it is medicine for the soul and cheers you up. It is even more exciting when the whole family watches with you, and have the same kind of feelings, too. If one should pay money to go see a movie, you want to leave the wonderful movie, inspired, delighted, and feeling good.

"Great job!" I told him after I finished reading. "You are growing into quite the writer. If baseball doesn't work out, maybe plan B would be to go to Hollywood and make this change."

He laughed. "We'll see."

We celebrated Mitchell's thirteenth birthday on September 12. He was officially a teenager. Brad and I had a special surprise, which we wrapped in a shirt box and gave it to him to open. We could tell by his disappointed face that he thought he'd gotten more clothes. But then he opened it. Much to his surprise, we'd gotten him four tickets to the Dodger game in Los Angeles, with a two-night stay in a hotel. But the tickets didn't show the entire surprise.

Brad made a special arrangement with his friend and teammate from back in AA ball—Fernando Valenzuela, who was now a retired pitcher from the Dodger organization and well known for his screwball pitch. Brad got Fernando to give us a special behind-the-scenes tour of Dodger stadium, the locker room, dug out, and museum. This was such a special day for Mitchell. He was so happy the entire time. We were glad we could give this experience to him, since we had no idea what screwball pitch was about to hit us all next.

Age 12, Sedona, Arizona, shopping with Matthew for western wear.

Age 12, first time sailing a boat,
as Matthew and Brad look on.

Mitch 7th Grade School Photo

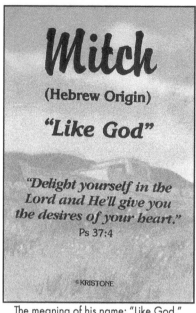

Mitch

(Hebrew Origin)

"Like God"

"Delight yourself in the Lord and He'll give you the desires of your heart."
Ps 37:4

©KRISTONE

The meaning of his name: "Like God."

Age 13, on his travel ball team, pitching a no hitter.

Mitch's home run as he was showing off the sweet swing he was known for.

Team celebrates their tournament win.

Celebrating win with Dad.

Enjoying his 13th birthday at Dodger Stadium with Matthew, Brad, and Fernando Valenzuela.

A 13th birthday he would never forget.

Chapter 8

Something Is Not Right

"Mom, I have a bad headache," Mitchell said one day when he came home from school near the end of his seventh-grade year.

"Okay, honey," I said. "Let's take your temperature and get you into bed." I thought maybe he was coming down with the flu or something, but he didn't have a fever. I gave him a pain reliever and told him to lie down and rest.

After a couple of days, he still was complaining of a headache, though he still had no fever. I didn't want to keep giving him pain relievers, especially since it hadn't gone away, so I called the pediatrician to schedule an appointment. The only time we ever went to the doctor was for wellness check-ups since Mitchell rarely got sick and had no prior medical issues.

The pediatrician looked him over and listened as we explained his symptoms. "I think you should see an allergist and have his eyes checked, to rule out those issues as a cause for his headaches," he said.

I immediately made appointments with both an allergist and eye doctor and started a check list to rule out each issue. But they didn't see anything unusual. So I made appointments with other doctors. Still nothing relieved Mitchell's pain. As each month passed, Brad and I could see that something was seriously wrong with our son. We noticed that he had slowed down in sports and could not breath very well. During one basketball practice, his pain was so great that he bent over with hands on his knees trying to recover.

"Go tell the coach that we need to take him home," I told Brad. I was very worried. We'd never had to take him out of practice. Mitchell was always the star athlete. "Something is seriously wrong, Brad, and I don't know what it is."

In September 2004, as Mitchell was starting his eighth-grade year, his ability to concentrate diminished. He had always been a top student and very disciplined with his studies, but the pain was so severe that he could not keep up. A month later, on October 4, we checked him into the local children's hospital to have the medical team there do an evaluation and run tests. He was hospitalized for three days as the staff ran tests and monitored him.

I was grateful they were able to manage his head pain with IV meds. But they found nothing concerning in his test results, so they released him to go home. We were baffled.

He returned to school, but things didn't improve. One day he came home after school and collapsed on the front yard. I heard him cry out for me, as I looked out the window and saw him lying on the grass in pain. I yelled, "Mitchell!" I dashed outside. I cradled him in my arms and yelled for Brad to help me get him into the house.

Brad carried him inside and placed him gently on the couch. We took his temperature, gave him fluids, and observed him for any other distress he may be in.

"What are you feeling, sweetie? What's going on inside you?" I asked,

"My head," he said in groans. "It hurts so bad."

"I just don't understand. Why is this happening? And why can't anybody figure out what's causing it?" I said, desperate to help my little boy.

We checked him back into the local children's hospital for another complete workup. This time they performed more tests, MRI scans, CT scans, and an extensive blood workup. But yet again, the tests all came back negative/normal with no diagnosis.

They released him with more pain relievers, which seemed to alleviate his pain but not eliminate it completely.

"But what is causing all this head pain?" we asked the doctors over and over. They only shrugged. The pain had become chronic. I knew the solution wasn't just to have him continue to pop pain relievers.

After he was released from the hospital, we knew Mitchell could not go back to school with the headaches, so we arranged with the school district to provide him an at-home teacher. Brad and I hated pulling him out of the school setting, because we knew how much Mitchell loved being with his friends. However, at this point, we had to think of his health and comfort first. Rumors began to spread in the school community that he was at death's door. I tried to set the rumors straight whenever I got wind of them, but rumors are contagious and evasive. It didn't help that our straight-A, 4.0-GPA student now struggled with his schoolwork even with the private teacher.

I took him to the optometrist, who suggested he wear glasses in case eyestrain was the cause. We had him fitted with new glasses, but those didn't help.

We continued to manage his head pain, thinking he suffered from migraines. In December, we took him to a neurologist, who suggested that we try a Botox treatment, which was then a new treatment option for those suffering from migraines. We were skeptical giving this to a fourteen-year-old boy, but we were desperate for some relief for him.

"Sweetie, the doctor will give you injections to help block the nerves," I explained. I could see Mitchell's concern. He hated needles. "If we don't try, honey, we won't know if it works."

He nodded, and the doctor injected him ten times along the base of the neck and the forehead.

The neurologist told us to return in a few months and to document any improvements. "Also try to keep his mind off his pain," he said. "Keep him busy and distracted."

We got in the car and drove home. "Grandpa's eightieth birthday is coming up," I told Mitchell. "We can take a road trip to Arizona and do some other traveling if you're up for it."

He simply nodded, with his head on his pillow against the window.

Later that week, we packed for our trip, and off we went. As we drove, I smiled brightly and looked at the boys. "Grandma and Grandpa Bobek are so excited to see you—and all your aunts, uncles, and cousins will be there too."

I glanced at Brad. We knew seeing his cousins would bring a smile to Mitchell's face and keep him distracted.

While we were in Arizona, Brad and I watched him constantly. We were discouraged that the injections didn't totally take away the pain. We could tell he was not himself, but he was putting on a brave face. I asked our family members to please pray for Mitchell and for us as we tried to figure out what to do for him next—and that God would bring someone who could take his case and help us. I was grateful to see our family join our quest to find answers.

That summer we drove the boys to Yosemite National Park to go fishing, hiking, and enjoy nature. Mitchell was a trooper, but as the doctor said, we were trying our best to keep him distracted. One night as we got ready to go to sleep, we heard banging noises coming from the parking lot. Brad and I peered out the cabin window to see a black bear rummaging through the garbage cans. This was the first time we'd seen a bear in the wild.

"Boys! Quick, get up and come look," I told Mitchell and Matthew. "It's a bear."

Even though they looked scared, they came over to peer out the window. "Cool," they both said.

With the end of summer, Mitchell was entering ninth grade. We still kept him home with a teacher. He tried to keep up, but he struggled more and more. The teacher began to find lessons that he could listen to or that she could read to him, which seemed to help a bit.

His school work wasn't the only thing frustrating him. He missed playing ball and hanging out with his teammates and friends. It was as though life was moving on, and he worried that they would all forget about him.

One day our doorbell rang. Mitchell's coach stood there.

"Hello, Mrs. Thorp. The boys on the team miss Mitchell and wanted to give him this present." He handed me a matted and framed photo of the

Carlsbad High School freshman baseball team. The coach and each player had signed notes of encouragement around the picture's matting.

My heart overflowed with gratitude that these boys hadn't forgotten Mitchell at all. "I know Mitchell will love this. Thank you from the bottom of our hearts. This means a lot."

I immediately took the photo to my son. "Look here, Mitchell, what the coach just dropped off for you. All the ballplayers are wishing you to get well soon and miss you very much."

He looked at it as I held it up. A mixture of joy and sadness covered his face. I could tell he was pleased by their thoughtfulness, but it magnified the ache of missing out on being with his teammates and playing the game he loved so much.

The following week we had another special delivery. Mitchell's teacher had all the students create get-well cards and messages for him. I pulled out the stack from a big envelope and began to read all twenty messages, showing him all the creative artwork on the covers.

One boy wrote, "I heard about you from my teacher. Sorry you are in lots of pain. I hope the doctors help you get better. I also heard that you play baseball. I like to play baseball, too. I hope you get to play baseball again. I also hope you keep your strong spirit. You are really brave."

"You have so many friends who miss you and love you and want you to get better. Even new friends!" I know the notes of care made him feel loved.

Thanksgiving came around and we drove to Sedona, Arizona, to visit my sister Cheryl and her husband, Bob. Our friends, Gina and Larry, and their three children, Molly, Jack and Kara, wanted to join us. They booked a cabin near my sister's house. Brad and I thought it was a great idea since Jack was one of Mitchell's best friends. We knew Jack would keep Mitchell distracted, and it was good for him to have a friend to talk to.

Mitchell loved to hike the different trails. But I worried about him, especially with the trails not being smooth or paved. Even though he used his walking stick, I wanted to make sure he wouldn't fall or collapse.

"Jack, would you please walk with Mitchell and shadow him?" I asked his friend. "I don't want him to fall."

We decided to take the flattest and easiest trail that day.

At the end of the hike, Jack reported, "He was a trooper hiking. He was hurting, though. He said he just doesn't understand why he has all this head pain."

I sighed. "Thanks, Jack. Yeah, we don't understand either."

Despite the pain we had a wonderful Thanksgiving together, creating memories with family and friends. Life, however, has a way of throwing curve balls at us. When we returned home, we noticed that Buddy, Mitch's dog, was not doing well. He wasn't eating and he looked weak. I immediately took him to the vet.

I can't believe all this is happening at once.

"Buddy is suffering from a heart condition," the vet announced. "We can perform surgery, but this will only buy Buddy a little more time."

"My son is also very ill and in a lot of pain," I told the doctor. "And this is his dog, so please perform the surgery to help us keep Buddy alive as long as possible."

I hugged Buddy and watched as they took him away. Then I got in the car. "Why is this happening to us!" I wailed and screamed at God. "Why are we under attack like this?"

I had to pull myself together. *What do I tell my son about his dog?* I could not bear to tell Mitchell his dog was dying. I felt if Buddy died, that would make Mitchell too depressed and cause even more tension and pain. But I knew I had to tell him the truth. Somehow.

As I pulled up to the house, Brad met me in the driveway. I told him the sad news, and that I agreed to have them perform the surgery on Buddy's heart to keep Buddy alive as long as possible. "Let's pray right now that God gives us the words to say to Mitchell, so he won't feel so devastated."

We walked in the house, and I went to the couch where Mitch was resting. His eyes sought mine, and my heart ached for my sweet boy.

"I have to tell you some news, Mitchell," I said as softly and gently as I could. "Buddy was born with a heart defect. The vet is performing surgery on him, and they are doing everything possible for him. We need to love Buddy as long as we have him."

His eyes grew sad, and I blinked to keep my tears from forming. I sat next to him and held him close. Then Brad and Matthew joined in, and we sat together in a big group hug and prayed.

As parents, we were frustrated, afraid for our son, and questioning why our faith was being tested to the limits. We were doing everything in our power to help Mitchell and to figure out how to get him well. We would search and pray daily for answers and for doctors who could bring some hope and clarity.

One day I sat and read my Bible and ran across two passages that stuck with me: "Cast your cares on the LORD and he will sustain you" (Psalm 55:22) and "Trust in the LORD with all your heart and lean not on your own understanding; in all your ways submit to him, and he will make your paths straight" (Proverbs 3:5–6). We had to keep trusting in our Lord that he would help us, even when we did not understand why this was all happening. Our fears and our anxieties were constantly rearing their ugly heads, and yet we clung to God, trusting for Mitchell's healing.

Mitchell and Grandpa Bobek at
Grandpa's 80th birthday celebration.

Mitch hiking with Jack.
Though still in pain, he was a trooper.

Fishing trip to Yosemite to help distract from his pain.

Mitchell crying in head pain, with his dog, Buddy, by his side to comfort him.

Part 3
The Nightmare Continues

Chapter 9

Seeking Alternative Health Solutions

Mitchell had been in the hospital two times with this mysterious condition, and we were no closer to discovering the problem. With our frustration and desperation growing, we decided to expand our search to include holistic and integrative doctors and therapists who, we hoped, could relieve his pain.

We obediently followed each expert's advice, checking off all the boxes. Our family rarely visited a doctor except for the occasional earache and check-ups, so to be plunged into this huge and scary world of medicine and alternative treatments felt overwhelming. We just wanted a simple answer and a simple treatment. We could not understand why no one seemed able to give us one.

The one doctor we hadn't gone to yet about Mitchell's headaches was now next on our list—his orthodontist. Mitchell had worn braces for the three-and-a-half years and was due to get them removed. Honestly, we hadn't thought his braces might contribute to his headaches, since he'd never had a problem with them before. But perhaps as he was a growing boy, they may have triggered muscle tension.

The orthodontist did a complete evaluation. "Has he had any issues with his braces or jaws since wearing these?"

"Well, he did get hit in the jaw after a dog-pile incident on the field after his final big game win last year," I recalled. "He came to me when he was bleeding because his braces caught his upper lip. I iced it down and gave him some pain reliever. But he didn't display any other concern or discomfort. If he had, we would have taken him to the ER."

He nodded. "It was a good thing he had the braces on, since they probably saved his teeth from being knocked out."

When he didn't find anything abnormal, he recommended that we take Mitch to see a TMJ specialist. TMJ, or temporomandibular joint syndrome, is a disorder of the jaw muscles and nerves. The temporomandibular joint connects the jawbone and the skull. Its most prominent symptom is headaches.

On October 26, 2004, we sought treatment at the TMJ Therapy Center, which specialized in TMJ disorders, orofacial pain, and sleep disorders. They wanted a comprehensive list of Mitchell's complaints, so we listed them all: limited mouth opening, jaw pain, locking jaw, jaw clicking, headaches, fatigue, facial pain, ear pain, dizziness, eye pain, back pain, and ringing in the ears.

The doctor recommended a treatment plan, which required additional imaging and testing, since he believed they needed to orthopedically realign his jaw. This, he said, would lessen myalgia (muscle pain), improve range of motion, reduce inflammation, reduce adverse joint loading, strengthen the musculoskeletal system, and reduce his overall pain. It sounded good to us.

Mitchell left the room for the imaging and some muscle stimulation to relax the muscles around his jaw. After that, the specialist provided Mitchell with mandibular orthopedic appliances to wear. He suggested that we start Mitchell on a soft diet—eating such foods as scrambled eggs, oatmeal, yogurt, soup, smoothies, mashed potatoes, fish—and physical therapy on an as-needed basis.

"Stabilization is the goal toward maintaining muscle comfort and joint stabilization of the mandible," the doctor told us. "Bring him back within eight-to-ten weeks for his new appliance therapy. I predict his prognosis is good." With that announcement, he signed off on the paper.

His confidence was contagious, and we now felt that we were getting somewhere.

Time marched on slowly with Mitchell's pain continuing, though. We kept looking for signs of improvement and continued with all the TMJ protocols and action plans. But his pain didn't lessen. We wondered if some alternative health practitioners could alleviate the pain, along with what we were already doing. We sought out a naturopath and chiropractor who recommended we see an acupuncturist to get Mitchell treated with cranial sacral therapy to help manage his pain.

No matter how crazy or unconventional the treatments seemed, we left no stone unturned to help Mitchell.

Next, we began to see Kim, a nutritionist friend of ours who partnered with an osteopath doctor, a licensed physician who practiced medicine using both conventional and "whole person" approach to medicine. Kim began to educate us on diet, nutrition, heavy metal toxicity, and Lyme's disease.

"Lyme's disease?" I said. "Why do you think it might be that?"

"Something else is going on here. He is displaying some kind neurological disorder and inflammation in the head region that could be linked to something like Lyme. I'd suggest testing for it. It won't hurt and, if nothing else, at least you can rule it out."

We began researching and then testing. On November 16, 2005, Mitchell had his first test, this one for heavy metals. We followed that with a Lyme's disease test, then a hair analysis. The Lyme's disease test came back normal, although Kim warned us that false negatives could happen. The heavy metals and hair analysis revealed high levels of arsenic, cadmium, and lead. All toxic.

How is that possible? I wondered.

Matthew, Brad, and I immediately tested our levels. All three of us were in the normal range, so we knew it was not in our water or food at home.

Is it something at school? Maybe the school's water fountains were toxic, or if the pipes were old, maybe they were leaking into the water.

Besides the TMJ issue, this was one of his first tests that showed some abnormality. But it just didn't make sense for him to have heavy metals in his system.

When we shared this information with his pediatrician, he didn't seem alarmed. "Metals can be found in many things like the foods we eat and our environment." He didn't address how to treat it, only suggesting that we make an appointment with an osteopath—the same doctor Kim had recommended.

The osteopath diagnosed Mitchell as having heavy-metal toxicity coupled with a viral infection, which affected the central nervous system.

"But why are our levels normal and Mitchell's elevated?" I asked.

"Some people's bodies excrete heavy metal or toxins more than others. Our goal now is to remove these metals from his body, so it can be restored to its original function."

So on to new protocols and treatments, hoping this would clear everything up.

Mitchell went through several therapies, including chelation and infrared sauna to detox the metals from his body.

While I didn't begrudge all the time and effort Mitchell's care was taking, I was struggling to keep up with everything, as it was becoming 24/7 care. I had to help him with all his needs, including feeding him, as he was slowly losing his ability to feed himself, which frightened us the most. And his appetite was dwindling.

"Honey, you need food for energy and to get your strength and health back," I coaxed.

He tried to comply, but he just wasn't "feeling it," as he said.

Then walking became much harder. It was a sad day when we came home with a wheelchair. Mitchell saw it and felt the same way.

"I know, sweetheart, but this will help Mom and Dad push you around and not make it so hard on you and us," I said, sensing his anguish. "Let's not give up on trying to walk, though. We will still work on that, okay? Don't give up!"

That night I felt scared out of my mind. Something else was going on here besides his TMJ and the heavy metal issues.

"I need a little time to myself to clear my head and pray," I told Brad and headed outside for a walk. I wailed and cried out to God from the deepest part of my soul. "No mother should have to go through this kind of pain, watching her son suffer and slip away," I prayed. "If something doesn't happen soon to reverse this, he could die."

I thought about Jesus and what his mother had experienced. She'd had this same pain and grief as she helplessly watched her son suffer and die on the cross. Not that I was suggesting Mitchell's illness was anything like Jesus' suffering on the cross, but the thought made me feel less alone. God himself was a Father. He understood my pain. I knew I had to release all this emotion and fear so I could be strong for Mitchell.

I pushed my shoulders back. *We are not going to give up hope on him. We are going to keep fighting.*

When I returned, I walked into his bedroom. His eyes were sunken and his body skeletal.

Still, I smiled. "Don't give up, my warrior son," I told him. "We are going to figure this out with God's help and guidance. We are praying for a breakthrough."

Even though Mitchell was taking up so much of our time and energy, it didn't mean the rest of us weren't suffering. While I was covering the home front, Brad was doing his best to hold up the financial end of everything. He was working double time to help us make ends meet. Doctor and hospital bills were piling up. Even so, the financial stress, plus Mitchell's health, began to put a real strain on our marriage. We snipped at each other too often and for no good reason.

Matthew wasn't immune to what was happening, either. His grades began to slip as he could not concentrate with all that was happening at home. I asked Matthew's school counselor to keep an eye on Matthew and let me know if she saw anything we needed to know about. We also made Matthew's baseball coach aware.

Thank goodness for team sports. Matthew's teammates worked hard to encourage him. Being surrounded by friends and playing baseball were good distractions for him.

Word began to spread again, as the community heard about Mitchell's worsened condition. People wanted to help in any way they could—delivering meals, picking up Matthew for his games and practices, mowing the lawn, and so much more. We were amazed that people showed how much they cared about us. It reminded me of Galatians 6:2 that says we are to "Carry each other's burdens, and in this way, you will fulfill the law of Christ."

When I felt the most helpless, I found myself praying for strength. "What does all this mean, Lord?" I asked so many times. "Why are we going through so much suffering and heartache? Is it a test to our faith?" So many questions and no answers.

To make everything worse, despite Buddy's surgery, Mitchell's dog didn't survive much longer, so Mitchell had the added anguish of saying goodbye to him. We knew how sad Mitchell was, and we all were in mourning over Buddy. But as parents, we could not bear to have Mitchell deal with one more thing.

"Why, Lord, why have you forsaken us?" I prayed. "Why are we going through this? Please, Lord, heal my son!"

The more I prayed, the more I felt as though my prayers were not being heard. I thought about Psalm 22:1–2: "My God, my God, why have you forsaken me? Why are you so far from saving [my son], so far from my cries of anguish? My God, I cry out by day, but you do not answer, by night, but I find no rest."

Even though it felt as though God was absent, I knew he never left our side. We had just entered a dry season of life. I kept hoping and praying this season would end soon so we could get back to normal with our two boys. We reached out to all the local community churches to put Mitchell on their prayer lists. Everywhere our extended family lived in the United States, Mitchell was on their church prayer list. We even took him to healing services where the pastor laid hands on him and prayed.

Even so, we saw no positive change in our son.

A month after Buddy passed, Brad and I felt it was time to get Mitchell a new puppy. We took him with us to the breeder to pick one out. "This will never replace Buddy, and you will carry him in your heart forever, but getting a new puppy you can bond with will help you in your healing," I told Mitchell on the car ride. I knew that getting a new puppy was like bringing new life into our home, something positive to look forward to. Brad and I also agreed that this would help distract him from his head pain.

We held Mitchell's arm as we sauntered to the cage where all the pups were. The breeder opened the door, and all these adorable golden retriever puppies surrounded Mitchell. The aides gave him a chair to sit on as we held him upright. He managed to pet a few, and we waited to see which pup bonded to him the most. We figured once that happened, we had found the one, as dogs know how to bring healing and comfort.

Sure enough, soon a perfect little pup came over and lay on Mitchell's shoe. "This is the one," we told the breeder.

Brad helped Mitchell back to the car. I placed the puppy in the back seat with Mitchell so he could hold him. "What do you want to name him?"

"Um," he said, trying to think of a name. Finally, he said quietly, "Let me sleep on it."

"Fair enough," I said.

The next morning, Brad helped Mitchell down the stairs for breakfast. "Mom, I want to name him Joshua."

I looked at him in surprise. "Wow! Mitchell, God must have spoken to you in your dreams. That is the perfect name for him." Joshua 1:9 was our favorite Bible verse, and we repeated it often to help us all stay strong: "Have I not commanded you? Be strong and courageous. Do not be afraid; do not be discouraged, for the LORD your God will be with you wherever you go."

I smiled at his choice. "Mitchell, you are the strongest and most courageous boy I have ever met. And you are making others stronger as they see what you are enduring."

Our little Joshua was exactly what we needed to remind us to not give up, to not give in, for God would be with us in whatever we would face. And Mitchell definitely needed Joshua's presence.

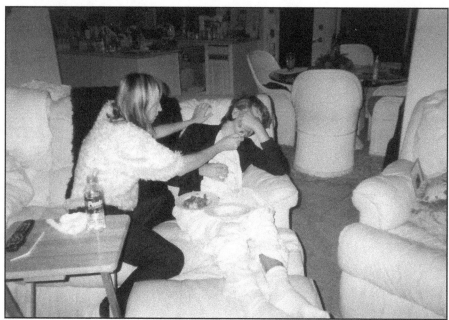

Feeding Mitchell because he could no longer feed himself.

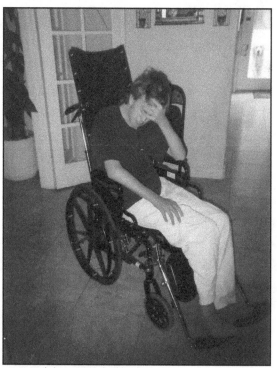

Sad day as Mitchell had to rely on a wheelchair
since his ability to walk had weakened.

Mitchell with Joshua, his new puppy.

Chapter 10

Searching for Answers

Our search for answers and a diagnosis was our never-ending quest. We were juggling so many different issues with Mitchell, we had to tackle each situation as it came. After several months of treatment, instead of his pain being relieved, it continued to increase. We were at our wit's end and couldn't understand why *no one* in the medical community could get a handle on what was happening to our son.

We had our craniosacral session one day, when the therapist recommended that we see one of the most reputable craniosacral doctors in the country. That would mean we would have to fly to Florida. We researched and called the center to see if this doctor would even see him. When he agreed, we were so desperate, we decided to take this leap of faith and go. We were to be there for two weeks of therapy.

Mitchell made it through the first week, but into the second week, while being treated, he had a myoclonic seizure. His body began to tremor.

The doctor stopped treatment and encouraged us to take Mitchell back home and hospitalize him.

My fears went into overdrive. What if he didn't make it through the flight? We'd be more than thirty thousand feet in the air for most of five hours. If something terrible happened, we'd have no way to get him immediate help.

But we knew we had no other choice. Placing him in a hospital in Florida wasn't a solution since they didn't know his medical history.

We decided it was better to take the risk and pray for God's hand of mercy to get us home.

We boarded the flight, buckled in, and prayed all the way.

As the plane's wheels landed in San Diego, I uttered a silent prayer of gratitude and then turned my attention to getting Mitchell back into the local children's hospital.

He underwent MRIs, lumbar punctures, blood workups, and a very complete series of tests. But still the neurologists, psychiatrists, hospital physicians, and others brought into this case, had no answers for what was happening to our son. They stabilized him and, after five days of observation and testing, they were ready to release him. But he wasn't any better.

His appetite was still decreasing at an alarming rate. Within those two weeks, he lost thirty-five pounds and was unable to feed himself, walk, or speak.

The lead doctor on Mitchell's case recommended that we take our son either to Mayo Clinic or UCLA research hospital, because his case was far more complicated than they had ever seen.

Three months before our trip to Florida, we had scheduled an appointment with the UCLA Pain Clinic in Los Angeles. We had hoped they could provide us with the answers we so desperately needed. But they had been booked for six months out! So, we figured we would get the treatment in Florida and then, upon our return, wait three more months until July to get him there. Mayo's wait list was about the same, and we felt that was too far from home to fly back and forth. In quiet desperation, in May 2005, we took Michell home and prayed he would make it until his appointment at UCLA.

"God, just give us an answer," I begged. "We just need to know what this is so we can treat it. Please!"

I was angry and frustrated and confused. I felt the doctors and the medical community had abandoned us. I wanted them to understand our desperation. They could shrug their shoulders and go home to their healthy families, to their normal lives. We couldn't.

Since the medical community wasn't helping, I put Mitchell's story out in the newspaper to see if anyone had similar symptoms or knew of anyone who could give us information that might help. Social media was almost nonexistent at the time, so print media or word of mouth were the only real ways to get the information out about this mysterious and perplexing illness.

We got no help there either.

After six months of our waiting in anguish, the day finally came when I drove Mitchell to the UCLA Pain Center. Mitchell's pain was so intense that the myoclonic seizures became constant and the tremors continuous.

"This boy needs to be in the hospital," the doctor announced, and admitted him into a renowned children's hospital in the LA area.

By now, Mitchell's pain was so severe he spent most of his time unconscious.

I gave the doctors Mitchell's medical book, which by then was quite large with all his previous records of hospital stays, treatments, and blood work. This way they could review what had already been done.

The doctors performed a further workup and series of tests and hooked him up to a seizure machine to monitor his seizure activity.

We felt helpless. Watching our son suffer, while waiting for the test results, and holding onto a glimmer of hope, was gut wrenching. A part of me was dying inside. Brad confessed that he felt the same.

As a mom, my job was to help my children and make things better for them. This was so out of our control, all we could do was surrender our son to the doctors and to God.

As we waited for the test results, the doctors recommended putting in a feeding tube, as he was losing too much weight. We agreed, and they performed the surgery.

While in surgery, I went outside the hospital and found a garden area with a park bench tucked off to the side. I lay on the bench and cried my eyes out.

"Please help us, Lord! My son needs you. I need you. I cannot carry this anymore." We'd been dealing with this mysterious illness now for two years, and I was physically and emotionally drained.

With my head face down to the bench, sobbing, I didn't hear a woman approach.

"Are you okay?" Her compassionate voice made me cry fresh tears.

"No, I am not okay," I said, hiccupping the words. "My boy is having surgery right now. Thank you for asking. I just need this time alone."

She smiled kindly and left me be.

I was hoping and praying for Mitchell's miracle healing. But the stress had so tested us beyond our endurance; only a miracle could save us, too. The emotional, physical, and financial stress bankrupted us and nearly caused Brad and me to divorce.

Brad and I took turns staying at the hospital so Mitchell would never be alone. I stayed during the week while Brad worked, and Brad came on the weekends so I could go home to rest and recover. It was a battle for survival; our son was fighting for his life, and we were fighting right alongside him. Since Mitchell could no longer speak, we had to be by his side 24/7 to advocate for him. We spent many nights walking the halls or in the medical library looking for answers.

The doctors arranged for Brad and me to meet with their team. We could tell they were as perplexed as we were. They told us about all the tests they had done, which were over and above what had been done previously. Then they told us the course of action to take next.

As we waited days then weeks with Mitchell still in the hospital, many of the test results came back negative-normal.

"What is causing all this pain?" I said to the team of doctors at another team meeting a week later in July 2005. "This is crazy."

We all could see that our son was an active, healthy young man until something happened. He was truly suffering and not thriving. *Something* was going on.

"We just aren't finding any answers," one doctor said.

"Could you look into other possibilities?" I asked. "What about testing for Lyme's disease, since his symptoms mirrored many of the markers that others have suffered from."

The doctors looked unconvinced but agreed to do a blood test.

"And what about his hormones, serotonin, and dopamine levels?" I pressed on. "Can you test further about the heavy metals or a mitochondrial disorder?"

I'm glad the team offered to have this meeting with us, but I was surprised that this was a research hospital, yet Brad and I were the ones doing all this extra research.

The doctors could no longer give us the hope we so desperately sought. I now understood what they mean by *practicing* medicine. When they have a tough case like my son's, so many give up or misdiagnose it.

Because they could not find a physical cause, the doctors began to suggest that Mitchell had a psychological issue and wanted to bring in the psych team.

That pushed my buttons. "You think my son *wants* to be like this? That this is all in his head?" I grabbed a photo of Mitchell swinging his baseball bat from my purse and shoved it on the conference table toward them. "Look at this photo. He would rather be on the ballfield playing baseball with his friends. He is in pain! And according to your findings, the myoclonic seizures are due to his pain, so *what is causing all this head pain?*" They heard the desperation in my voice loudly and clearly. I found out later that on Mitchell's medical records they wrote, "Beware of the mom."

I didn't want to get aggressive, but nobody was advocating for my son. No one seemed to grasp that this wasn't a hypothetical study. So if I had to become more forceful to help them understand the severity, so be it.

Even though Brad and I knew this was not a psychological issue, we agreed to let them do their tests. Mitchell did his best, despite his current condition.

Their conclusion? This was not psychological. But they did think he was suffering from depression.

I bit my tongue. I really wanted to tell them, "You think? Due to his constant pain and no relief, you think he's going to feel happy?"

The neurologist research team wanted to bring in a renowned, now-retired neurologist to look at Mitchell. The following week, when he walked in the room, I was struck by his gentle and grandfatherly demeanor. He was around eighty years old, and his bedside manner was refreshing.

He looked over Mitchell's records and asked the doctors about the tests they performed. Finally, he looked up from the records file. "I want to see this boy clean. Get him off all medications. I want to get a baseline look with all of that out of his system."

I thought this was the best news I'd heard yet, as they were masking his symptoms with drugs.

As they began weaning him over the next few days, Mitchell's myoclonic seizures started to subside, and his tremors disappeared, too.

They also began to feed Mitchell through the feeding tube for the first time—he'd been receiving his nutrition through a tube in his nose, which was painful, and he continually pulled it out. I could tell through his body language and facial expression; he was not happy with the G-tube in his stomach either.

"This is only temporary, honey," I said, trying to reassure him. "It's just until you can start to eat by mouth again."

After thirty days in the hospital, we faced a difficult decision: We received no straight answers and faced the real possibility that Mitchell had little time left. The doctors told us there was no more they could do.

"If there is nothing else you can do for him, then when can we take him home?" we asked.

"I don't think that's a good idea," the lead doctor told us. "It would be best for him to remain with us. I'd suggest that we put him in our psychiatric ward."

"What?" Brad's voice rose angrily, and his face turned red.

They wanted to take our son away from us. We knew he would surely die—alone—there. If they placed him in the psychiatric ward, they could end up working to strip us of our parenting rights, then we would have no say in what happened to our son. We may not even be able to see him!

"You informed us that this was not a psychological problem," I said, trying to keep my temper in check. "So why would you take this course of action?"

No one would answer.

"That's not an option," Brad said. "So, what other options can we do to care for our son and take him home?"

We were scrambling mentally to know what to do next to protect our rights with our son. We asked for time to put a team of doctors and specialists together for him upon our return home. But still, they wouldn't budge.

We called a family friend who was also an attorney and explained the situation. Brad told her, "They already told us and documented in Mitchell's medical file that it is not a psychological disorder. So how can they keep him and put him in a psych ward?"

She agreed to help. She warned us to be careful about everything we said going forward, since many parents had lost parental rights over questioning medical decisions.

Her warning terrified us.

She explained that hospitals were so worried about being sued that they made it difficult for parents—especially in difficult cases like ours.

"You think that as parents you have the right to make medical decisions for your child? Think again," she said. "This right is increasingly being taken away. Be aware that they can remove a child from fit parents during a hospital visit, due to a disagreement or question. They also can do an intrusive investigation without evidence. Despite legislative gains in some states, most judges still rubber-stamp intrusive investigations into homes where no evidence exists of abuse or neglect, just because one medical professional disagrees with the judgment of fit parents."

I swallowed hard as she continued.

"As wonderful as our modern medicine is, and as helpful as most doctors are, they are not perfect. Sadly, medical error is the number three cause of death in our country, according to a 2016 report. And even the best doctors are rarely in a better position than a loving parent to make the difficult decisions for a child."

"Oh wow, we had no idea," Brad said. "We will work with them, and hopefully, they will work with us."

"Don't you worry, I will get him home," she assured us.

We were already stressed out over our son's condition, and now we had to deal with the stressors that came from trying to get him released from the hospital. And I was even more scared! I began praying to God to let him come home.

How was it possible that they could dictate to us how to care for and handle our son? How could they wield such power? Who authorized that?

We contacted our nutritionist, the osteopath doctor we worked with before, a physical and occupational therapist, and our family pastor and asked them to submit in writing that they would be handling Mitchell's care. In addition, our attorney immediately sent the hospital a letter. It took just a week for the hospital to finally agree to release our son to us once we had his care lined up at home.

They wanted to transport him via ambulance back home, which was an hour and half away, and which we would have to pay for. They would not let us put him in our car.

We were terrified that the system could take our son away from us and put him into a situation where we knew he would surely die, so we complied with their final demand.

"Can I at least ride in the ambulance with him?" I asked, holding my breath. They agreed.

After more than a month, we left the hospital with a diagnosis of neurodegenerative disorder of unknown etiology. Basically, that was a fancy sounding label that meant they didn't know what it was or what caused it.

Though we felt angry and scared, we did find a few blessings from his hospital stay: we gained a feeding tube, and the medical staff helped him break the cycle of his myoclonic seizures.

The doctors' final statement to us was to take him home and make him comfortable. We knew what they meant: palliative/hospice care.

I rode with Mitchell in the transport vehicle while Brad gathered everything from the room and loaded it into the car to follow us. Not until we pulled into the driveway of our home did I breathe easier. I was relieved to be there, and I know Mitchell was too. A person cannot heal in a hospital with all the distractions, bells, beeps, and nurses coming and going.

Walking into our home felt like walking into a warm hug. Matthew and Mitchell's dog, Joshua, raced to welcome Mitchell home. The emergency medical team settled Mitchell in his bedroom, they had us sign the paperwork, and then left. I crawled in next to Mitchell and held him. He managed to sink his head onto my chest, and we lay there close together.

"I'm so happy to be home. I hope you feel the same too, sweetheart," I whispered into his ear. "We have some great people lined up to take care of you and to holistically get your body healed."

Mitchell inhaled deeply. "Food," he managed to whisper. For the first time, in a very long time, Mitchell spoke.

My eyes grew big. *He's still in there.* I knew he must have been starving and just wanted food. I jumped up and headed to the kitchen, where I grabbed applesauce. I tried to get him to eat it, but his swallowing muscles were not working well, and he gasped. So I got his feeding tube going asap.

That night when we had Mitchell comfortable, I turned on the monitor so we could hear any distress. Brad and I crawled into bed together. I had the best sleep I'd had in a month.

The next morning, our first visit was with the osteopath and nutritionist. They both arrived and went right to work, knowing that time was of the essence. They looked at all his recent hospital records and notes.

The nutritionist knew he was on a feeding tube and asked to see the ingredients in the can formula the hospital used. She scanned the label. "I wouldn't give this to my dog!" she announced. She put together what we called "Mitchell's formula." It consisted of us juicing organic greens and a whole list of nutrients, vitamins, and other ingredients to help him on a cellular level as well as to maintain and put weight back on him. She adjusted and added to this formula weekly as she monitored his blood work.

The osteopath put him on different remedies that we were to give him around the clock. His first goal was to help him out of pain. He was the only doctor who felt confident enough to say that Mitchell had some potential underlying mechanisms of neurological inflammation, immunosuppression, and infectious disease, so the doctor was going to get the inflammation down and then go from there.

Brad put together a master schedule on a clipboard with all Mitchell's remedies, feedings, bathing care, physical and occupational therapy, and homeschooling. This was for all of us to follow each day around the clock, like nurses do in the hospital. This way we knew what the last person did and what the next person needed to do.

Though he still could not open his eyes, it appeared that he could lift one eyelid halfway. He still couldn't talk except for the one word he had managed to get out. Oh, how I longed to hear his voice and to talk with him like we used to. We desperately needed to know from him about what was happening and how we could help even more.

We became experts at reading his body language. The therapists and schoolteacher recommended some type of instrument that Mitchell could use to communicate with us. However, his fine motor skills were nonexistent. So we began simply: We asked him to tap the bed with his fingers if an answer was yes and not to tap if no.

Though we were relieved and happy to have him home, we still worried about his care—and the costs. The hospital bill went above a million dollars. Fortunately, we had good insurance. But even with good insurance, we were still responsible to pay over a hundred thousand dollars. And that was just the UCLA hospital bill. We had the previous healthcare bills, and now we faced home visits with doctors, therapists, and nutritionists.

As his parents, we were willing to go to the ends of this earth to help our son. So, if we needed to sell the house and lose everything to do that, we would. All that mattered to us was getting Mitchell better. We refused to give up on him. We kept fighting, and we asked him to keep fighting too.

Fighting didn't take away the agony of watching our child suffer, however. Many days I collapsed to my knees, crying out to the Lord, "Why is our precious son having to suffer like this? Why has this affliction come upon him and us? Please, God, help my son! Help us understand what to do next." In those moments, I often felt the Lord led me to read the Bible.

"Lord," I said in response, as I flipped through the pages, "speak to me."

I landed on Romans 8 and began to read: "Now if we are children, then we are heirs—heirs of God and co-heirs with Christ, if indeed we share in his sufferings in order that we may also share in his glory. I consider that our present sufferings are not worth comparing with the glory that will be revealed in us" (verses 17–18).

I leaned back in my chair and thought about what I'd just read. I had no idea why this passage jumped off the pages at me, but I had a feeling that future glory was about to be revealed through Mitchell and us.

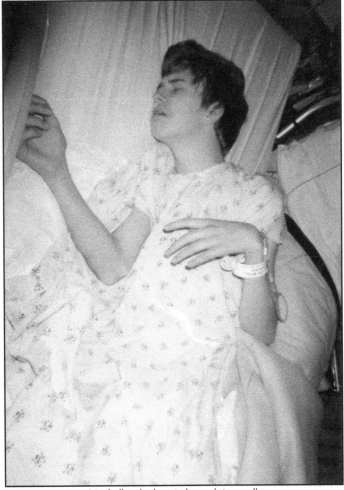

Mitchell in the hospital, not doing well.

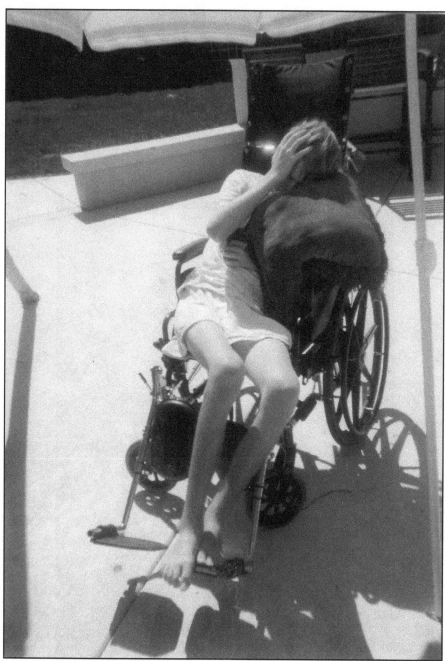

Finally home and getting some vitamin D sunshine.

Chapter 11

Surrendering to God

I stood at the kitchen counter blending Mitchell's "formula" of fruits, vegetables, and vitamins and felt the weariness spread over me. I hadn't even been up an hour and I was already yearning for rest. Time wasn't stopping for us to catch our breath and get caught up on all the things we let slip. It became a chore just to swing my feet out of bed in the mornings. And I didn't stop until my head hit the pillow late in the night.

But Brad and I kept pressing on. We were like two pit bulls holding on to each end of a towel and not letting go, determined to fight for our son, no matter what it took. To be honest, I *couldn't* let go. I felt if I eased up, I would lose Mitchell. And I couldn't stand to consider that.

How long could I keep going at this pace, though? That night, about two days after we brought Mitchell home, I was gripped with such anguish, I fell to my knees and wept. No matter how much I tried, I simply could no longer muster the strength to keep going at the pace and intensity I had been. I was so very tired and had nothing left in me.

"Okay, God, I surrender," I cried out, sobbing with my head to the floor. "I can't do this anymore; I have no control over this, even though I keep acting as though I do. I can't heal my son. I can't bring peace to this house.

Only you can do those things. You must take control. I surrender my son to you wholeheartedly."

I had done all I could do and said all I could say. I had exhausted all the options and still found myself and our situation without remedy, comfort, or resolution. On the floor that night, I realized that I had been fighting, but it was to try to control everything on my own. I thought of the scripture in which Jesus said, "Take my yoke upon you and learn from me, for I am gentle and humble in heart, and you will find rest for your souls" (Matthew 11:29). I had been working against God instead of with him. I needed to let him handle things.

If I wanted rest for my soul, if I needed strength and power to keep going on, then I needed to surrender my will and my way to God and let him carry the burden.

I'd fought against that kind of surrender, because I was afraid, I wouldn't like the way he would choose to handle the situation—and the outcome. But how foolish I'd been to think that I could actually handle it better than he could!

For I am gentle and humble in heart, and you will find rest for your soul.

That's what surrender promised. To hand over my will to him in trust and faith, believing that even in my bleakest moments, the presence of God would be within me and all around me.

I knew I had to surrender myself to God—and I had to surrender my son too. Whatever my need or desire was for my son, my first step was to surrender the outcome. It was not enough to merely say that I had to let go of the situation. I needed to trust in my heart that all would be well. I had to release my expectations, let go, and recognize that Mitchell's highest good was even now unfolding in amazing and unexpected ways.

As my tears slowly dried, I began to think of the ways God had moved in our family. We had learned to be resilient, to persevere and adapt to whatever was presented before us. Staying in the present was all we had; we took one minute at a time. We did not have the energy to see too far into the future. But that was actually a good thing. Too often we could focus on the past or the future and forget to enjoy the beautiful present that offered itself to us fully right then. As much pain we all were in, we had grown even stronger in our faith. We did not turn our backs on God.

After that night, God honored my prayer. I had accepted his yoke, and I found his gentleness to be exactly what I needed to bring rest for my weariness. I began to see the clear distinction of when I was fully surrendered to God and when I began to sink back into wanting my own way. I began to adapt to the twists and turns of life and not resist them. When I faced a new challenge, I focused first on pausing and praying, remembering that if God was for me and my family then who could stand against us? I affirmed in my mind that I could greet any change or challenge with resiliency, strength, and courage. And peace and rest began to return as I took each day, each moment, at a time, trusting God with it.

To keep battling day in and day out, to keep remaining hopeful and not let the enemy get a foothold over me took perseverance. I often thought of what our soldiers must endure in war—battling for life, hoping and praying that they will one day return safely to their loved ones. God was growing perseverance in me and my family.

In Romans 5:1–5, the apostle Paul talked about perseverance and what it comes from and what it produces:

> Since we have been justified through faith, we have peace with God through our Lord Jesus Christ, through whom we have gained access by faith into this grace in which we now stand. And we boast in the hope of the glory of God. Not only so, but we also glory in our sufferings, because we know that suffering produces perseverance; perseverance, character; and character, hope. And hope does not put us to shame, because God's love has been poured out into our hearts through the Holy Spirit, who has been given to us.

I often lay next to my son in his bed, holding him and comforting him, praying over him. I spoke life into him day and night. I put on inspirational messages by different pastors that he could listen to, getting the Word of God deep into Mitchell's soul to help strengthen his spirit to keep him fighting another day. I played soft worship music for him to listen to. I whispered to him that we would not give up hope. But above all, each day, I surrendered my son to God.

His facial expressions at times revealed frustration and anger, and who could blame him? I often asked the Lord to take this cup from him and give it to me instead. I could never imagine having to live with this torture for so long. I couldn't stand *one* day with head pain much less living with it for years. But I would take it all if it meant he could find relief. The pain was taking its toll on his frail body.

One evening, Brad and I were in Mitchell's room and his pain level seemed to be worse. He took what strength he had and hit the bed pillow with his fist. Then he motioned with his hand to the heavens as if to tell us that he wanted to go to be with his Father in heaven.

My momma bear came out. "No, Mitchell, keep fighting! We are praying for your miracle healing. We will get this figured out. Be strong and courageous, my love. You are such a warrior. Please don't give up."

I grabbed my Bible and began reading encouraging scriptures to him. "We are more than conquerors through him who loved us," I quoted from Romans 8:37, and from Philippians 4:13: "I can do all this through him who gives me strength."

I read from 1 Peter 2:24: "He himself bore our sins in his body on the cross, so that we might die to sins and live for righteousness; by his wounds you have been healed." Finally, I turned to the Old Testament and read from Psalm 107: 20: "He sent out his word and healed them."

Even in our direst circumstances, God gave us the faith to hold out hope for Mitchell. We were looking beyond the circumstances and trusting in God to inspire us and to help us find good amid all of this.

As the days and weeks passed, we slowly began to see improvements. It was a slow process. Actually, we could not see the change as much as others did when they visited. They told us how much better he looked from the day we brought him home from the hospital. This encouraged us, and we believe that we must be on the right track, and that we needed to keep doing what we are doing.

My sister Cheryl and my aunt Sharon, who both lived in Arizona, called to let me know they wanted to see Mitchell and us. Sharon had a strong walk with the Lord and had worked as a missionary for years. She was a prophetic woman.

"I have heard from the Lord that it is time for me to come over to see Mitchell and you all," she told me over the phone. "I'm not sure what will come of this visit; I only know God told me to come."

I was thrilled that they were making the trip, and I knew Mitchell would be too.

When they arrived, I felt such relief to see family, as we had been isolated for so long. We all hugged and chatted, then gathered around Mitchell's bed.

"I am speaking to your spirit, Mitchell," Sharon said in a tender voice. "I am calling your spirit forward to listen. "God hears your cries, and he sees your pain and suffering, and he will heal you. I am calling your spirit back into your body, as you want to leave it."

The Holy Spirit was speaking through her to him. I was amazed at what she was saying to our son, as I never told her that he would motion to the heavens as though he wanted to be with the Lord.

"It is not time yet," she continued.

I could tell by his body language that Mitchell was listening and comprehending, spirit to spirit. When she prayed with him and left the room, his body and facial expressions were relaxed. I could tell his spirit was at peace.

Brad and I were so happy they came. The timing was spot on—of course it was! This was all in God's perfect timing and will.

The osteopath and nutritionist had placed Mitchell on a detox to rid his body of all the medications and the heavy metal toxicity. It would also help with a viral infection he believed Mitchell had, which affected the central nervous system. As part of the detox therapy, we purchased an infrared sauna. Brad always carried him in and sat with him as the heat from the infrared lights drew out toxins. Mitchell also began chelation therapy, which also helped to remove the heavy metals from his system. He had hyperbaric oxygen treatments, which a friend of the family insisted on paying for. We continued with these therapies, hopeful that they would help his body heal.

As the weeks went by, we noticed Mitchell stopped grabbing his head as much. His tremors and seizures stopped, and he spent more time awake. We rejoiced in these glimmers of hope.

All of this happened at the same time as he hit puberty! He was growing from adolescence to being a young man. He was getting taller by the minute. But because he lost so much muscle mass, and what muscle he had atrophied, he still could not stand up or walk. We purchased a standing frame to help him feel what it was like again to put weight on his legs and feet. He could only tolerate it a few minutes at a time and could eventually stay in it thirty minutes a day. One day, he indicated that he wanted to slide out of his bed to the floor. We helped him down to see what he would do next. He began to scoot, using his upper body strength. He stopped when he got to his dog, Joshua, where he lay next to him, cuddling.

Brad and I looked at each other in amazement. This was real progress!

Mitchell still kept his eyes closed, although it appeared he could still lift that one eyelid halfway. And he still could not speak. I failed to understand what had caused that—and again, as with everything else, no one could tell us why.

"We just need to get all those metals out of his body," I told Brad one night. "If that happens, then all his bodily functions will start to heal."

Not long after Sharon returned home, we received a beautiful letter from her:

Dear Brad and Beth,

It has been such a privilege to be with you the past few days and to see your commitment and hard work. I'm aware that you are at the "end," and in your "releasing," God has been "panting" for your surrender. That [may make you believe] that somehow God could have interrupted your suffering but instead waited for your surrender. That is not the truth. One of my main gifts in the Lord is to direct members of the body of Christ to their purpose and help them (either by prayer or direct ministry or both) to take their position "on the wall," so to speak. Each of our positions on the wall is to defend some aspect of life here on earth and take it away from the enemy—whether it be in sports, education, health care, car mechanics, etc. I believe God has given me insight into some of the unanswered questions of our suffering.

Every one of us comes into this world with an anointing to "take the land" in some area . . . to destroy the works of the devil. Our purpose is the same as Jesus' purpose when he came . . . to destroy the works of the devil.

The enemy is aware of the anointing on each life and works to destroy that purpose that threatens his kingdom. He has authority over any area that is not "surrendered," because we are still working from a point of our own natural strength. God cannot take that authority away from the enemy until we lay down our right to stand in that "self" strength (surrender). We do not even realize the natural strength that we have within us.

We cry out to God that we "can't take any more" or "I give this to you"—but until it actually is that you literally *cannot* do anymore, God's hands are tied to deliver. Of course, it isn't that God doesn't have you encompassed in himself during this time, but the breakthrough comes with surrender.

I don't like using Job from the Bible because it is used so often. However, you can tell from the story that his purpose is to love God no matter what. He was greatly blessed before the enemy came after his "anointing." When he came after it, God told him that he could not kill Job, but he thrashed him terribly. However, after Job learned to lay down everything in his own strength, he fulfilled his purpose and was blessed greater than ever.

Job's life was an extreme case. You are living an extreme case. The enemy is after your family's anointing, not just Mitchell's. They are connected. What is happening has nothing to do with God's hand. He is and has been sending all kinds of warriors to aid you in your journey to surrender. I believe [the day I was with you] was a big turning point in your journey. God's presence was everywhere with us. God is orchestrating great change all around us. You are entering into a new season. I want to call you to "come up." Search within and you will find that you are being strengthened.

It has come from many sides over the years that Mitchell has something "big" to do in this world. My dear friend, Angela (which means messenger of truth), who is a prophet, came forth with this prophecy when we were praying for Mitchell. She declared with great strength, "Mitchell is not to leave this earth. He has a *giant* (not a word I hear her use) purpose. We must stand for him to establish his purpose here on earth. He will have great influence on many people, including adults and children and even animals." (She commented that she didn't know what animals had to do with anything, but the Spirit wanted her to include that.) She did not get any of that from me. I have only spoken of his condition.

I had received from the Lord the same strong urging the night before. A few nights later the Lord woke me in the night and told me to go to Mitchell. I would have come whether Cheryl had been coming or not. The Lord told me to go and *influence* the atmosphere (the atmosphere of the heavenlies around you where the enemy reigns) and fight for Mitchell and your family. . . . For ten days I have been screaming around my house, "Mitchell Thorp, you may not leave. God has a purpose for you in this earth realm, and you may not make that decision to go." An attitude of praise and thanksgiving, no matter what, is what takes you to God's gate and opens his strength to you. You are not thanking God for the awful things that are happening to Mitchell and your family. You are thanking God for being God and for loving you and saving your family's soul, etc. Whatever you can find to be thankful for opens you up to receive from God.

Whenever you are in strife and disagreement, God cannot work. Love is what never fails, but all else will. During these times of intense stress, the enemy loves to turn us one against the other. If he succeeds, God is once again pushed to the outside. Even in your intense fatigue, victory is in laying your life down for the other. God will strengthen you when you do not consider yourself "entitled" but, instead, serve the other. I know these are things that you know, but being reminded in the middle of distress may bring clarity to some situations.

Once again, I am honored to serve you in any way I can. I will continue to *war* for you as will all my other warriors. Victory is on the horizon. Look for the light there. It may seem very little, but it will grow bigger as you love and praise and continue to surrender.

I love you all so,

Your Sister in Christ,

Sharon

I wiped the tears from my eyes as I read the letter to Brad. Her prophetic words over the whole situation deeply touched us. In the middle of a battle and under attack, we'd found it difficult sometimes to see the whole picture. Her letter encouraged us to keep laying it all down at the foot of the cross each day, releasing any anxiety about always winning or being in control. As I held Brad's hand, I looked him in the eyes. "Let's pray that God's divine love continues to enfold us and strengthen us," I told him. I meant every word.

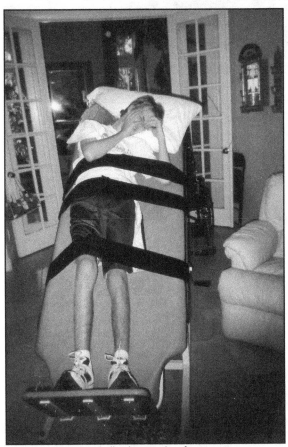

Mitchell in his standing frame.

Mitchell scooting over to lie with his dog, Joshua.

Part 4
A Glimmer of Light

Chapter 12

The Community Shows Up for Mitchell

The path that lay before us was veiled in uncertainty, and the only thing we could do was cling to God, trusting him to guide us through Mitchell's journey. I often found comfort in Isaiah 41:13, "I am the LORD your God who takes hold of your right hand and says to you, Do not fear; I will help you."

I thought of it like being a child in a crowded city. The child feels lost and confused with so much sensory overload that he or she becomes lost and confused, until the adult takes the child's hand and guides that one to safety. I found that taking God's hand was like this, too. Even though we did not know the way we should go next, we knew the One who is the way, and we trusted Him to direct our steps.

One day, out of the blue, our friends Terri Healy and Tom Watson visited us. As I opened the door, I was so surprised and happy! I hadn't been able to socialize anymore and seeing friendly faces felt wonderful.

After hugs and greetings, we settled in the living room. "So, what brings the two of you by?" I said.

"Tom and I were talking last week," Terri said. "We want to help your family. We can get the community involved in a walkathon to help raise funds for you, to help pay off the insurmountable medical bills you have. What do you think?"

Brad and I looked at each other stunned.

"This would be a miracle!" I said.

We were both in awe and humbled that they would do something like this for us.

"How and when were you thinking of doing this?" Brad asked.

"Tom and I have begun discussing the who, what, where, and when questions, and we are putting a plan into place," Terri said. "Tom is excellent at organizing all these details into a spreadsheet and timeline. We were thinking to have the walkathon on Saturday, May 6. Would that work with your schedule?"

May 6 was only four months away.

"Yes, we will make it work!" Brad said.

My mind began to race. I appreciated the offer, but I hesitated to ask for help and money—and to open up our personal lives to so many people. "I have no idea how we'll pull this off! Where will we have it? Who would even show up, much less contribute?"

Terri smiled kindly. "Beth, people *want* to help, but they don't know how. This will give them an opportunity to give back. I don't want you or Brad to worry about a thing. This is where faith steps in. Faith is knowing it can be done, an inner conviction, the profound knowing that comes before reality confirms it."

"You are my faithful friend indeed," I told her, as a sense of relief poured from the heavens upon us.

They went right to work. She told us we just needed to show up the day of the event. They began planning in earnest, creating flyers and posters, organizing volunteers, reaching out to the city for park approval, writing a press release, and submitting it to all the local newspapers to bring awareness to the event and to Mitchell's condition. The press release even gained the attention of a community news writer who put together the following piece:

> "Walkathon to Help Ailing Teen Ballplayer"
>
> by Linda McIntosh—Community News Writer
>
> Baseball always meant a lot to Mitchell Thorp. He started playing T-ball when he was five years old and soon became an all-star baseball player traveling with his

team across the country. His father, Brad Thorp, was a minor league pitcher for the Los Angeles Dodgers in the early 1980s and coached Mitchell's team and his brother for years. But Mitchell, 15, was struck by a mysterious illness two years ago and had to stop playing ball.

He cannot walk, talk, or see and has been fighting intense pain. Since 2004, Mitchell has been to doctors around the country to try to find out what's wrong. Now, Mitchell's teammates are rallying the community to stand behind him. The Carlsbad Youth Baseball league is hosting a walkathon to raise money to help the Thorp family with doctors' bills that have run into six figures.

The three-mile fundraiser walk around Poinsettia Park will be May 6. Hopes are that at least 1,000 walkers will step up to the plate and together help raise $100,000 to pay off their last medical bill, and that is with good insurance. Tom Watson, the event organizer, along with Terri Healy, said, "We want to alleviate some of the financial burden, but we also want to bring attention to Mitchell's condition in hopes that new information might turn up that would shed light on a cure." . . .

"I knew him before all this, and he had the sweetest spirit. He's a fighter," said Kim Schuette, a nutritionist who has been working with Mitchell's formula that she created special for him. Now, Mitchell can somewhat open his eyes and scoot on the floor to get around. He cannot speak yet, but understands what people say. "It's the progress we're holding onto," Schuette said.

The day of the event finally came—May 6, 2006. We arrived at the park with Mitchell. I wasn't sure anybody would show up! But then when we arrived and saw the crowd, I became anxious. My spirit was picking up that Mitchell was feeling the same.

"Mitchell, many people love you and came out to support you and the family," I told him. "Mrs. Healy and Mr. Watson organized this event especially for you. Mom and Dad need for you to be strong and courageous as we get you out of the car and to the staging area. If it becomes too much for you, Dad will take you home, okay?"

Brad lifted Mitchell out of the back seat and into his wheelchair. We wheeled him through the crowd. Everybody began to clap for him. I began to cry and noticed that Brad and Matthew were also trying to hold back their tears.

We were amazed that more than eight hundred people showed up. We were so moved that people cared that much about our family and Mitchell. Tears kept flowing down my face.

After we got to the staging area, two of Mitchell's former classmates from Aviara Oaks elementary and middle school greeted the crowd. They both gave an emotional tribute to Mitchell. Mitchell's nutritionist, Kim Schuette, followed and gave an update on Mitchell's medical condition and treatments.

While this was going on, I could tell Mitchell was struggling. This was the first time he'd been out of our house in months. I worried that it may be too much for him to handle. I could tell he was trying to hang on, but I couldn't blame him for his discomfort. He was a trooper to stick it out as long as he could.

We knew we would need to take him home soon, as the loud music would be overwhelming for him with a heightened sensory system.

"When the walk kicks off, tap your leg with your fingers so I know that means yes to take you home, okay?" I told him.

We watched as the local high school lancer dance team performed several sets. The color guard came out, and we all stood in silence when a student sang the national anthem. The city council, attending on behalf of the mayor's office, congratulated the crowd for their attendance and support of our family, which exemplified the great and giving spirit of our community. At the end of the address, someone blared a horn, and the walk officially began.

I noticed that Mitchell was getting more agitated. "Please take Mitchell home with Aunt Cheryl," I told Brad. She had agreed to stay with him until we returned.

So Brad took them both home and returned to the park long before all the walkers finished.

Each participant received a T-shirt and a ball cap with Joshua 1:9 imprinted on the inside of the bill. I felt overwhelmed to see this sea of participants all wearing items in support of our family.

The walking route went throughout Poinsettia Park, with four round-trip loops creating the three-mile course. At the end of the walk, several grand prizes were awarded to the individuals and teams. Then, event co-chairman Tom Watson thanked the committee members for planning and carrying out the walkathon.

Brad and I addressed the crowd, thanking the community for the tremendous support and giving hearts—many of whom we never knew, who just read about our story and wanted to help. Both of us were so humbled by their generosity, we teared up as we spoke.

I wanted to leave the crowd with an understanding of our faith and what kept us persevering and fighting. "I do not know where you all are in your faith walk and relationship with God, some of you may not even know him. Regardless of where you are at this moment, know that you are not alone and that you can only walk this walk with faith and hope that the Lord is with you and me and Mitchell. The Lord knows what we all are going through, and he will see us through. If you all can remove your caps and look under the bill, I will read the Bible verse we've written there so you can take it with you and memorize for when you need it."

I began to read out loud. "Joshua 1:9 has been our Bible verse through our journey. It says, 'Have I not commanded you? Be strong and courageous. Do not be afraid; do not be discouraged, for the LORD your God will be with you wherever you go.'" I looked out at the crowd. "A simple but a very powerful command. Hang on to this verse when life gets tough and throws you a curve ball. It will give you strength and courage in whatever you are experiencing and walking through."

As I stepped away from the microphone, the audience began to clap and cheer. I looked out again at the faces and could tell the words had touched them. I knew God was pleased.

The community raised seventy thousand dollars to help us work towards paying off our $100,000 hospital and medical bills. How and why were we so blessed? Our close friends and the hand of God were with us every step of the way. We were putting our faith into action. This day forever changed us, and we knew someday we wanted to be able to pay it forward.

One of many volunteers helping that day

Terri and Kim Healy, the event's organizers

Tom Watson event organizer for Mitchell's walkathon.
Photo courtesy of Kristina Chartier Photography.

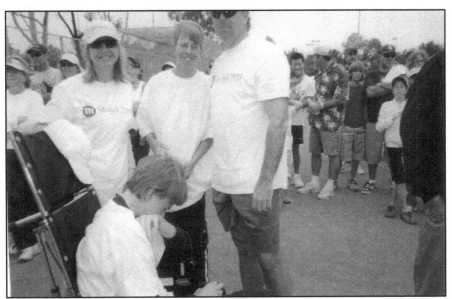

Surrounded by a crowd as we walked into the park.

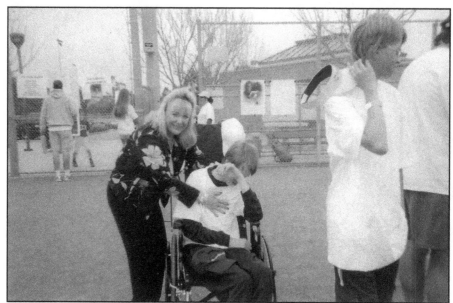

My sister Cheryl comforting Mitchell.

Chapter 13

Receiving Celebrity Attention

"Hello, my friend! I have some good news for you," our friend Gustavo said in an unexpected phone call about three weeks after the walkathon. Gustavo was the chief marketing and communications officer at Pomerado Health and Medical Center. "Dikembe Mutombo is in town. He is a famous NBA basketball player. He came to visit our hospital to learn about what it will take to build a hospital in his homeland of Congo."

"Okay," I said, wondering why I was given this information.

"I happened to talk with him about Mitchell and your family. He wants to help. He has a huge heart and is very philanthropic."

My jaw dropped.

"Hello? Are you still there?"

"Yes! I'm just in a bit of shock," I said and laughed. "This is wonderful news!"

"He would like to meet Mitchell and your family. Is tomorrow okay? He will be flying back home after that."

"That would be perfect."

We settled on his coming at 1:00 p.m.

"Oh, I almost forgot," Gustavo said. "A sportswriter from the *Union Tribune* will be coming, too. Is that okay?"

I assured him that it was and thanked him for all he had done for us. Then I hung up the phone and ran upstairs to tell everyone.

Another God moment and blessing! God helped orchestrate this through our friend and Dikembe.

"Brad, you'll never believe what is happening tomorrow! A celebrity NBA basketball player named Dikembe Mutombo is coming to our home to meet us and to visit with Mitchell."

Because Dikembe had never played on our local teams. We didn't know much about him, except that he was a famous NBA basketball star. That was enough to excite us!

We jumped on the internet and began to research about him before we told Mitchell. We learned that Dikembe Mutombo was born June 25, 1966.

He shares the same birthday as me, I thought. *We must be kindred spirits.*

He had played eighteen seasons in the NBA, playing for the Denver Nuggets, Atlanta Hawks, Philadelphia 76ers, New Jersey Nets, New York Knicks, and Houston Rockets. He was commonly regarded as one of the greatest shot blockers and defensive players of all time, winning the NBA Defensive Player of the Year award four times, as well as being an eight-time All-Star. Outside basketball, he has become well known for his humanitarian work.

"Oh, my goodness," I said out loud as I kept reading. "He is seven feet, two inches tall and wears a size 22 shoe!"

Brad, Matthew, and I went into Mitchell's bedroom to share the exciting news. I read everything about Dikembe to Mitchell. He seemed excited and impressed.

The next day, May 21, 2006, Dikembe appeared right on time, accompanied by Gustavo and a community sports writer named Gigi Alford.

"So great to meet you," Brad told Dikembe, extending his hand in greeting. "And thank you for coming to meet us and our son Mitchell. I know it will mean a lot to him."

Dikembe smiled warmly and shook Brad's hand. Then he turned his attention to me. "This must be the mom I heard much about."

"I hope all good!" I said, and we laughed.

"Of course," he said, shaking my hand. I was amazed by how large his hand was. It swallowed mine.

After we made all the introductions, Brad escorted Dikembe to the living room where Mitchell was seated in his wheelchair, with Matthew close by.

"Does he understand what we say?" Dikembe asked Brad.

"He does. He just cannot speak or walk, and his vision is distorted."

Dikembe bent down to look Mitchell in the eyes. "Hello, Mitchell, I'm Dikembe Mutombo. I play basketball with the Houston Rockets. I'm here to help you and your family. I know your struggle has been hard and probably discouraging but I want you to keep on fighting and not give up."

Dikembe looked at our other son. "What is your name?"

"Matthew."

Matthew was awestruck.

"I brought both you boys an autographed basketball."

"Wow! Thank you," Matthew said. "I know my brother is happy, too. We will put it in his room where we can display it with his trophies."

After spending some time talking with the boys, Dikembe sat next to me on the couch and looked at me. "I'm surprised to see a smile on your face since being confronted with so much adversity."

I looked into his eyes. "You know where that strength comes from?"

Dikembe nodded. "I know your family has very strong beliefs,"

"This journey has been long, and it is hard, and you cannot walk this walk without faith in God. I rely upon this inexhaustible spiritual strength by plugging into the Man upstairs. When I carry a heavy load, my muscles can tire and my bones grow weary, but my spiritual strength is unlike my physical strength. Spiritual strength is limitless. When I'm tempted to give up, I tap into this strength to stay the course and maintain my endurance. Jesus taught this, that one who does not have faith in God will be easily knocked down, like a house built upon sand. Someone with strong faith is like a house built upon a strong foundation of rock, able to withstand whatever comes its way."[4]

Dikembe listened closely and nodded thoughtfully.

"Well, enough of me!" I said, knowing he hadn't come to hear a sermon. "Since we are exchanging gifts, we have a gift for you."

He looked surprised. I handed him a gift bag. He pulled out one of Mitchell's baseball caps with Mitchell's favorite Bible verse inscribed under the bill. He began to read it out loud. "Joshua 1:9: 'Have I not commanded you? Be strong and courageous. Do not be terrified; do not be discouraged, for the LORD your God will be with you wherever you go.'" He nodded. "Powerful." Then he placed the cap on his head.

"Let's take Mitchell and Dikembe out to the boys' basketball court," Brad said. "I know they both would love to see you dunk a ball."

"Yeah!" Matthew said. We all felt excited.

"Well, all right then, let's go," Dikembe said, his face lighting up.

We all walked to the basketball court toward the back of the house. It was a beautiful sunny day. I wheeled Mitchell out and parked him on the side of the court.

Brad handed Dikembe one of the autographed balls.

Dikembe dribbled a bit and began to shoot free throw shots. We cheered him on with each shot. After a while, with great flare, he dribbled the ball around the court, then dunked it.

We all shouted and clapped.

"I was so inspired by your son and your story," he told Brad and me, after he handed the basketball back to Matthew. "I could not help but respond."

He pulled out a check from his pocket and handed it to me. "I want to donate this check to you all, to help with Mitchell's medical costs, as I heard they are quite high.

"That's so generous," I said. "Thank you from the bottom of our hearts. This will help a lot. May God bless you a hundred-fold for your giving." I threw my arms around him in a big hug.

Our time with him went by so quickly, and before we knew it, he needed to leave for the airport. We escorted them all to the door and said our goodbyes.

As we closed the door, Brad and I looked at each other in amazement. "This is another gift from God," I said. "We could not have orchestrated this if we'd tried."

We were so humbled by this man's kind gesture to give to a family and child he did not know. We felt a little guilty accepting the money, especially because I knew people in his homeland were suffering too.

What a role model he is, I thought.

Our family gathered together to talk about what a special day it had been.

"What was the one thing that stood out to you?" I asked everyone.

"How tall he was!" Matthew said.

"Brad, what about you?"

"I would have to say that he is a gentle giant and kindhearted."

"Mitchell, what did you notice?" Since I knew he couldn't answer, I gave him some answers. "I saw you looking down at his feet. Were you amazed that anyone could wear a shoe that big?"

We laughed.

"For me, I would say it was a soul connection that I could speak into Dikembe's spirit, and he could speak into mine," I said. "This was another unexpected blessing God gave to all of us. God created this divine appointment that we should all meet."

The next day, we read the article that Gigi wrote, titled: "NBA's Mutombo Joins Fight in Carlsbad Teenager's Battle to Overcome Mysterious Illness." We were curious to know what she observed and how she reported the story. She started the piece:

Only a mother could understand what her son, unable to speak or communicate his thoughts was thinking at the time. As NBA star Dikembe Mutombo leaned toward Mitchell Thorp, his mom knew her boy was doing his best to focus his dizzy and spinning vision on Mutombo's size 22 shoes. "I knew he was looking at (Mutombo's) feet," Beth Thorp said. "I had to say that to get a rise out of him."

Then she went on to describe the visit, as well as what was wrong with Mitchell. She finished the article by saying:

> Named one of the most generous athletes in a Foxsports.com article earlier this year, Mutombo lived up to his reputation, donating $5,000. . . . "It's a blessing people can help us," Beth said. "We're able to stay where we are and focus on the healing rather than the stress over the finances. Otherwise, we'd be selling the house." . . .
>
> One friend who shared the moment with the Thorps told Mitchell's father, Brad, who played minor league baseball in the Dodgers organization, that Mitchell may decide to play basketball instead of baseball once he's recovered.[5]

I smiled as I finished reading and reflected on the previous day's events. I believe we are all part of this big universe as we connect one soul to another. The ripple effect phenomenon where there is a constant flow of giving and receiving is at work in our universe. So, whenever we make the decision to give, we are also getting something in return—love and joy.

I realized that even the air we breathe illustrates the law of circulation at work. Plants release oxygen we must have to live, and as we exhale, we transform it into the carbon dioxide they need to thrive. Without the exchange of giving and receiving, neither can survive.

I was amazed by how God had shown up for us yet again in such an unexpected way. He knew our journey had been long and difficult, and he knew our financial struggles as we had spent everything on Mitchell's care. I felt grateful both to Dikembe and to God. Having a lot of money like Mutombo does not mean much unless he could do something good with it to bless others. He had—and I knew he was going to be blessed in return.

This was another sign that we had received, and one day we wanted to have an opportunity to give back. As the apostle Paul encourages us in 2 Corinthians 9:6–8:

> Remember this: Whoever sows sparingly will also reap sparingly, and whoever sows generously will also reap generously. Each of you should give what you have

decided in your heart to give, not reluctantly or under compulsion, for God loves a cheerful giver. And God is able to bless you abundantly, so that in all things at all times, having all that you need, you will abound in every good work.

We looked forward to the day when we could begin to repay the blessings we'd received, knowing that our generosity would fill our hearts as we, in turn, can bless others. We appreciated how others had opened their hearts wide to the dynamic flow of life, generously giving what they had to share of their time, talents, and treasures. As a result of their giving generously, not only did we receive abundantly, but they also did too. Even more than financially, the gifts of joy, love, and peace were ours. Even though we still struggled with Mitchell's condition, God was filling our spirits with his love and care.

NBA basketball player Dikembe Mutombo visiting Mitchell and our family.

Brad and I enjoying a laugh together with NBA basketball player Dikembe Mutombo.

Chapter 14

A Divine Appointment

Months had gone by since Mitchell's walkathon and Dikembe's visit. It was now September 12, 2006—Mitchell's sixteenth birthday. We were happy to see that he continued to make small improvements but felt disappointed that he was still not well.

When family or friends came to visit, they always commented that he looked better from the previous time they had seen him. Brad and I were both pleased to hear their observations, as we were doing everything within our power to get him the help he needed.

Each time we tried something new in his treatment, we played the wait-and-see game. We felt good that all of our hard work after leaving the hospital was paying off, but still not seeing him back to normal was heart wrenching.

Mitchell hit another growth spurt. While he was in his standing frame, Brad took a tape measure and stretched it out to see how Mitchell was growing. He now measured six feet two inches tall.

Though we were pleased to see he was still growing at a healthy rate, we realized that with each growth spurt, it was getting harder for us to move and carry him. Fortunately, Brad was big and strong to lift him. Brad would simply put him over his right shoulder and carry him up and down the stairs to bed and basically everywhere we needed to take him. I was grateful that Brad did all the heavy lifting; I could not have done that on my own.

We celebrated Mitchell's birthday at home with his cousin Kelly and her two children, Andrew and Rebecca. Andrew adored Mitchell. He looked up to him as a big brother—they both were old souls and kindred spirits, even though they were both so young. I wasn't sure how much the children knew about Mitchell's condition, except that he was not well.

We all sang "Happy Birthday" to him. Mitchell buried his head in his hand, to squint through his fingers. He was trying to open his eyes to see the cake and candles burning before him. The light was too bright, and so his brother comforted him when he noticed Mitchell struggling. Mitchell had always protected his brother; now the roles were reversed. Matthew's kind heart wanted to reassure Mitchell that he would be there for him and help him.

"Let's see what goodies we have for you," I said, drawing his attention to the presents.

Matthew picked up each present and opened it for Mitchell—a signed and framed Tiger Woods golf photo, some autographed baseballs and photos, and clothes.

I would have loved to have thrown a big bash for Mitchell. Sixteen years old! The year he should be getting his driver's license and starting to date. So much excitement should have been ahead of him. But because of his sensitivities and exhaustion level, a big celebration was out of the question. Though we celebrated with our family, I ached that our son was in this shape—with no cure yet.

By December, Mitchell's progress was still slow and steady. The doctor ordered glutathione injections, saying he was low in it.

"What is that?" I asked.

"Glutathione is critical for immune function and controlling inflammation," he explained. "It is the master detoxifier and the body's main antioxidant, protecting our cells and making our energy metabolism run well. Plus, it improves quality of sleep and combats stress from sleep apnea."

Later, that day Brad commented, "After all the hospital stays, why was there not one doctor who knew this or could recognize that these injections could possibly help?"

It definitely made us wonder.

We agreed to the injections, but as Christmas was approaching, we decided to stop this treatment for a few weeks to give him a break—Mitchell always hated needles and turned white as a ghost. So refraining from the shots was like a little Christmas present, though he knew he'd need to receive them again soon.

He also continued to respond well to the hyperbaric oxygen treatments, which he received at least twice a week. It seemed to help alleviate the awful headaches. As when I asked him to tap his fingers if it was helping, he did. However, this did not cure him after sixty sessions of treatment.

During this month, he also had a series of blood panels taken, along with some other tests. Once again, we found ourselves awaiting the results, hoping these tests would reveal another piece to this mysterious puzzle and give us direction.

Even with the progress, he still suffered from some paralysis, still could not speak, and his vision was still disturbed from the dizziness, muscle weakness, and atrophy. And he continued to suffer from ataxia, along with some pressure in his head.

Our medical support team proved to be great, but with each new step, we were reminded that Mitchell's healing was complex and multilayered. Too often it was more of a do-it-yourself guessing game, with a daily and some-times hourly focus on what was causing the symptoms and how could we best address them.

While our son had very good non-mainstream doctors on board to help him heal, the constant shifts in his health required Brad and me to continue to be Mitchell's own doctors, therapists, researchers, and diagnosticians. Here we were, several years later, and we were still searching and filing away new ideas of possible causes as Mitchell's symptoms waxed and waned.

Over time we got really good at reading his nonverbal body language. Spending so much time with him, I felt as though God had miraculously linked our spirits together so I could understand what Mitchell was trying to communicate. I could feel deep within my soul what he must be feeling. I knew in my spirit that he wished he could be back to his normal self. I knew he must have wondered, *Why is this happening to me?*

I knew I needed to cling to hope and give him the hope that he would make a full recovery.

The year had been long and difficult, as so many of the others had been since we'd started on this unwelcomed journey. I needed an escape. I knew Mitchell needed that too. He needed to get outside in the fresh air and sunshine where he wasn't lying cooped up on his bed in his bedroom. So, when Brad got home from work, I met him in the driveway with my arms filled with snacks, a blanket, and plenty of sunscreen.

It was time to go for one of our favorite outings. We loaded Mitchell in the back seat of the car, packed his wheelchair, and piled in. We headed for a walk along the boardwalk at the beach.

It felt wonderful to hear the waves crashing against the shore and know that God's power was a greater force than anything in the world—including Mitchell's illness.

As we pushed him in his wheelchair, I saw people's expressions as we passed. I wasn't sure what they were thinking or if they simply had pity in their eyes for us. I quickly shrugged it away, as I was more concerned about my son's enjoyment.

We came to our spot. I locked the wheelchair in place, and then we sat and looked out over the ocean. Feeling the gentle breeze against our skin and the warmth of the sun, listening to the ocean waves crash to the shoreline, smelling the salt water in the air. It was healing for him, and for me, too.

I looked over at him. *What is he thinking?* I wondered. I couldn't imagine being trapped in a body that once was so healthy to now being confined to a wheelchair and needing everyone's care to keep him alive. My heart ached for him.

On the way home, I stopped at another favorite place of ours—what we called our lookout point. It sat high on a cliff above the shoreline. From this vantage point we loved to watch the spectacular sunsets. The look-out point was a great area where people flew their remote airplanes, taking flight off the cliff.

Mitchell had always enjoyed watching the planes fly around. Before his illness, Brad and I had purchased a remote-control airplane for him to fly, but he never had a chance to use it. The plane sat in his room on his shelf.

We arrived at lookout point and parked, rolling down our windows to listen to the waves crashing below the cliff and to watch the planes fly. After a few moments, a man walked by carrying a plane.

He glanced into our car and spotted Mitchell, who had his head leaning against the car door with his window open. Then he looked at me and smiled.

"Nice airplane you have there," I told him. "My son likes airplanes. I bring him here often so he can see the planes being flown off the cliff."

The man listened thoughtfully. "Is it okay with you if I show him my plane and the controls?"

"Absolutely!" I got out of the car and opened the door so Mitchell could see the plane, as the man explained how it operated and then showed him the controls.

We watched him take his plane and lift it off the cliff and into the air.

"Wow, that's so cool, isn't it?" I told Mitchell, and then thanked the man for being so kind.

I knew my son had a deep desire to fly planes. "You will fly a plane one day," I told him.

It was just the perfect break we needed—including the divine appointment God orchestrated. "Thank you, God," I whispered on the way home.

That man wasn't just there to fly his plane. God had placed him there, at just that time, to remind us that even in the midst of the hardest days, he still surprises us with his love and comfort. He gives us strength when we need it.

Mitchell's 16th birthday with his cousins Andrew and Rebecca.

Mitchell celebrating his 16th birthday with his brother, Matthew.

Lookout point where we watched sunsets and listened to the ocean waves.

Chapter 15

Racing Against Time and Testing Our Faith

Another year passed without any real progress. We had now traveled a five-year journey to find a cure for our son, and we knew we were racing against time. I felt as if our son was like sand slipping through our fingers. Without question, this process had been expensive and draining. It became wearying to continually throw all kinds of treatments against the wall, essentially, to see what may or may not stick. We faced constant roadblocks. It was like taking one foot forward, two steps back. We felt as though we'd been pushing a boulder up a mountain, the weight of it taking its toll on him and us.

Without a doubt, we knew we would keep on fighting and hoping for answers and a diagnosis. But still, we felt mainstream medicine had let us down. We knew Mitchell wasn't the first person who had ever gone undiagnosed or misdiagnosed. But we'd hoped that the doctors would have persevered to get to the root.

In the midst of all that, we still worried about Matthew, and did our best to make sure he didn't get lost in his big brother's shadow. And our marriage, though not on the rocks, was definitely treading water. It simply had to take a backseat—we didn't have energy to give to each other as much as we both needed. But fortunately, we were committed to each other. And God somehow continued to give us just the strength we needed to get through each day.

In February 2008, Mitchell took a turn for the worse. He got sick with the flu. Because his immune system was out of whack, he struggled to get over the virus. Over the next couple months, he struggled to keep any food in his system. After three emergency room visits and still no answers on why he couldn't keep his food down, one gastroenterologist gave him a gastroparesis diagnosis, which means the stomach shuts down and becomes unable to process food.

So on April 28, Mitchell had a surgical procedure to take his G-tube and make it a J-tube, which fed directly into his small intestine. Though this procedure was life-saving, and he was able to come home with us after a few days, we began to despair that Mitchell was in serious trouble. We knew having a J-tube was not a good sign for him to keep thriving.

On May 3, Mitchell suffered his first seizure in a long time, and we admitted him back to the hospital. By this point, he was now down to eighty-four pounds.

The medical staff worked hard to help his body control his seizure activity, and we were grateful to see him slowly come around. But then he started suffering from sleep apnea, which occurs when the brain doesn't send proper signals to the muscles that control breathing. This was so alarming, it threw the medical staff into overdrive. They moved Mitchell to ICU, where he remained for two weeks.

We continued to encourage him to fight, and I knew he was trying, but his central nervous system was starting to affect more and more areas of his body.

Mitchell stayed in the hospital for four weeks while the doctors continued to try and to figure out what was going on with him. They ran many of the same tests from the previous hospital stay and were genuinely stumped that all the tests kept coming back negative, normal.

How could they explain the unexplainable?

On May 30, Mitchell was discharged from the hospital. He was able to put ten pounds back on and could now sleep again throughout the nights. The days, though, held understandable anxiety and frustration for him.

We returned to the idea that he might be suffering from a TMJ problem, something we'd put on the shelf for a while due to all his hospital stays. We knew from his last x-rays that his discs were displaced from a previous injury, and they needed to be corrected at some point, though we still did not know if this was part of his pain.

In June, we heard about a doctor who was in town for a conference and had heard about Mitchell's case through our osteopath. Dr. Ochs developed the LENS, Low Energy Neurofeedback System, a specialized type of brain mapping. LENS is basically a functional EEG to see how the brain is operating and what parts are affected. We learned that he was interested in taking Mitchell under his wing as a case study.

Could this be the cure we've been hoping for? we wondered.

Dr. Ochs wanted Mitchell to undergo LENS therapy. He explained to us what LENS therapy did. "We believe that the LENS appears to positively impact slow brainwave activity. It also works to break up the rigid, self-protective way the brain has of responding after physical or psychological stress or trauma," he said. "During any kind of trauma—physical, infectious, toxic, or emotional—the brain protects itself from seizures and overloads by releasing neurochemicals. Unfortunately, this protective response also reduces the brain's overall functional capacity. Long after the trauma is over and the danger is past, the 'protection' may still remain. The person, therefore, becomes stuck in various kinds of disabilities due to this reduced neurological flexibility.

"The LENS appears to have an effect in helping to restore the brain's natural flexibility. The difficult part, as it relates to Mitchell's case, is that trying to treat him when he is still undiagnosed means there are no real guarantees of success."

We were used to hearing that disclaimer. But if this new therapy offered even the slightest chance of helping Mitchell improve, then we knew we had to take it.

Dr. Ochs said we would give Mitchell the therapy twice a day—once in the morning and once at night. Then he showed us how to use the LENS therapy unit. We could do the treatment from home, since advances on the internet and neurofeedback equipment now allowed clients to receive neurofeedback remotely from anywhere in the world. The devise had a few electrodes that we placed on different parts of Mitchell's head. We turned it on and let the system begin. The doctor promised no side effects, saying that the brain did all the work, and it would actually be calming for Mitchell.

Brad and I stayed hopeful.

"We've tried just about everything we know to do, and nothing has worked. Let's see if this does," Brad said.

"Be sure to record any differences you see," Dr. Ochs said.

We obediently followed Dr. Ochs's directions and prayed we'd see results.

Mitchell continued to fight the unknown, which amazed me—the strength and bravery this young man had. There were days, however, when I saw in his frail body and by the look of grief on his face that he wanted to give up. I wept and prayed in sorrow for him. I kept encouraging him, telling him we would not give up on him.

But why wasn't he getting better? Why was *nothing* working? And worst of all, why wasn't God stepping in to cure him—or to at least help us diagnose the problem?

I began to feel as if God had turned his back on us, that this was some kind of cruel way to test our faith to the highest degree. But I felt that way only at my weakest points. I knew the truth. When adversity hits, we humans tend to think we must have done something wrong, that God must be punishing us. This is a wrong ideology, because the Lord is a loving and kind Father, and our relationship with him transcends all our circumstances. So, when I began to think those wrong thoughts, I dug deep and continued praying.

One day I came across a story about butterflies that strengthened my soul. Mitchell and I loved butterflies, so I knew this would be a good story for him to hear as well. As I lay in bed beside him, I began to read.

Once a little boy was playing outdoors and found a fascinating caterpillar. He carefully picked it up and took it home to show his mother. He asked his mother if he could keep it, and she said he could if he would take good care of it.

The little boy got a large jar from his mother and put plants to eat, and a stick to climb on, in the jar. Every day he watched the caterpillar and brought it new plants to eat.

One day the caterpillar climbed up the stick and started acting strangely. The boy worriedly called his mother, who came and understood that the caterpillar was creating a cocoon. The mother explained to the boy how the caterpillar was going to go through a metamorphosis to become a butterfly.

The little boy was thrilled to hear about the changes his caterpillar would go through. He watched every day, waiting for the butterfly to emerge. One day a small hole appeared in the cocoon and the butterfly started to struggle to come out.

At first the boy was excited, but soon he became concerned. The butterfly was struggling so hard to get out! It looked like it couldn't break free. It looked desperate! It looked like it was making no progress.

The boy was so concerned he decided to help. He ran to get scissors, and then walked back (because he had learned not to run with scissors). He snipped the cocoon to make the hole bigger, and the butterfly quickly emerged!

As the butterfly came out, the boy was surprised. It had a swollen body and small, shriveled wings. He continued to watch the butterfly, expecting that, at any moment, the wings would dry out, enlarge, and expand to support the swollen body. He knew that in time the body would shrink and the butterfly's wings would expand. But neither happened. The butterfly spent the rest of its life crawling around with a swollen body and shriveled wings.

It never was able to fly, as the boy tried to figure out what had gone wrong. His mother took him to talk to a scientist from a local college. He learned that the butterfly was *supposed* to struggle. In fact, the butterfly's struggle to push its way through the tiny opening of the cocoon pushes the fluid out of its body and into its wings. Without the struggle, the butterfly would never ever fly. The boy's good intentions hurt the butterfly. Butterflies need adversity to become what God intended them to be. So do we.[6]

I held Mitchell in my arms as tears rolled down my face.

Not what we want, God, but what you want. I don't understand your plan, but I know I can trust you. Somehow you will redeem all this pain, I prayed. I knew, ultimately, God had the final say on what he had planned for Mitchell and for us. We had to keep surrendering it all to him.

Someone once told us that we are like Job in the Bible that bad things kept happening to us, one thing after the other. This was not what I wanted to hear! But this person's words motivated me to go back to the story and read more about him.

Job was a very wealthy and successful community leader and businessman with huge holdings of livestock and real estate. He was also a righteous and devoted follower of God. One day the angels presented themselves before the Lord, and Satan came with them.

The Lord said to Satan, "Where have you come from?"

Satan answered, "From roaming through the earth and going back and forth in it." In other words, Satan had been looking for someone he could devour. He'd been looking to stir up trouble, misery, and sin.

God said to Satan, "Have you considered my servant Job? There is no one on earth like him; he is blameless and upright, a man who fears God and shuns evil."

I stopped reading and considered that. God knew what Satan was up to and still he pointed Job out. I believe this happened because God knew Job's faithfulness and inner character.

Satan said, "Does Job fear God for nothing? Have you not put a hedge around him and his household and everything he has? You have blessed the work of his hands so that his flocks and herds are spread throughout the land. But stretch out your hand and strike everything he has, and he will surely curse you to your face."

And the Lord replied, "Very well, then, everything he has is in your hands, but do not lay a finger on the man himself."

And with that, Satan put poor Job through a trial of adversity. Job's herds were stolen, his servants were murdered, and *all* of Job's children were killed by a sudden tornado that struck the four corners of the house, collapsing it on his children. On hearing this news, Job tore his robe, shaved his head, and fell on his face before God. He told God, "Naked I came from my mother's womb, and naked I will depart. The LORD gave and the LORD has taken away; may the name of the LORD be praised" (Job 1:21).

Job underwent a kind of Joseph-calling experience, turning tragedy, hardship, and torment into God's glory in the end, which helped to serve and rescue so many. Through Job's trial of adversity, he grew in strength, perseverance, wisdom, and faith. His perspective of God was transformed by his suffering.

I sat back and thought about our circumstances. Had I fallen victim to believing that somehow as children of God, my family and I should be immune from trouble and tragedy? Had I assumed that we somehow had the inherent right to live long, easy lives and die peacefully in our sleep one day?

It was clear to me that this mystery of my son's illness was not a mystery to God. But for whatever purpose, he had chosen to let it remain a mystery to us. As the Bible says, "As the heavens are higher than the earth, so are my ways higher than your ways and my thoughts than your thoughts" (Isaiah 55:9). Such knowledge is higher than the heavens. And yet I could be assured of something else higher than the heavens: "For great is [God's] love, higher than the heavens; your faithfulness reaches to the skies" (Psalm 108:4). The Bible says that our "future is in [his] hands" (Psalm 31:15, NLT).

I may not understand or like what was happening to my son—to our family. But I could be assured that even in the mystery of it all, the Lord was continuing to walk with us, never leaving us alone, always being faithful. I just needed to remind myself of that once again.

Butterflies are deep and powerful representations of life. Not only are they beautiful, they also have mystery and symbolism. They are a metaphor representing spiritual rebirth, transformation, change, hope, and life.
Photo by Beth Thorp.

Chapter 16

Our Darkest Night

It had been ten long, grueling months since Mitchell had been released from the hospital in February 2008. All the progress we'd made before his hospital stay disappeared! He needed to put back on all the weight he had lost, and we continued with the same protocols as before, though it took months to get him back to where he had been. We continued with the LENS therapy. The brain mapping showed changes, so we knew something was working, but we did not see any physical difference in Mitchell's condition.

When we asked the doctor about it, he said he believed Mitchell's brain was tightly locked in this stance for survival. His brain thought it was doing the right thing and now couldn't get out of it. He suggested trying HE (high efficiency) protocols to see how Mitchell would respond.

We agreed, though both Brad and I felt extremely frustrated that we kept jumping from one protocol and treatment to the next with no real physical change to Mitchell's overall condition.

I began to have this gnawing sense that we needed to get his discs put back in place on each side of his jaw, as this was the one thing we had never pursued, since all his other health conditions and hospital stays kept pulling our focus in those directions.

We heard about a doctor in Dallas who specialized in this type of procedure and was willing to perform it on Mitchell. We had several phone consultations with him about Mitchell's condition and mailed him the most recent doctors' notes and blood work. He gave us some dates to consider for putting Mitchell on the schedule, however, he warned us that he would not attempt this procedure until Mitchell's blood counts were high enough and he was strong enough to go through surgery.

He told us that he had dealt with many difficult cases before and was confident that the disc issue could possibly be one of the reasons for Mitchell's head pain. Once again, our hopes raised; though this time, I felt more cautious.

"If we do this, then we have to get Mitchell down to Baylor Hospital in Texas, since that's the only place this doctor does surgery," I told Brad. "Is it worth what we'd have to put Mitchell through? We've done just about everything else we know to do."

"I know, honey," Brad said. "Mitchell *has* gotten stronger. He has put on more weight and his blood count is up, so maybe it's time to see if this will help him."

We agreed to move forward. We scheduled his surgery date and began thinking about how to get there. We couldn't travel by plane, because Mitchell needed to be able to respond to commands and walk on by himself from the wheelchair to his seat, which he could not do. We decided our best option was to rent an RV and drive him to Texas.

I began to talk to Mitchell about next steps to help him with his displaced discs. I explained to him that we had put off this procedure for far too long and if we didn't do it, we would never know if this might be the cure we'd been seeking.

"We've seen so many doctors with no cure or diagnosis," I told him. "We will be taking you in an RV to Texas, since that's the only way to get you there."

I looked into Mitchell's eyes and waited for him to speak, to somehow communicate with me. But, of course, he couldn't. *How I wish you could talk to me and tell me what you're thinking and what we should know!*

Two weeks later, Brad and his good friend, Kim Healy, with whom he'd coached for many years and who was the father to Brandon, Mitchell's best friend, drove up to the house in a big RV. Kim had volunteered to join us on the trip. He would help Brad drive, while I sat in the back tending to Mitchell. Meanwhile, my mom had flown in to stay with Matthew.

I could tell Mitchell was aware of what was happening, because whenever Kim spoke, Mitchell looked up at him, recognizing his voice.

Kim was super positive and encouraged Mitchell as he talked to him about the journey ahead and this next treatment that could hopefully help him.

The morning we left, everyone helped us load up the RV with suitcases and Mitchell's medical supplies. My mom even helped make all the sandwiches, soup, fruit, and snacks for the road. We were finally packed. Mitchell and I were the last to board the RV.

Mitchell did surprising well on the eighteen-hour trip. Whenever I saw him in discomfort in his wheelchair, I alerted the men who lifted him to the bed in the back, where I lay with him, holding him close to me.

All our friends and family were on the prayer alert team to intercede for us on this journey and throughout the surgery. We finally pulled up to the hospital the following day, Tuesday, November 18, 2008. We got Mitchell checked in to a room for his procedure the following day, and then we met with the doctor who examined him and explained the procedure to us. We handed over Mitchell's medical book of records to make the doctor aware of all the previous doctor and hospital visits.

"If you think, medically, we should not proceed with this procedure, please let us know now, and we will turn around and go home," I told him.

"No need. He's young, and he'll be fine. If we don't fix these discs, he'll continue to have pain."

Trusting the doctor's medical expertise, we felt we had no other choice but to proceed.

I was sure Mitchell felt anxious. Brad and I found the hospital chapel, where we sat and prayed that everything would go well, and Mitchell would be fine. Each minute that passed felt like an eternity.

Finally, a few hours later the doctor found us. "The procedure went well. Mitchell is being monitored in the recovery room."

Brad and I sighed with relief.

The hospital staff eventually took Mitchell to his room to recover, where nurses came in occasionally to check in on him.

Brad and I stayed by his side, continuing to encourage him and feeling hopeful that this would finally be the success we'd been hoping for.

At midnight, Brad yawned and stood. "I'm going to get some sleep in the RV. I am exhausted and only had four hours of sleep last night."

"Okay, honey," I said. "I'll be here with Mitchell. I can rest on the pull-out chair here."

We were both drained from this whole ordeal.

After Brad left, I tried to keep my eyes open, but I soon fell asleep.

A nurse entered Mitchell's room around 3:00 a.m. to check his vitals. I was vaguely aware of her entrance.

Suddenly a loud alarm blared from his bedside.

"Code blue," an announcement came, followed by Mitchell's room number.

Medical staff rushed in and surrounding his bed, scrambling to get a pulse from him.

I began to scream, "No, Mitchell! No, Mitchell! Come back!"

"Get her out of here," a nurse said, and someone took my arm and forced me to a nearby waiting room where I fell to my knees praying and wailing.

I tried calling Brad, but he didn't answer, so I called my sister Cheryl. She was my rock and a strong spiritual force when I needed it. As soon as I heard her drowsy hello, I began screaming and crying again. She stayed on the phone with me as she prayed out loud, asking God to spare Mitchell's life.

"Hang on, Mitchell. Come back, Mitchell," she said as she prayed.

Thirty or forty minutes later, a somber nurse stepped into the waiting room. "I'm so sorry," she said. "We tried everything we could to bring him back. He's gone."

I collapsed to the floor with my head between my knees and wailed in pain and grief.

"We've called the doctor, and he's on his way. Where is your husband? Do you want me to find him?"

"He—" my voice cracked and I could hardly speak. I whispered, "He's in the RV parked outside."

"I'll walk out there with you, okay?"

I nodded slowly, and we walked down the hall toward the elevators, past Mitchell's room. The room that only moments before had been a scene of chaos. The room that now stood as silent as a sepulcher.

"We'll clean him up, Mrs. Thorp," she said. "Then you and your husband can go in and see him."

In the stillness of the night, I stepped to the RV and banged on the door hard several times to wake Brad. He finally came to the door. His eyes looked groggy, but with one look at me, he became fully awake.

"Mitchell's gone," I said, as I fell into his arms. "He's dead."

Brad grabbed me, and we ran to Mitchell's room. When we entered, all monitors were turned off and the nurses had cleared him of all his tubes.

Mitchell was lying still, his beautiful blues eyes open with a blank stare.

We fell to our knees next to his bed as Brad grabbed his hand. And we prayed and wept until the sunrise came and our strength was gone. Everyone gave us the time we needed. No one interrupted or bothered us. For the brief bit of time, it was just Mom and Dad and our child. A child who would never again speak, or smile, or walk.

We knew we couldn't remain in the hospital room. We had to make plans. Had to think about next steps and who to notify. But I just couldn't muster the strength to do it. I couldn't think straight. I could only stare blankly ahead of me.

My son, my precious firstborn, was gone.

The doctor finally came and expressed his sorrow, though he was unable to offer an explanation.

"Why was my son not in the ICU?" I said angrily. "You knew his condition before he went in. He should have been monitored better."

But the doctor only offered more condolences and then left.

Brad pulled his wits about him and started notifying family. "I want you to fly to Tucson to your sister Linda's home," Brad told me. "I'll make arrangements to have Matthew and Mom fly to Tucson on Sunday. I won't get to Tucson until late Saturday. We can tell Matthew then what has happened." We knew word would start traveling fast, and we did not want Matthew to hear this news from anyone besides us. He needed to be with us to grieve. We needed to mourn as a family.

Brad planned to drive the RV back with my brother OJ, who lived in the Houston area. Since Kim had flown home after we got to Dallas, OJ agreed to fly to Dallas Friday night to help Brad drive the RV.

That Friday afternoon, Brad drove me to the Dallas airport and dropped me off. As I waited for my plane, I felt as if I were drowning in shock. It all felt like a bad dream, and I kept waiting for someone to wake me up. I kept my head down and could not look at people in the eye. I found a seat away from people. On the overhead television, the local news talked about how a mother had left her baby on the steps of a police station.

It struck me to the core, and I felt sick to my stomach.

God, this is not fair. I loved my child and did everything I knew to do to save him, and yet here is a mother who wants to dispose of her child like waste.

As if out of the depths of my spirit, I held out my right hand and said, "Mitchell, I'm calling you here next to Mommy to take my hand." If anyone saw me, they probably thought I'd lost my mind. I didn't care. I felt in my heart that Mitchell's spirit was with me, and I continued to hold out my hand for him to take. I waited patiently until I felt the warmth of his spirit take my right hand. I knew God in his grace had allowed me that bit of comfort.

"Let's go, Son," I said, and we walked onto the plane together.

Whether this was Mitchell or my guardian angel, I may never know. But I do know I experienced a heavenly presence with me.

I sat next to the window and settled in, pleased that I had the row all to myself. "Mitchell, we're going home."

Then I stared outside and grieved the loss of my son, as tears rolled down my face.

My sister Linda and my brother-in-law Dave met me at the airport in Arizona. We hugged as a group and cried. They graciously let me rest in their guesthouse as I waited for my mother and Matthew to arrive.

Though my mother knew the news, Matthew did not. He knew only that he was going to spend Thanksgiving with his aunt and uncle in Tucson.

Brad and OJ drove straight through to Tucson—more than fifteen hours—and finally pulled in Saturday around 10:00 p.m. Brad withdrew to the guesthouse for a long sleep.

Telling Matthew was one of the hardest things Brad and I had to do. Matthew did not know we were in Tucson. When he arrived Sunday afternoon, my sister told him to come to the guest house to find a surprise. When he opened the door and found us there, his eyes grew wide and he smiled. We hugged him close, tighter than normal, and saw that he was slowly realizing something wasn't right. He became awkward and his face registered fear.

"Let's sit on the couch, honey," I said. *Holy Spirit, please give me the right words to say to him.* I took his hands in mine and looked into his eyes. "Mitchell did not make it. He passed away to be with the Lord. I believe the Lord took him home to heal him, because he has suffered far too long. No one could figure it out here on earth. You know we tried everything we knew to do. I'm sure if Mitchell were given a choice to go back into his earthly body full of pain or take the Lord's hand to heal him in heaven, I believe he made that choice to go home to be with his father in heaven."

Matthew looked at his dad, then back at me. Tears welled up in his eyes, matching ours, as Brad and I put our arms around him we all cried.

Afterward, Matthew became like a zombie, a shocked looked covered his face, and he walked around aimlessly or sat on the couch and stared. And yet again, my heart broke, knowing I couldn't take away his hurt or grief either.

Thanksgiving was one day away, and I was not feeling thankful about anything. I couldn't be around people, so I stayed in bed and slept all day.

The following day, my sister offered to get me a massage. "My massage therapist has healing hands and is willing to come to the house," she said. "It may help you to relax."

I reluctantly agreed, though I wasn't sure how a massage would help me feel less grief.

The therapist arrived and set up her massage table. As I rested, she began to work on my muscles, releasing the tension throughout my body. But I fought it. I didn't feel right relaxing when my son had just died. That felt almost like a betrayal.

During the middle of the session, as the therapist continued to work my muscles, I heard Mitchell's voice for the first time in years.

"Let it go, Mom," he whispered in my ear, clear as day. I knew it was his voice. A mother can recognize her child's voice, even in a crowd.

His voice and words so startled me that I sat up abruptly.

"What happened?" the therapist asked.

"I heard my son speak to me."

She smiled.

I lay back down for the rest of my treatment and allowed myself to relax my muscles. Hebrews 4:16 drifted through my mind: *"Let us then approach God's throne of grace with confidence, so that we may receive mercy and find grace to help us in our time of need."* In his mercy and grace, God allowed me to hear my boy's voice, as I so longed to hear him speak again. I knew I couldn't have my son back with me. But to hear his voice was a beautiful gift that brought comfort and strength.

RV trip to Texas hospital.

In the hospital where Mitchell passed away.

Part 5

A Life Honored

Chapter 17

Speaking Beyond the Veil of Heaven

Thanksgiving was a struggle. Mitchell had just passed away, and Brad, Matthew, my mom, and I were in Tucson with my sister Linda and her husband, Dave. Meanwhile the other half of the family was in Sedona at my sister Cheryl's and her husband, Bob's, home. That day none of us felt particularly good. We grieved and ached over Mitchell.

God, help us get through this day, I prayed that morning. *I miss my son so much.*

God and Mitchell showed up in a big way. That afternoon, while we were outside, I glanced into the sky and stopped in my tracks. There, in the distance, was a beautiful double rainbow. I couldn't help but smile through my tears.

Mitch is having fun with the Lord! I thought, remembering that Mitchell had always loved to paint and color. *He's painting the sky with God!*

The next day Cheryl called to check in on me. "Something happened here yesterday that is amazing," she said.

She told me that her daughter, Kelly, along with Kelly's husband and their two children Andrew and Rebecca, were there in Sedona too. Andrew, who was six years old, saw two big arching rainbows and quickly ran out on Cheryl's balcony. "Mombo, Mombo!" he yelled, his name for Grandma Cheryl. "It's Mitchell's rainbow! He's telling us he's okay."

I was stunned. They'd seen the same rainbow at the same time as we had! "Only through the mouths of babes," I said. "Children can see and hear the voice of God."

"I have lived here thirteen years and have never seen a rainbow, much less two of them," Cheryl said.

God and Mitchell displayed for us to see through our spiritual eyes not one, but two full arching rainbows, over the red mountain and over the church of the Holy Cross. This church had been one of Mitchell's favorite places we visited. We had all hiked the trails together, and Mitchell had used his walking stick like a shepherd's staff. God and Mitchell were communicating with us all, to tell us the Lord's promise that he has our son, and he took him home to heal him.

How perfect that God chose a rainbow. Before Mitchell got so sick, my world of fashion dictated that I learn color and how to wardrobe clients in their best colors according to their skin, hair, and eyes. Since I was a specialist in color analysis, I always found color fascinating to learn, figuring out what colors meant, and why people were drawn to certain colors. So as I considered this rainbow, I knew it had another significant meaning. Rainbows are a beautiful phenomenon that bear significance across different religions and cultures. In the Bible, we need only to look in three places to discover the meaning of a rainbow and what certain colors may symbolize—Genesis, Ezekiel, and Revelation. In the Genesis account, a rainbow appeared right after the great worldwide flood. It symbolized God's mercy and his covenant with all creation in which he vowed never again to destroy the world in such a way:

> God said, "This is the sign of the covenant which I make between Me and you and every living creature with you, for everlasting generations: I set my rainbow in the cloud, and it shall be the sign of the covenant between Me and the earth. . . . [And the waters shall no more become a flood to destroy all flesh]" (Genesis 9:12–13, 15, HBFV).

In Ezekiel, the prophet's first vision from God, known as the "wheel in the middle of a wheel" vision, compares the glory of God to what he saw.

The wheel-like image seems to represent the universe, the path we travel through this world, and the afterlife, and it stands for the enduring connections between this world and the next, the power from above and below: "Like the appearance of a rainbow in the clouds on a rainy day, so was the radiance around him" (Ezekiel 1:28).

Rainbows appear again in the book of Revelation, which foretells the end of human rule on earth and the coming of Jesus to set up his kingdom. The first mention in Revelation appears when the apostle John uses it to describe the glory and power of God on his throne:

> I looked, and there before me was a door standing open in heaven. . . . A rainbow that shone like an emerald encircled the throne. (4:1, 3)

At the time I did not question why we saw two rainbows, but later I wanted to know the significance. I found out that a single rainbow signifies a human descending from heaven to earth. A double rainbow, due to its reversal of colors, represents the movement from earth to heaven and is considered to be a sign of future success.

Every rainbow consists of seven colors—red, orange, yellow, green, blue, indigo, and violet. In my search for biblical meanings of rainbow colors, I could not help but find these meanings that were also attached to certain archangels. I learned that red has the longest wavelength and resembles Archangel Uriel—representing wisdom and energy. Orange combines the colors before and after it (red and yellow respectively). It represents creativity and the ability to enjoy ourselves. Yellow relates to Archangel Jophiel—representing the brilliance of thoughts and wisdom. Green relates to health, love, and wealth. It also connects with Archangel Raphael—representing healing. Blue associates with Archangel Michael, the leader of all archangels. It also represents spirituality and denotes the spirit world and connection with water. Indigo represents the bridge between the subconscious and conscious worlds. And violet is associated with Archangel Zadkeil, who represents mercy. Violet also means divine inspiration and imagination.[7]

After researching the symbolism, I felt even more comforted by the beautiful rainbows we saw.

But God's signs to us about Mitchell weren't finished. Cheryl told me about something else that had happened that Thanksgiving Day.

After viewing these two beautiful arching rainbows, the family returned inside to eat dinner. They all sat and prayed for Mitchell and us and the whole family. It was hard at first to be thankful as they were all grieving in their own way, but to witness what they had just seen gave them hope. They gave thanks to God for his mercy and grace as he wrapped his loving arms around Mitchell to take him to his eternal home.

Halfway through the meal, they heard a loud crash in another room. Kelly went to investigate, with Andrew following. Kelly found Mitchell's walking stick laying on the floor. She found that odd, as Mitchell's walking stick had been securely leaning against the corner of the wall and no one had been in that room.

Young Andrew had taken over Mitchell's walking stick a while before and had tied around the stick some Native American beads that spelled out his name. When Andrew saw the walking stick, he noticed two of his beads—D and R—had broken off the stick and were on the floor.

Kelly picked up the stick. "Let's see what it says now," she told her son. "I bet Mitchell is trying to tell us something."

Kelly read the new word: "ANEW."

She yelled to the others to come see what the loud noise had been about. They were all amazed.

"Let's put Mitchell's walking stick in a safe place so we can present this to Brad, Beth, and Matthew when we see them," Cheryl said. "This will bring them hope that they know where he is and that he is a new creation in heaven."

As Cheryl told me about this, tears streamed down my face. I knew Mitchell's spirit was alive and well, and that he was speaking to us beyond the veil of heaven to let us know that he was okay, and that God had him and Grandpa—my father—who passed six months before Mitchell.

A veil separates heaven and earth, and the heavenly dimensions are truly all around us. Knowing that fact brought me such healing, hope, peace, and intense comfort. I realized that God opened our spiritual eyes, mind, and heart so we could see through that veil to witness the miraculous signs and wonders we needed.

Later as I read my Bible, I came across 2 Corinthians 3:16–18: "Whenever anyone turns to the Lord, the veil is taken away. Now the Lord is Spirit, and where the Spirit of the Lord is, there is freedom. And we all, who with unveiled faces contemplate the Lord's glory, are being transformed into his image with ever-increasing glory, which comes from the Lord, who is the Spirit."

Where the Spirit of the Lord is, there is freedom. Mitchell was finally and truly free, indeed.

Mitchell's rainbow in Sedona, Arizona, arching over the Holy Cross Church.

After the stick fell, the D and R beads broke off.

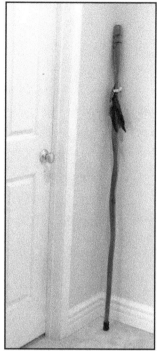

Mitchell's walking stick.

Chapter 18

Final Journey Home

The day after Thanksgiving my amazing husband pulled himself out of the deepest pit of his grief to start communicating with the family about Mitchell's funeral. We couldn't put the planning off any longer. Just about everyone in the family stepped up.

Mitchell had now been gone a week. Jesus the Master Healer took Mitchell home to heal him. Mitchell's strength and courage led him in a new direction, on a new journey with our Lord—one without pain, burden, or uncertainty. He fought so hard for five years and left this world on his and the Lord's terms.

I like to believe that when the angels came to his bedside, his spirit felt the manifestation of his healing immediately. His spirit could not be contained in his broken-down vessel. He was willing to let go and let God heal him, since he knew that no one on earth had the answers to make him well. God set Mitchell free from his pain, as he had suffered enough.

So many of us were praying for his miracle healing here on earth, but God had a different plan. God sovereignly controls our lives. Nothing occurs that does not pass through his hands and is ultimately used for his glory and good. Still, it was not what we would have chosen. It is never the will of the Father who is in heaven that any child should perish—Jesus loves children. As Matthew 19:14 tells us: "Jesus said, 'Let the little children come to me and do not hinder them, for to such belongs the kingdom of heaven'" (ESV).

God has so much compassion and mercy for the suffering: "The LORD is close to the brokenhearted and saves those who are crushed in spirit" (Psalm 34:18). God's ways are not our ways; the mysteries of the Lord are beyond our earthly comprehension. And even though we do not understand or see the bigger picture or like the earthly outcome, we can trust God, because he is good.

Mitchell believed for complete freedom from a body that had been holding him captive for too long. I remember so clearly when he was still with us and would motion up to heaven, communicating that he wanted to go home—his eternal home. We were crushed from the anguish we felt that no one on this earth could diagnose or heal our boy. Yet we were not without hope, and we would not give up on him. I believe Mitchell was given a choice to stay or finally go home, and as hard as it was to leave his family and friends, he wanted to be out of pain. His larger-than-life spirit could not be contained any longer. I know in my heart my son wanted to be set free—free to fly on eagles' wings over the rainbow.

And while his freedom was just beginning, our grief was, too. Brad contacted the funeral home to arrange for Mitchell's body to be flown from Texas back to California. Cheryl called the church to set a date for a service, Kelly put together the slide presentation of Mitchell's life, Brad picked out the music and got my input, and others organized flowers and refreshments.

I wanted to help, to do something, but my grief was so great, and I felt helpless. I could barely function. I stayed in bed, grief stricken, still in shock and disbelief. I just did not have it in me to be around anyone. I curled into a fetal position, retreating into my shell of grief.

My sweet Matthew also needed attention as he was mourning the loss of his brother. He stayed close to me, and we comforted each other.

"Why didn't God save him?" Matthew asked.

A tough question to face when you are in the midst of grief. "He didn't have enough strength or fight left in him to keep going," I told him. "God had to take your brother home to heaven to heal him and make him anew—a new creation free of pain and suffering."

The following day we said our goodbyes to family, and Brad, Matthew, and I drove the RV back to San Diego.

Mitchell's funeral service was the following week, on December 4, at North Coast Calvary Church. The church was newly built and decorated for Christmas. We would be the first family to hold a funeral service in the new church.

As the days slowly passed, we received a copy of Mitchell's autopsy. Texas state law required an autopsy after surgery to determine cause of death. We could hardly bring ourselves to read the report. We scanned through the medical terminology, trying to figure out what it meant. But from what we could gather, it was unclear whether the morphine administered may have also contributed to the cause of death, the report said, "particularly in light of the decedent's neuromuscular disorder." We landed at the bottom of the report to learn the final results: The chief medical examiner signed off the cause of death as *undetermined!*

All the unanswered questions remained and would be left that way. Hanging on by a thread, only by God's grace did we manage to keep going.

One night in my grief, God spoke deep within my soul, *"This is not the end, only the beginning."* I had no idea what that meant, but I knew God did, and I would just have to trust him.

On the day of the funeral, I dreaded getting out of bed. I dreaded seeing my son in a casket. I dreaded being forced to grieve publicly. But I knew this day wasn't about me; it was about honoring the life and memory of Mitchell.

The church had a large auditorium, which held eighteen hundred people. We had no idea how many would come, but we knew that word had spread quickly. We were stunned to find that the whole auditorium was packed—some people even had to stand in the back. We were amazed at the outpouring of love from everyone in the community. Family, friends, coaches, teachers, pastors, doctors, therapists, teammates from Mitchell's and Matthew's teams, as well as people we did not even know, came to come show their respects.

With that many people in the auditorium, I was amazed that we could hear a pin drop through the whole service. It was so beautifully orchestrated. Brad and I were thankful to our family and friends who helped organize the service; without them this out pouring of love would not have happened or been as impactful. As everyone took his or her seat, the service started with the song, "I Can Only Imagine," by Mercy Me.

My whole body trembled, as though I were having an out-of-body experience. It was like I was there, but I was not. Brad held my hand to calm me down.

After the song, Pastor Orville Stanton, North Coast Calvary's caring pastor, welcomed everyone and offered an opening prayer. Orville often came to our home and prayed for Mitchell and us, so it meant a lot to have him participate in this service. Next, their youth pastor, Derek DaPena, gave a reading and prayer for youth. Then we listened to another beautiful song, "On Eagles Wings," by Will Fledgecock.

Kim Healy, who'd driven with us to Texas, gave a touching testimony, offering his perspective about Mitchell and our family's grueling journey and how we persevered.

Family friend Angela Moskovis-Kazmarek performed Josh Groban's, "You Raise Me Up." Then my sister Cheryl, Mitchell's godmother, reflected on Mitchell's life and began the photo presentation, all orchestrated to some of our most meaningful songs—the ukulele version of "Somewhere Over the Rainbow," by Israel Kamakawiwoʻole, and "Finally Home," by Mercy Me. I do not believe there was a dry eye in the place.

With so much emotion in the atmosphere, Lead Pastor Jason Graves from Daybreak Church delivered a powerful message on Joshua 1:9. He shared how strong our faith was and our perseverance in never giving up on our son.

"We knew this journey was hard and long for you but especially for Mitchell," he said. "This journey was remarkable and inspiring to witness, as it has touched the hearts of so many of you in the community. That is why you are here. The strength and courage that Mitchell had to go through and what he had to endure was beyond words. He is remarkable young man."

He continued talking about how talented Mitchell was in baseball and lightened the mood as he shared about Mitchell's and Matthew's world series wiffle ball games that they would play from sunup to sundown in the backyard—and how Mitch painted a scoreboard on a four-by-six piece of plywood and named the back yard Thorp Field.

To our surprise, Pastor Jason had taken the top part of the scoreboard with the words *Thorp Field* and had it professionally framed. He presented it to Brad and me. We were deeply touched. He then asked Brad and me to stand.

"God is well pleased with you two, good and faithful servants," he told us. Then he asked the audience to applaud. Everyone stood and began clapping, which coaxed a fresh round of tears from us. After what felt like an eternity, the pastor asked everyone to sit, so the service could continue. They played the song "There Will Be a Day," by Jeremy Camp. One of our friends told us afterward that the heavens parted during this ceremony, as Mitchell's life brought so many closer to God.

Pastor Jason gave final remarks and a closing prayer. Finally, we listened to the closing song, "Arms of An Angel," by Tullamore Gospel Choir.

As the service ended, many stayed, not wanting or ready to leave. We stood for a procession line that had started so everyone could say something to Brad, Matthew, and me. This went on for a couple hours. One woman I did not know stood crying before me. "You make me want to be a better mother," she said.

I began to console her. It was a strange moment; it should have been the other way around, with her consoling us, but if God had brought her here to understand what it meant to be a better mother, then I would let the Lord work.

I knew one thing with certainty: God was going to use this tragedy for his purpose and his glory—somehow, someway. And if this woman was any indication, he had already begun.

the
Mitchell Thorp
Journey

September 12, 1990

to

November 19, 2008

"Have I not commanded you? Be strong and courageous. Do not be terrified; do not be discouraged, for the Lord your God will be with you wherever you go."

-Joshua 1:9

Front cover to memorial service program.

I'M FREE

Don't grieve for me, for now I'm free
I'm following the path God laid for me.
I took His hand when I heard Him call
I turned my back and left it all.

I could not stay another day
To laugh, to love, to work or play.
Tasks left undone must stay that way
I found that peace at the close of day.

If my parting left a void,
Then fill it with remembered joy.
A friendship shared, a laugh, a kiss.
Ah yes, these things I too will miss.

Be not burdened with times of sorrow.
I wish you sunshine of tomorrow.
My life's been blessed, having knowing you all.
My family, my friends and all my dogs.

Perhaps my time seemed all too brief.
Don't lengthen it now with undue grief.
Lift up you heart and share with me.
God wanted me now; He set me free.

December 4, 2008
North Coast Calvary Chapel

Worship

Opening Song. . . . . I Can Only Imagine
by: MercyMe

Welcome . . . . Orville Stanton
Caring Pastor, NCCC

Opening Prayer . . . . Orville Stanton
Caring Pastor, NCCC

Reading & Prayer for Youth . . . . Derek DaPena
Youth Pastor, NCCC

Song . . . . On Eagles Wings
by: Will Hedgecock

Testimonial . . . . Kim Healy
Family Friend

Solo . . . . You Raise Me Up
by Josh Groban
Soloist: Angela Moskovis-Kazmarek

Reflections of Mitchell's Life . . . . . . Cheryl Porter
Godmother and Aunt

Message (Joshua 1:9) . . . . Jason Graves
Lead Pastor, Daybreak Church

Song . . . . There Will Be a Day
by: Jeremy Camp

Closing Prayer . . . . Jason Graves
Lead Pastor, Daybreak Church

Closing Song . . . . Arms of An Angel
Tullamore Gospel Choir

The family invites you to join them in the north side of the
Family Center Room at NCCC for refreshments
immediately following the service.

Program for the service.

Back cover showing God and Mitchell's rainbow.

Chapter 19

Last Goodbye

On December 5, we arrived at the funeral home on the day when we would have a private service at his burial site with only family and close friends. Before everyone started coming, Brad and I spent time alone with Mitchell. The funeral director escorted us to a room for a private viewing to say our last goodbye. Flower arrangements surrounded the casket. Soft music played in the background, but my mind barely registered it. My only focus was on my firstborn son, lying still in a casket.

My knees felt weak as we approached him. He looked so peaceful, like he was sleeping. It was too much for me to bear, and I fell into a nearby chair.

The extended family all wrote goodbye letters, and Brad placed those, along with Mitchell's baseballs, his favorite baseball jersey, and other items he had cherished in his casket with him. Then Brad pulled a letter out of his jacket pocket and unfolded it. This was his letter to Mitchell. After he had arrived in Tucson from Dallas and had gotten some sleep, he'd woke up at 4:00 a.m. and written this farewell letter. He leaned over and took his son's hand. My heart ached for Brad as I watched his hand shake slightly.

He cleared his throat, then began to read.

Mitchell,

You have provided our family with a lifetime of memories. Your enthusiasm for life was infectious. You were filled with joy as you played all your sports and as you focused on your academics. Your smile was a gift. It brought joy and happiness to all those who loved you and all those lives you touched in a special way.

You were perfect in many ways, just like the perfect game you pitched when you were twelve. And to see you come home with straight As on your report card and to see how proud you were of your accomplishments brought smiles and tears to our faces.

The last five years for you have been the hardest struggle anyone could ever imagine. Your life, lived with courage and strength, will stand tall with the Lord today. You will be missed so much, but knowing that you are out of pain now and knowing you are with the Lord gives us comfort. Your memories and your spirit will go on forever. We will embrace your precious memories to help us fill the void, and your spirit will live on in our hearts to help others.

Your mom and I enjoyed so much the way you and Matthew set up Thorp Field in the backyard with a scoreboard that you handmade and all your team hats lined up on the ledge from all the major league teams. This was a source of pride and joy for us to watch. You boys would play wiffle ball daily until the sun went down and would not give up until the last two teams played a world series and a winner decided. Both you and your brother loved the game of baseball, and you played the game until you could not play anymore.

Your dream of playing professional baseball may been cut short, but you have given us a lifetime of lessons on how to live to the fullest. Mitchell, you never gave up, no matter how painful and difficult things would get. You were our warrior son, so brave and strong. You fought to the very end, and you transitioned from this world to the next on your and the Lord's terms.

No one should ever live their last five years in constant pain and suffering. We, your family, and friends, suffered along with you but we could never imagine the pain and devastation you felt each day. Your constant struggle and fight for life brought strength and courage to us all. The outcome of trials and tribulations we all suffered was not what we had hoped and prayed for. But your love of life, family, and friends, and the courageous way you lived, are memories that will always be there to comfort us and strengthen us.

We will miss the daily routine during these past five years, and the void it will leave for the family will be hard to fill. Matthew has been so loving and supportive of our commitment to get you well. He loves you and misses you so much. Please help Matthew, as he is hurting. Be his guardian angel. Strengthen him and give him the courage to get through life without you in it.

As we go forward, we will take the many lessons you and the Lord have provided us and, until we meet again in heaven, the love, and precious memories of you will carry us on. We will miss your love, your laughter, and your passion for life. We hope and pray that many hearts will be touched and that we will bring hope to the hopeless, courage and strength to the weak, and transformation through faith in the process. We will miss you and carry you in our hearts forever.

Love,

Dad, Mom, and Matthew

I sobbed as I listened to him read to our son. My mind raced. *Please, someone, wake me from this horrific dream.*

Brad had to help me get up from the chair and walk over to his casket, where we both kissed Mitchell's forehead, and then walked out to join the procession, which was about to start. I was so grief stricken, I felt as though someone had stabbed me in my heart. I could hardly breathe. We watched as Mitchell's casket was loaded into the hearse, and we went to his burial site.

The pallbearers carried his casket to where he would be laid to rest, and then our pastor, Jason Graves from Daybreak Church, gave a brief, but beautiful, message and prayed to release Mitchell's spirt to God. Afterward, we watched as dozens of white doves were released into the air, symbolizing his spirit being set free.

As hard as it was to let go, I felt comforted to know that God created us to change into a better state of being when we go to be with him in heaven.

Two Scriptures came to my mind as I lingered at the graveside:

I consider that our present sufferings are not worth comparing with the glory that will be revealed in us. (Romans 8:18)

He will wipe every tear from their eyes. There will be no more death or mourning or crying or pain, for the old order of things has passed away. (Revelation 21:4)

Such wonderful promises.

Then I thought about Hannah in the Bible, who said, "I prayed for this child, and the LORD has granted me what I asked of him. So now I give him to the LORD" (1 Samuel 1:27–28). Her words were my own. I, too, had prayed for this child, and the Lord granted me what I had asked for, even if it was for just a little while.

Now I had to give him back to the Lord.

Our last family portrait together.

A father's love for his son.

The dove release.

Chapter 20

Dealing with Grief and Questioning Why

After the funeral, Brad and I walked into Mitchell's bedroom and looked around. An emptiness filled our spirits. I grabbed his pillow and clutched it, taking in the smell of him. Brad wrapped his arms around me, and we wept.

Questions kept circling in my head. *Why was our precious child taken from us? Why did he have to suffer so? Why could no one figure out what was wrong and heal him? Where were you, God, when we prayed for a miracle?*

After I hurled accusations and questions heavenward, I knew the best place to go was to God's Word. I left Mitchell's room and got my Bible. I opened it to the book of Jeremiah. The Old Testament prophet Jeremiah was known as the "weeping prophet" because he carried so much grief over his people, the Jews. They were a conquered people, suffering under tremendous burdens.

I began reading Jeremiah 31: "I have loved you with an everlasting love; I have drawn you with unfailing kindness. I will build you up again, and you . . . will be rebuilt" (verses 3–4).

Even with that promise, I wrestled with God over the injustices I felt. Once we meet Mitchell again in heaven and see all the joy and glory, all these questions will no longer matter. But they matter now.

The following morning during my prayer time, I read scripture that stopped me: "Record my misery; list my tears on your scroll—are they not in your record?" (Psalm 56:8). I felt God tell me, *Beth, I have counted all your tears. So don't be afraid of them or of the reasons for them. They will not be wasted. I'm calling you to trust me. I know what I am doing!*

As the days passed and my heart still carried the heavy weight of grief, I began reading books about heaven and the afterlife, looking for comfort and hope. But mostly I retreated from everyone. I slept a lot and did not want to face the world.

Weeks passed, and my retreat continued. I didn't know how to take that knife out of my heart. The pain was so deep, I could not stop the bleeding. A part of me died with my son.

I knew I was heading down a deep black hole if I did not seek help. I called our spiritual counselor, Bertha Hernandez. "Brad and I need help, someone of your expertise who can deliver us from all this pain of grief. Can you give us some counseling—and maybe Matthew, too?"

"Yes, of course!"

We scheduled a time the following Tuesday.

After the call I felt good to have taken a first step for my family. Now I needed to tell Brad about it. I was not sure how Brad would respond, as I knew it could be difficult for him to open up his soul to someone, but he agreed.

So, I ran back to my room and read the Bible and drank in God's Word. As I studied, I realized I needed to trust in the Lord with all my heart and lean not on my own understanding, as Proverbs 3:5 says. But it was difficult. To me, letting go in my mind felt as though I was letting go of my child for good. And I couldn't bear that thought. A part of me *wanted* to hang on to grief, because I felt that kept me connected to him. I was afraid to let go. But I knew deep down, I had to—that was the only way I could find healing. I had to surrender the need to understand and accept that we did not have the whole picture. I had to accept that I knew he was in heaven and that he was out of pain and suffering.

I had to accept what the apostle Paul said in 1 Corinthians 13:12: "Now we see things only a reflection as in a mirror; then we shall see face to face. Now I know in part; then I shall know fully, even as I am fully known." He goes on to say in 2 Corinthians 4:18: "So we fix our eyes not on what is seen, but on what is unseen, since what is seen is temporary, but what is unseen is eternal."

The more I studied, the more I realized that if I wanted to find healing, I had to watch out for the ways the enemy of my soul would attack me. One of his attacks was to keep me withdrawn and away from others who could bring strength and comfort. The enemy wanted me to grieve in unhealthy ways and to blame God for what had happened. He wanted to destroy our lives through our grief.

Satan, the fallen angel who prowls the earth to see whom he may devour, has always determined to ruin people's lives. He is not a cartoon character in a red suit with a pitchfork. The Bible says he is a personal force of evil who comes to steal and kill and destroy (see John 10:10). Satan wants to steal our joy, kill our desires to continue, and destroy our peace—and one of the best ways he does that is to keep us isolated and to torment our minds with "what ifs." That's what he'd tried to do with us. We had wrestled with him many nights when Mitchell was still fighting for his life. And he was trying to do this to me now, as I retreated from the world.

He is also the one who wants to keep our minds filled with guilty regrets. The Bible calls him "the accuser" (Revelation 12:10). He loves to whisper half-truths in our ears, charging us with things we "should have" or "could have" done.

In the midst of my questions and pain and hearing those accusations, I finally realized that as long as I remained shut off and withdrawn without real faith-filled comforters, he could keep me cut off from God's peace. The reality of Ephesians 6:12 finally sunk in: "Our struggle is not against flesh and blood, but against the rulers, against the authorities, against the powers of this dark world and against the spiritual forces of evil in the heavenly realms."

What the enemy meant to destroy; God meant for another plan. I knew I needed to overcome my grief—not remove it, but put it in its proper place and deal with it in a healthy way. That would be impossible without the help of our Lord Jesus Christ. I needed to draw near to him.

Many people respond in the opposite way when tragedy strikes. They stay away from God because they are angry with him, and that anger turns to bitterness and bitterness into hate. And yet God wants us to bring our anger to him—not for us to run from him. He is there with open arms just waiting for us to fall into. He wants to wrap us in his arms so we can begin to feel a comfort and warmth that will transform and heal our broken hearts. As Hebrews 10:22 says: "Let us draw near to God with a sincere heart and with the full assurance that faith brings, having our hearts sprinkled to cleanse us from a guilty conscience and having our bodies washed with pure water."

We all need to be more equipped when tragedy strikes. Some who do not have faith may turn to drugs and alcohol to numb the pain, but for those of us who do have faith, we need to stand firm on God's promises and his firm foundation to carry us through. If we choose not to do so, our world will crumble, taking us with it.

We have to constantly be on our guard, to be aware when the enemy manipulates our grief with deceptive thoughts. I realized that I didn't have to be held down by those thoughts that plagued me in those months after Mitchell's death. And I didn't have to be. That didn't mean that I was no longer going to grieve—but I wasn't going to stop living. I needed to take my thoughts captive (see 2 Corinthian 10:5). I needed to resist the enemy's lies and submit myself to God, with the promise that as I did, as I resisted the devil's schemes, he would flee (see James 4:7).

I shook myself out of my retreat and determined to get back to living. Mitchell wouldn't have wanted me to be this way. It didn't honor his memory. But more so, God didn't want me living this way. He had a plan for my life, and somehow Mitchell's death was part of that. So slowly I began to replace the questions and lies in my mind with truths from Scripture, and I begin to trust again. I memorized and recited helpful verses, such as, "Trust in the LORD with all your heart and lean not on your own understanding" (Proverbs 3:5) and "Let the morning bring me word of your unfailing love, for I have put my trust in you. Show me the way I should go, for to you I entrust my life" (Psalm 143:8).

I also took prayer walks to get out of the house. I enlisted help from Brad, my family and friends, and a spiritual counselor. I played worship music around the home and in the car and sang along loudly. And I embraced the knowledge that I had the power and authority through the name of Jesus Christ to rebuke the enemy, to make him get his hands off my family and me.

The apostle Peter wrote,

> Be alert and of sober mind. Your enemy the devil prowls around like a roaring lion looking for someone to devour. Resist him, standing firm in the faith, because you know that the family of believers throughout the world is undergoing the same kind of sufferings.
>
> And the God of all grace, who called you to his eternal glory in Christ, after you have suffered a little while, will himself restore you and make you strong, firm, and steadfast. To him be the power forever and ever. (1 Peter 5:8–11)

That scripture is exactly what happened to us. As I began to recognize what my unhealthy grief was doing, my husband and I determined that we would not let the enemy win. He messed with the wrong mama and papa bear, and we began to feel a new energy of strength and fight again. This supernatural power came from our Father in heaven.

If I let the enemy win, what would happen to Matthew? I knew I had to fight to get out of this dark pit of grief to help my other son deal with his grief and to be a wife to my husband who also was hurting. Grief is real, and it is a necessary process toward healing and restoration—but it must never take over.

"Those who hope in the LORD will renew their strength," Isaiah 40:31 tells us. "They will soar on wings like eagles." That's exactly what I needed to get myself out of bed every morning to face a new day.

I have read that an eagle, like many other animals, can sense a storm before it arrives. Eagles are the only birds that love the storm. When all other birds try to flee from a storm's fierceness, eagles fly into it and will use the wind to rise higher in a matter of seconds. The eagle sets its wings so the wind will pick it up and lift it above the storm. While the storm rages below, the eagle is soaring above it. The eagle does not escape the storm but simply rises on the winds to be lifted higher.[8]

This was the time to press deeper into God's words in the Bible, to let it speak to me and breathe new life into my spirit. He said he would give me his strength when I was weak. I needed it now. I needed him to help me rise above the storms of grief until he ultimately calmed it down.

An eagle conveys freedom, trust, and courage to look ahead.

Chapter 21

Healing and Restoration Begins

When people lose a loved one, either suddenly or after a long period of sickness, the emotions that follow will hit hard and at different times. I had to remember to be gentle with myself and patient with others, understanding that everyone heals and grieves at a different rate. Certain triggers that reminded us of Mitchell could set one of us off at different times and in different ways. We needed to be sensitive to everyone's timetable of healing and give each family member space to grieve in his or her own way.

I especially needed to be aware of Matthew's pain and grief, as he missed his brother. He was angry with God and would scream, "Why did you take my brother away?" He would throw and kick things. I even gave him a pillow to punch. He cried and had to release it in his own way. I had to respect and understand what he must be feeling, too, and that he needed help just as much as his mom and dad did.

"It's okay to let your emotions out," I told him one day. "God created us to have emotions. Even Jesus showed his humanity through emotions. He wept, he rejoiced, and he even got angry. God is not mad at you, Matthew, because you are angry or because you're questioning why. It isn't healthy to stuff these emotions within yourself, so let them go."

And he did.

The following day, I asked Pastor Jason, who performed Mitchell's service, to come to the house. He offered to take Matthew to lunch and then for a walk on the beach to talk about it.

As Matthew was learning to express his grief, I worried about my husband's struggle. Brad stuffed many of his emotions, which caused him intense suffering, taking a toll on his own health.

I knew we needed help; we were all falling apart. We previously attended the grief share program at our church. In fact, we took the program a couple of times. It helped us process and talk about our pain in a safe place, because everyone in the group was dealing with the same thing. After the second go-around, however, we felt the group was helpful, but we found it too painful to keep hearing about everyone else's sorrows. We needed to go deeper with our own trauma, having lived through five years of it. We needed a trained professional to help us find our way out.

Tuesday finally arrived and Brad and I thought, as we were driving to our appointment, that doing a one-on-one spiritual counseling session in private would be better for us as a couple. We had to find someone we trusted to bare our souls to. We needed someone who specialized in grief and Bertha was trained as a minister of healing and the gift of prophecy. We trusted her, since she knew what we had gone through and had even prayed over Mitchell and our family several times.

We met with her separately, and then together. She took us through a whole process of healing and forgiveness. We harbored much in our souls that we needed to release. Our session began with forgiveness. We both needed to forgive people, including each other for things in our marriage we'd said or hadn't said; the countless doctors for not finding a cure or answers; family members and friends who said things that hurt us; and God for not answering prayers in the way we wanted. As she took each of us through this exercise, the Holy Spirit began to work.

When the Holy Spirit met us where we hurt most, we could no longer contain our grief. We had to release all those emotions and pain. My husband was an emotional mess, on his knees, moaning and crying out. The same for me. We were both sobbing as the Holy Spirit, our Comforter, was working through us to guide us through the refiner's fire. We both needed this deep emotional release for the healing to truly begin.

God is always big enough to handle whatever we take to him. He will wait patiently for us as we rant and rave, cry, and moan. He will then speak to our souls and provide the comfort we need.

When it was over, Brad and I felt exhausted, but the weight we both had been carrying lifted.

"Many people dwell so much on the past when they are grieving," Bertha said. "Do not look into the past. That will trigger only regrets, guilt, and happier days when our loved one was with us in all his strength. Do not look too far into the future, as this will make you feel anxious about what could have been and the deprivation, you'll feel at facing those years without your loved one. The enemy tries to wreak havoc on your mind and emotions. Stay in the moment; this is all any of us have."

We all had cried so much over Mitchell's passing that we felt dried up. We had no more tears to shed. I knew my Lord collected all our tears and preserved them in a special bottle (see Psalm 56:8). And I found comfort knowing that someday God "will wipe away every tear from their eyes. There will be no more death or mourning or crying or pain, for the old order of things has passed away" (Revelation 21:4).

After our intense times with Bertha, our healing and restoration began, and our relentless crying stopped.

The following day, we both were totally transformed. I woke up and felt different, as though God wanted me to focus my grief for a bigger purpose.

"I do not want to do anything else on this earth unless it has eternal significance," I told Brad.

He looked at me and nodded. "I feel the same way."

Our priorities changed. Things that had been important before no longer held significance. God turned our priorities completely around. All that was important now was bringing people closer to Jesus Christ in a meaningful way through our testimony.

We both had an awakening with a fire in our spirits. We felt that the enemy had messed with the wrong mama and papa bear. What the enemy stole from us, we now knew God would turn into something beautiful. We did not know what that would be just yet, but God would reveal it in his time. And we knew that included ministering to others.

That didn't mean we stopped grieving Mitchell. Staying in the present took some practice because each moment reminded us that Mitchell wasn't there. But we determined to keep working on that, and in due time, we found more comfort living in the present rather than in the past and the future.

Occasionally when we heard the songs from Mitchell's funeral, or when we saw butterflies around our house, we would be reminded of him, saying, "Mitchell is with us," and we'd smile. Sometimes when I felt my son's presence, I lifted my hand, as if pressing against the veil between heaven and earth and, in my imagination, I saw us touching palm to palm.

I never doubted the reality of heaven, and I knew Mitchell was there. Jesus spoke about heaven in simple terms. He did not make up the concept to ease people's minds when they faced death. To Jesus, heaven was as real as could be. He said, "Do not let your hearts be troubled. You believe in God; believe also in me. My Father's house has many rooms; if that were not so, would I have told you that I am going there to prepare a place for you? And if I go and prepare a place for you, I will come back and take you to be with me that you also may be where I am" (John 14:1–3).

God loves us so much that he prepared this heavenly place for those who believe in him to spend eternity with him. This knowledge filled my heart, mind, and soul with hope. I knew that not only would I see God, but I would also see my son again.

Time marched on, and we felt God leading us every step of the way, giving us strength. Each day we healed a bit more, slowly but surely. Our hearts stopped bleeding. We moved ahead, not knowing for sure what each day would bring, but believing God would guide our way. The only way I could describe it was that we walked by faith. Hebrews 11:1 tells us that "faith is confidence in what we hope for and assurance about what we do not see."

To help strengthen our faith, we relied on the Bible to be our compass. It tells us that as believers we are different from others in this world because "we live by faith, not by sight" (2 Corinthians 5:7).

I constantly reminded myself that I do not need to see everything because God sees it all from the beginning of history to the end of time. We see only this sliver of time; we view all of time through the same cracked and ill-fitting glasses. We forget that God exists outside of time's minutes and millennia. Only he has the big picture.

I came to understand that God does not mean for us to mourn in the way the world mourns, without hope. We know where Mitchell is, and we rejoice that he is in God's arms. Even though we must spend a few years here, as we are all spiritual beings having a human experience, we know that every disappointment here is designed to create a deeper longing in us for heaven.

Our family decided to focus on the life we had left, while anticipating our rich reward in eternity. Heaven will be such a wonder place for us. We will have no more suffering, and we will see Jesus face-to-face. It is so glorious to think about that. As the apostle Paul encouraged, "Since then, you have been raised with Christ, set your hearts on things above, where Christ is, seated at the right hand of God. Set your minds on things above, not on earthly things" (Colossians 3:1–2). It helped as we remembered to keep one foot on earth and one foot in heaven, but always focusing on our true home.

Our eternal home is heaven.

Chapter 22

How God Speaks

God knows specifically what each of us needs and will speak to us and provide just the right thing at the right time to bring healing and peace to our souls. The transformation Brad and I experienced didn't mean we no longer grieved. My grief popped up again when I looked at my son's obituary in the local paper. I could hardly bring myself to read it. My hands shook so much, the paper was all over the place. As grief overtook me, I closed the paper and put it down. But through my tears, the front headline jumped off the page at me, as if God and Mitchell were telling me this is what I needed to do to help with my healing: "Rescued Horses Help Others Heal."

I'd ridden since the age of five and had competed in horse shows most of my life. I loved being around these magnificent animals, but life and circumstances kept me away from them for many years. God knew that I was so used to taking care of Mitchell 24/7 for the past five years that to stop and not take care of someone or something was out of my norm.

I began to read about the Pegasus Rising Project and how its founders, Cynthia and Tony Royal, rescued this herd of twenty-seven Arabian horses that were living in deplorable conditions. It took fifty volunteers ten weeks to transport and relocate these rare and historically significant horses to San Diego. The horses had been in a suburb north of Sacramento, owned by an elderly couple who grew too sick and too old to care for them. The horses were malnourished, ungroomed, and teeming with parasites. Some of the nine stallions, seventeen mares, and their babies, lived alone in tiny pens with inadequate fencing, and with many horses up to their ankles in mud and their own waste.

These Arabian horses, originally from the Middle East, came to the United States during the Reagan era. President Reagan petitioned to bring a champion stallion to America. The stallion used for breeding on US soil had won races abroad equivalent to our own Triple Crown.

Now the Pegasus Rising Project gave the horses a healthy home and a place to be rehabilitated so they could help heal people who experienced emotional trauma.

Wow, this is what I need.

What were the odds for that story to be in the same paper as my son's obituary? I felt destined to walk this next path. I cared for, fed, brushed, exercised, and loved on these beautiful horses. As I was healing them, they were healing me, until one day, two years later, I put down the shovel and felt I was finished.

With God leading me there, I wondered where else God would lead and how else he might speak to me. I wanted to hear more from God, so I picked up Mark Virkler's *Four Keys to Hearing God's Voice*. In the book he explained the four keys:

> **Key #1:** Recognize God's voice as spontaneous thoughts, ideas, words, feelings, or visions that light up your mind.
>
> **Key #2:** Quiet yourself so you can hear God's voice. Remove yourself from outer noise.
>
> **Key #3:** Look for vision as you pray: "He said, 'Listen to my words: When there is a prophet among you, I, the LORD, reveal myself to them in visions, I speak to them in dreams'" (Numbers 12:6).
>
> **Key #4:** Journal your prayers and God's answers.[9]

Virkler said it is always a good idea to test whether an image is from ourselves, Satan, or God. "Find its origin, test the spirit (1 John 4:1). Examine its content, test the ideas (1 John 4:5) and see its fruit, test the fruit (Matthew 7:15–20). If it is self, it is born in mind, a painting of things I have learned. If the image is obstructive, negative, fearful, violates the Word of God then it is from Satan. God's visions will be a living flow of pictures coming from the innermost being after your quiet time praying and focusing on Jesus. It will be instructive, upbuilding, comforting, vision accepts, testing, power, peace, good fruit, enlightenment, knowledge, and humility."[10]

As I opened my spiritual eyes, I recognized that God continually showed up for Brad and me, reminding us that he was with us and cared about us. One of those signs happened one day when we went for our nature walk along our lagoon. We often walked there with our golden retrievers and the boys as they were growing up. On this particular day, we took our two dogs and headed out. After a few minutes, I felt a strong sense to stop. It was one of our favorite spots.

"Why are we stopping?" Brad asked.

I shrugged. *Wait and be still,* the spontaneous thought came through my spirit.

As we stood still, a monarch butterfly began flying around Brad and me. I thought the two dogs would have startled the butterfly, chasing it away, but they didn't. It stayed there flying around us. We watched as it landed on a wood post. I quietly knelt and extended my finger, hoping it would crawl on. It did!

I slowly stood to show my husband, and it flew away. But soon it returned and brushed Brad's head a couple times, as though to get his attention. Brad's face lit up.

"Be still and wait to see what happens next."

The butterfly landed on Brad's right shoulder and sat for a few moments. God seemed to be showing us what he knew we needed to see.

"God is letting Mitchell show us that his spirit is free as a butterfly," I told Brad. "To land on your right shoulder and to sit there is astonishing! Do you realize this is the same right shoulder you used to carry Mitchell up and down the stairs when he was sick? Mitchell wants you to know how much he loves you."

That day on the trail, my husband saw the veil lifted from his own eyes. We both had to wipe away the tears. I thanked the Father, Son, and Holy Spirit for letting us see this through spiritual eyes.

When Mitchell was still with us, we would sit outside and see butterflies flying around us in our backyard. Often, I would tell him that one day God would set him free from all his pain. I always thought the healing would take place on earth. But God had other plans. I felt God was showing us again that Mitchell was indeed free from suffering.

God speaks to all of us if we listen and open the eyes of our hearts. I often asked God to open my spiritual eyes so I could see more clearly. And he did. It may have been a spontaneous thought or a dream. Or he would speak through others. Or we would receive a sign that only we recognized as our family moved through the healing process. Our hearts where still broken, and in our brokenness, God never left our side.

One day God directed my steps to Mitchell's bedroom where I came across one of his notes tucked inside his treasure box. He had written it at a time when he was still able to pick up a pen. It read, "Thank you, Mom and Dad, for all you have done to find help for me. I love you so much. Mitchell."

Tears rolled down my face. "Thank you, Lord, for letting me see this note." It was what I needed that day—to be reminded of how much Mitchell loved and appreciated us."

I also began to recognize how God used his followers to deliver a message. He spoke to my aunt Sharon, a prophetic woman. In May 2009, six months after Mitchell's passing, we were attending my cousin Eric's wedding at Churchill Downs, in Kentucky, when she gave us a letter. In our hotel room later that evening, I opened the letter and read.

The timing for this letter is to be read when their spirits can receive it. I just saw this vision for Beth Ann and Brad and wrote it down soon after. Mitchell's suffering is over and gone. It only exists in them. As they release it, there will be great authority to help others in these situations. Mitchell was sent for this very purpose. The work done in Brad and Beth Ann between February and November was very important. That is why his purpose was held to the earth for that time.

Something was accomplished in them that "took territory"—something they and God had to do. If Brad and Beth Ann can give Mitchell to Jesus and realize that he did fulfill his purpose, their grief will lift, and they will see him as the great gift to the world that he was and is. There was a grace for them to live what they experienced. And they did. Now there is destiny in the balance. When they are able to release the hopes they had for him and see that his purpose was fulfilled, they will open within themselves a new vision for their own destinies, and they will be able to embrace the walk God is ready to unveil.

God spoke to us through her. Little did we know what was about to unfold as God was taking us on a new journey.

I wanted to let go of the pain and sorrow, not the love and memories. At times I wished I could forget about his death, but that would mean I'd have to forget about him, and I never wanted to forget about Mitchell. Death leaves a heartache that no one can heal except God; love leaves a memory no one can steal.

I wanted to hear from God, and he graciously answered. Jesus told us, "I will ask the Father, and he will give you another advocate to help you and be with you forever—the Spirit of truth. The world cannot accept him, because it neither sees him nor knows him. But you know him, for he lives with you and will be in you" (John 14:16–17).

And his words are true. The Holy Spirit was our advocate, our comforter. And he led us, along with the apostle Paul, to say, "Praise be to the God and Father of our Lord Jesus Christ, the Father of compassion and the God of all comfort, who comforts us in all our troubles, so that we can comfort those in any trouble with the same comfort we ourselves receive from God" (2 Corinthians 1:3–4).

Butterfly landing
on my finger.

The butterfly landed on Brad's finger
and then flew to his shoulder.

Thank you mom and
Dad for all the help
you have done to find
help for me, I love
you so much, Mitchell

One of the last notes Mitchell wrote to us at Christmas.

L to R starting in back row: Me, my sister Patty, my sister Linda;
front row my aunt Maine, my aunt Sharon, my sister and Mitchell's godmother Cheryl

With my aunt Sharon.

Rescued Arabian horse project.

Chapter 23

If You Build It, They Will Come

Six months after Mitchell's passing, in May 2009, two of our friends from the baseball community, Tom and Dave, asked Brad if we would like to pursue renaming of one of the ballfields in Mitchell's honor.

Brad was surprised and touched. "That is a super idea," he told them. "That will be a great way to keep Mitchell's legacy alive. And it will come full circle, since Mitchell named our backyard Thorp Field."

He was excited as he told me the news. But then he began to think about it more. "This may not be as easy as I first thought." He explained that we would have to present our case and proposal before the City of Carlsbad Parks and Recreation Committee. If they approved, then we'd go before the mayor and the city council and present our case to them.

As we discussed it, we knew we wanted to pursue this, even though we both understood the challenges.

Brad drafted the proposal and put it in a PowerPoint presentation.

"Here, honey. Listen to this," he said, after he completed it. He began to read what he'd worked so long and hard on:

We would like to thank you all for the opportunity to present our case to you. The subject is to rename Field 1 at Poinsettia Park to Thorp Field. We would like to propose an on-going living memorial and fund to help other kids play baseball.

Mitchell ate, slept, and drank baseball since he started picking up a ball at age two and started playing at age five. He grew up well known and respected in the La Costa Youth Organization (LCYO). Mitchell's father, Brad Thorp, was a pitcher in the Los Angeles Dodger organization. He was a board member and coach for many years with both LCYO and Carlsbad Youth Baseball (CYB). He continues to help CYB with pitching clinics and assists the pitchers at Carlsbad High School (CHS).

Mitchell's journey was reported widely in the media as we tried to find answers, in and out of different hospitals, with no diagnosis to his mysterious medical condition. He fought with all his might to stay here with us. His battle was long and hard, and ended with his passing on November 19, 2008. Mitchell's journey has touched many hearts in this community and throughout the United States.

Many Carlsbad citizens have signed our petitions in support of changing the name from Field 1 to Thorp Field. We would like to propose that the city honor and recognize the significant contributions that Brad Thorp and his son, Mitchell, have made to the public life of the citizens of Carlsbad and to the baseball community.

We bring before you some of the benefits and reasons for this rename request.

1. Mitchell's first walk-a-thon was on this field. The event raised nearly $70,000 for his medical expenses.
2. The proposal has the support of the baseball community of Carlsbad. LCYO, CYB, and CHS have all expressed a willingness to support the effort, and believe it is in the best interests of the community. These organizations are the primary users of Poinsettia Field #1.
3. We would like to continue annual events, like a walk-a-thon, baseball tournaments, and trainings to raise funds to help underprivileged kids play baseball, a perpetual scholarship for other young players to play the game Mitchell loved so much.
4. We can fund and help supply equipment for those who cannot afford it.

5. A fund has already been put in place and Mitchell's website is still up and running.

6. We can adopt the field and help maintain it.

7. It is good for the city to show good will.

On behalf of Mitchell and his entire family, we would be honored to see the Mitchell Thorp journey continue for the benefit of others.

Brad finished and looked at me. "What do you think?"

I was blown away! "You put a lot of thought and vison into this, honey, and I think it is a great way to honor our son. When do you need to present it?"

"Next week."

Wow, that was soon! But I was proud of the way he jumped on this effort.

"Can I ask a big favor? Can you present this?"

I blinked in surprise. "Wow. Okay, I was not expecting you to ask me to do that."

"You're a much better speaker than I am, and I might not be able to get through the first words without bursting into tears. Plus talking about myself seems weird."

"What makes you think I won't do the same? I'm still grieving too."

He smiled and shrugged. "I think you can do a better job."

I thought about it for a minute. "I will do it for our son."

Somehow, God's strength would get me through.

The week flew by, and before we knew it, the day arrived for us to give the presentation to the Parks and Recreation committee. My spirit was churning and knew this was where faith came in. I had to step up to the plate and put my faith into action that God would ease my fears and give me strength. Faith is knowing that something can be done, an inner conviction that comes before reality confirms it.

I can do all things through Christ who strengthens me, I thought, quoting Philippians 4:13, as Brad and I walked down the hall to the committee meeting room.

The committee quickly approved the proposal, and we both sighed with relief. We had crossed the first hurdle; now we had to present to the city council, which was crucial, since they had the final decision.

Later that month, I struggled, as I was still grieving, and I did not want to be around people. I could hardly speak to anyone without bursting into tears. How could I stand before the mayor and city council?

But I knew our request was important. *It's just like God to push me outside my comfort zone*, I thought.

Brad parked outside the city hall. Before he opened his car door, I took his hand. "Let's pray together for God's strength and invite the Holy Spirit to give me the words to speak. I'm just so weary with grief."

He smiled kindly and squeezed my hand.

"O Lord, please fill my words with your words," I prayed. "That whatever I say will touch the hearts of all those sitting on the city council."

Somehow, when we are weak, God makes us strong.

We walked into the meeting and waited our turn on the agenda. I felt my heart beating faster and faster, and I kept taking long deep breaths. I kept silently reciting Joshua 1:9: *"Have I not commanded you? Be strong and courageous. Do not be afraid; do not be discouraged, for the LORD your God will be with you wherever you go."*

When my time came to speak, Brad and I stepped to the podium. I took a deep breath and paused as I looked at each council member. Then I began to speak our case.

I presented the PowerPoint presentation and spoke from my heart. My voice quivered at times as I tried to hold back tears. Somehow, through the grace of God, I was able to pull it together.

I knew God already was going before us, and he already knew the outcome, even though we did not. God was lifting me and carrying me, as he is so faithful to do.

After I spoke, a few council members wiped tears from their eyes.

I thanked them for their time, and they in turn let us know that they would consider the matter and give us their decision in a few days.

A few days later, a council member called. "Mrs. Thorp, we have some good news. The city council has approved your request to rename Field 1 at Poinsettia Park to Thorp Field. Congratulations!"

I felt genuinely excited for the first time in a long time. "Thank you! This means the world to our family, and I know it would to Mitchell, too."

As soon as I hung up the phone, I jumped for joy into Brad's arms, and we celebrated the news. I was riding high all day. I kept thinking of Mitchell and our favorite movie to watch together, *Field of Dreams*. In the movie, Iowa farmer Ray Kinsella, played by actor Kevin Costner, hears a mysterious voice in his cornfield saying, "If you build it, they will come."

Despite taunts of lunacy, Ray builds a baseball diamond on his land. And out of the rows of corn come the ghosts of great players, led by "Shoeless" Joe Jackson. But, as Ray learns, this field of dreams is about much more than bringing former baseball greats out to play. Ray realizes that a mysterious ball player was his father when his dad was young. Welcome to this place where reality mixes with fantasy and dreams can come true.

"My sweet Mitchell, we did it!" I said out loud. "We have your field. It is already built. I know in my heart people will come. I don't know when or how, but people will come."

We then got busy creating the field signage for the big reveal.

On November 19, 2009, one year after Mitchell's death, Thorp Field was formally dedicated in a ceremony at Poinsettia Park in Carlsbad. The city agreed to a formal ribbon-cutting ceremony to commemorate this special day. We invited family, Pastor Jason, close friends, and the baseball community. They pulled down a covering that hid the sign on the backstop of the ballfield and then revealed Mitchell's plaque on the concrete score table. The press even came and published an article in the local paper titled: "Fitting Tribute: Poinsettia Park Ballfield Named in Memory of Former Player" by Elana Cristiano.

After the ribbon-cutting ceremony, in front of a few dozen onlookers, Matthew, who was now seventeen, threw out the first pitch on the field.

As our symbolic "home field," Thorp Field is the site for our annual signature events. This day brought both sadness and gladness as our family climbed a big milestone in getting the city to approve renaming the field that Mitchell played so many games on.

This day gave my family and me a big step forward in our healing. Matthew could bring some closure to his pain. Brad felt this was a great honor to recognize Mitchell and a way to bring baseball scholarships to the community. I recognized that not wanting to face other people again was not in my or my family's best interest or God's vision for us. I knew in my heart that God wanted us to have joy again; it would just take us more time to get there.

I could see that with God's healing touch and guiding hand, we were able to turn the ashes of death into beauty for God's glory.

I began to push myself to engage in life again. I think having to speak in public was the start. I attended my Bible study group, which I had been absent from for too long. One lady welcomed me with a hug and told me that she saw a bright light around me.

Her words intrigued me. "This is God shining light through you," she told me. "When your world seems dark and you trust God anyway, his light will brightly shine through you. Your display of transcendent faith weakens spiritual forces of evil. His supernatural light showing through you blesses and strengthens people around you."

"Thank you for sharing this with me. I do feel his warmth surrounding me, like a warm hug." I realized that I did feel God's love. God was protecting me, as he knew how fragile I was. He was wrapping his loving presence around me as I pushed myself into the world again. "He must have a covering over me."

My friend agreed.

After Mitchell went home to heaven, Brad, Matthew, and I had some very hard moments. We all had to adjust to a new normal. We had to mix things up differently. Life kept moving so fast, but we felt as though we were still stuck in time.

The 2009 high school graduation notices arrived at our home from Mitchell's class, which only put more salt to our wounds. The sadness that rushed over me of what could have been, the lost dreams and memories we would have had together, left a gaping hole. We had to learn to push through this pain again. Life is about overcoming for each of us, no matter what tragedy or trial we have been through; it's about how we face them and overcome them.

We may never understand why God allows certain things to happen. Believe me, I have asked him. It is human nature to think that when tragedy happens, we must have stepped out of God's blessing. But Isaiah 55:9 tells us, "As the heavens are higher than the earth, so are my ways higher than your ways and my thoughts than your thoughts."

We had many eyes on us in the community, as many people were deeply affected by Mitchell's death. People were amazed by our strength and resilience.

Looking back, I have found that during those dark times, God works in and through our lives, so we can be a witness for him. And I found strength in that, in God's words through the prophet Isaiah:

> I took you from the ends of the earth, from its farthest corners I called you.
> I said, "You are my servant"; I have chosen you and have *not* rejected you.
> So do *not* fear, for I am with you; do *not* be dismayed, for I am your God.
> I will strengthen you and help you; I will uphold you with my righteous right hand."
> (Isaiah 41:9–10, emphasis added)

Thorp Field, renamed in Mitchell's honor.

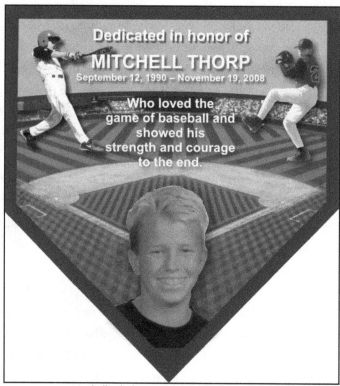

Mitchell's dedication plaque at the ball field.

Part 6

One Life Ignites Loving Change

Chapter 24

God's New Vision and Mission

Mitchell's life ignited loving change in us, as a new vision and mission began to unfold. At first Brad and I thought we would just have the ball field renamed in Mitchell's honor and provide scholarships to other young players to enjoy the game he loved. But soon we began to believe it might be more than that.

We felt God calling us in a new direction. And that meant our lives would begin to change. When we were both transformed, our focus changed to an eternal perspective. As Henry Blackaby wrote in *Experiencing God*: "You cannot go with God and stay where you are." Whenever God moves us in a new direction, we must change.

We realized that change would take us out of our comfort zone—nothing of great value is ever accomplished by staying in a comfort zone! To become what God had called us to, we needed to let him reshape us into a new creation. As the prophet Samuel told Saul, Israel's first king, "The Spirit of the LORD will come powerfully upon you, and you will prophesy with them; and you will be changed into a different person" (1 Samuel 10:6).

We knew God wanted to do the very same thing for us, as he does for all people to change them into new creations. He wanted to reshape us so we could reflect his glory in this dark world.

The days passed as we prayed and discussed where God may be leading us next—and we knew it would be as Christ's ambassadors: "We are therefore Christ's ambassadors, as though God were making his appeal through us" (2 Corinthians 5:20).

One night while Brad was at a meeting at our church, he learned about two young boys whom he had coached in baseball. One had Hodgkin's lymphoma and the other had non-Hodgkin's lymphoma. Both families were struggling to make ends meet as the medical bills and out-of-pocket expenses overtook them.

Brad heard God's voice speak to his spirit, *Start a foundation to help other families going through what you went through.*

That night he came home and announced, "God wants us to start a foundation."

I looked at him. "You want to do what?"

He explained about the boys and what he heard God tell him.

"But we know nothing about starting or running a foundation," I told him as my mind began racing with the logistics.

"Have faith my love," he said and smiled.

I laughed and shook my head. "You're right. Who am I to doubt what God has spoken?" *This must be what God meant when he told me months ago that Mitchell's death was not the end but the beginning,* I thought. "Okay, I'm on board if you are."

Our new mission and vision became larger. We serve a great big God; he doesn't do anything small.

We were now on a mission to store up treasures in heaven. As Jesus said in Matthew 6:19–20: "Do not store up for yourselves treasures on earth, where moths and vermin destroy, and where thieves break in and steal. But store up for yourselves treasures in heaven, where moth and vermin do not destroy, and where thieves do not break in and steal."

We had a choice: What would we do with all our suffering? Did we need to learn and share something? God's mission for us became clear. Even though we did not know the outcome, we walked in faith, knowing that God was walking right alongside us. So, we took the next steps.

Brad filed the paperwork to form a nonprofit organization. And on August 17, 2009, we officially became the Mitchell Thorp Foundation, a public 501(c)3 organization whose mission is: To support families whose children suffer from life-threatening illnesses, diseases, and disorders, by providing financial, emotional, and resources to their desperate situations.

When Brad returned home, he showed me the official document.

I looked at it and hugged him. We had stepped out in faith, giving up our past lives to start this foundation. God would use our experience with Mitchell to help others. What better legacy could we possibly have?

"Let's get on our hands and knees and give this foundation to God to run it the way he sees fit," I suggested.

We both knelt and committed the foundation to God, declaring him to be the CEO and asking him to direct our steps. We just needed to suit up and show up and wait in expectancy. Each step was a step of faith. We needed his guidance, wisdom, and discernment in our decisions. Now we were living a servant leadership role. We were ready to demonstrate God's love to help others who could not see the light at the end of the tunnel. We used what little money we had left from Mitchell's fund to start the foundation. For the rest, we had to step out in faith that God would provide.

God did provide just as we needed him to. Right after Mitchell's death, we filed a wrongful death lawsuit against the hospital and doctor. After two years with the lawyers for both sides negotiating, they finally settled. With the settlement money, we covered the attorney fees and paid off the medical bills, but more importantly, we had funds to help other children and families. We knew these funds would go only so far, and we needed a way to get others to donate to our cause.

We knew only too well the burdens families endure when they have a child with a life-threatening medical condition. They have loss of income, as one of the parents must usually quit his or her job to be the primary caregiver. That loss only exacerbates the financial burden as parents struggle to keep up with medical bills and household expenses on one income. And the emotional stress can be devastating. Other family relationships often take a back seat in a medical crisis. As the Johnson family described it, "There are so many extra layers of stress: worry over your child, navigating jobs, caring for other children at home, costs of medical care, hospital visits. And the list could easily go on." These stressors test families beyond their endurance, often bankrupting them financially, emotionally, and physically, and often leading to divorce or separation.

Brad and I jumped all in to start the foundation to help other families and children fighting for their tomorrows. Letting go of all fear and anxiety over money and security, we trusted that the Lord had a plan and a new purpose for us. As Philippians 1:6 says, "Being confident of this, that he who began a good work in you will carry it on to completion until the day of Christ Jesus."

Now that our foundation was official, Brad and I began planning our first event: the annual Mitchell Thorp Foundation walkathon. We decided to hold it on January 23, 2010. Though we'd already had a walkathon when Mitchell was still with us, the foundation had not been formed yet. The four-mile walk included laps around the park, beginning and ending at Thorp Field. We were so committed to our community after all they demonstrated to help our family, we knew we wanted to pay it forward. We knew that if each community could come together to help one another, the world would be a better place.

The week of the event came, along with heavy rains! As we monitored the weather forecast, we worried that the rain would wash out our foundation's first official event. We decided that the weather wouldn't ruin the day—we would move full steam ahead, regardless.

The sun rose gloriously on the morning of the walk, and some six hundred participants showed up at Poinsettia Park. Among them were the two families who were helped by the foundation, the Cassin's, and Johnson families—the ones Brad had heard about at church. Sadly, the Cassin's son passed away just weeks before the walkathon, but the Johnsons' son attended the event and cheered everyone on.

To kick off the event, Pastor Jason asked everyone to join hands and led in prayer. He thanked God for the day and the event, asking God to bless it and provide the funds for the families in need.

Tears streamed down my face as so many gathered. *Oh, my dear son, look what God and you have done. People have come!*

The city's Jazzercise leaders led the scores of walkers in stretches, and Carlsbad High School's Lancer's Dancers and Excalibur performed. The Boy Scout color guard presented the colors, and Sarah Elliot, a student from Carlsbad High School, led the enthusiastic throng in the national anthem. Carlsbad High cheerleaders provided motivation while a deejay kept the crowd moving and dancing along the way.

Support also came in many other forms. Carlsbad firefighters showed up in an antique fire truck and cooked hot dogs. Local businesses, such as BJ's, Annabelle's Coffee, and Jamba Juice provided post-walk refreshments. Henry's grocery store supplied snacks on the route; the Elks Club and Albertson's donated more than one thousand bottles of water; and the Kelly School PTA put on a bake sale, with all the proceeds going to the foundation. And at the end of the event, a local Daisy Troop volunteered to help with the recycling. We were overwhelmed by the community's support and enthusiasm.

At the end of the walk, everyone felt the air of excitement and the spirit of love. The Johnson family even acknowledged, "Being here gives us so much energy. The actual love and compassion are worth more than any money that they provide."

The walkathon was a huge success. We raised nearly $65,000.

Brad and I clearly saw God in action through us and how people were drawn to this cause and its message of hope. We knew from that day forward that this was our new mission in life.

Five months later, in June, I went to see the high school graduation—a year after Mitchell's class of 2009. I'm not sure why I felt drawn to go, as I knew it would be hard for me to see other students graduating since my son did not; I knew Mitchell had graduated to a different place—heaven. But still God prompted me to be there, so I went.

The whole football stadium was packed. I slowly found my place by the fence outside, looking onto the football field and the main stage. I watched and listened as the ceremony went on. Then the class president gave his speech.

I was stunned as I listened to him talk about the importance of helping others—and how the Mitchell Thorp Foundation made him and his class better people. He told the audience about the Mitchell Thorp Foundation and the mission.

Tears rolled down my face. I had no idea this young man's speech would be about Mitchell and the foundation and its effect on him and fellow students.

When he finished, I looked up to the heavens. So many people heard about the foundation for the very first time. Realizing that this student thought enough about Mitchell to include him in his speech touched me to the core.

Thank you, God. Was this what you needed me to hear?

I can't help but marvel at the way God moves and works in people's lives. Divine order has helped our life unfold from this tragic loss. Brad and I remember times when we did not know how a situation would work out; we just needed to trust that it would. Life is always changing, but the principle of divine order remains unchanged. I realize that order undergirds all situations and inspires us to focus on what is under our control and to release the rest. We have to surrender daily, trusting that the same power holding the planets in their orbits is supporting our lives too. And the more we trust, the more we have seen him unfold our highest good.

More than 1,000 participants, joined hands in prayer before the event.

National anthem sang at the opening ceremony.

City council presented check to the foundation.

Fire truck on display.

Participants enjoying their warm-up.

Carlsbad High Lancer Dancer team performed.

Brad and me.

Participants walking for the cause.

Chapter 25

Love of the Game

In keeping with our promise and mission, we wanted to honor Mitchell's memory by blessing other young players who love the game as much as Mitchell, Brad, and Matthew did. A few months after the walkathon, Brad and I investigated designing a unique plaque we could give to ball players who demonstrated many of the same skills and character that Mitchell had shown while playing the game.

"What about taking the design from Mitchell's plaque at the park, making it into a smaller scale, and listing criteria on the front?" Brad asked.

I thought that was a great idea, so we looked for a trophy shop that could do that.

Then we worked creating the criteria to win this honor. We finally came up with the four categories: the winner would have to be a good *sportsman*, have strong *baseball skills*, be a *student athlete*, and be an *outstanding citizen*.

"I think we have it!" Brad exclaimed.

We drove to the trophy shop to discuss our vision for this award—a smaller version of Mitchell's plaque with the ballplayer's name, division, criteria, and the year. The owner told us he could make that happen.

With our vision in place, we needed to honor some players! Besides the award plaque, each league would receive a $600 scholarship to help underprivileged children or anyone who simply couldn't afford to have their child play. Each league would have the funds to help cover that need.

Brad reached out to all the coaches in both Carlsbad Youth Baseball and La Costa Youth Baseball to explain about the award and how players could be nominated. Teachers, community members, other coaches, and individuals would write letters about the players and email them to the team coaches to vote on.

On May 22, 2010, we were to present the first ever Mitchell Thorp award on Championship Day during opening ceremonies. Before we began, I checked in to be sure Brad was prepared mentally and emotionally.

"I'm ready," he said. "I do this for Mitchell and to bring awareness to the foundation."

"Okay, honey," I said as I hugged him. "Mitchell is here. I feel his presence."

The president of the baseball organization announced over the loudspeaker, "We need all the coaches and players to line up in the outfield for the award presentation."

The young players scurried to their respective spaces. They were so excited to receive their team trophy for all their hard work. As thrilled as I was to give our award, the event was bittersweet because it reminded me of when our boys played ball and what could have been.

The president officially started the ceremony. "Welcome, everyone, to Championship Day. We are so proud of all these young ballplayers who put so much time and effort into a great season. Before we hand out your trophies by team, I want to bring to your attention a very special award. The coaches of each team selected one player from their team to receive the Mitchell Thorp award. It is very challenging to pick just one, and it is selected on the write ups that have been submitted from all the coaches. At this time, I would like to bring up the cofounder of the Mitchell Thorp Foundation, Brad Thorp, who, many of you may not know, pitched in the Los Angeles Dodger organization. Brad, come on up."

Brad stepped up to the microphone, with a few of our board members and me by his side. "I am happy to honor these outstanding athletes who have been nominated by their peers, coaches, teachers, and community members," he said. He talked briefly about Mitchell and why this award was so special. "This will be an annual award given to some lucky ballplayers."

All those precious little players, along with the coaches and families in the stands, listened intently.

Our son Mitchell was a young boy, just like all of you, who loved to play the game. He learned a lot about life through playing. He learned sportsmanship, being a team player, perseverance, winning and losing, and so much more. Tragically, on November 19, 2008, he was taken by an undiagnosed illness after suffering five long hard years. We called him our warrior son, as he was the strongest young man I ever knew and has made us stronger just knowing him," he continued. "Through the Mitchell Thorp Foundation, we provide grants to promising young athletes and award players who display outstanding sportsmanship and baseball skills, and who is a student athlete and an outstanding citizen.

Various fundraisers, corporate sponsorships, and grants support the Foundation's mission. Annually the foundation donates grant money to LCYO and CYB baseball clubs for those who cannot afford to pay to play the game Mitchell loved.

This award honors a player who has demonstrated these characteristics just like Mitchell:

* A passion for the game.
* The player should show a willingness to help others and to be a strong supportive teammate.
* The player should be a leader who has earned the respect of his teammates and coaches through hard work and dedication to the game.
* The player should also have a strong academic and community involvement.
* The player should demonstrate excellent baseball skills and the willingness to improve.

When each winner from each division was announced, Brad read the players' bios and accomplishments in baseball, school, and community involvement. Parents, grandparents, friends, and relatives listened. Cameras clicked away, and the local paper was there to document the moment.

With each player to be announced the suspense built as the names were called, shouts of joy from the stands and the teams. Everyone cheered as each player walked to the staging area to receive his or her award. To watch the children, stand by Brad while he read about each of them gave each a boost of confidence and strengthened their character further. We shook their hands and told them that they should feel proud of their accomplishments. We encouraged each to continue being a productive person and impacting the world they live in. We all gathered for separate and group photos. When the award presentation was all over, Matthew jogged out to the mound to throw out the first pitch for the championship game.

We left the park and looked at each other and smiled. We told Mitchell and God that this was a good day. We hoped we had touched and inspired the hearts of many people. The ripple effect has touched one person to another and has inspired them to achieve their goals.

Many people search their whole lives to find purpose and meaning. Ours, unfortunately, came to us through tragedy, but we endured and triumphantly turned it around. We know that God's divine spirit lives within us and that we can handle any challenge we face.

We decided we would not be defined by the tragedy but by the glory from it. Our strong, unwavering faith shows through our character no matter what is happening around us. Our commitment to each other, to Mitchell, and to Matthew is to fully express our spiritual nature, which inspires others.

We all display the very best of ourselves through our character. It is easy to let our light shine when we stay connected to God's light within. God loves you; he is inviting you to come to him and have a personal relationship with your father in heaven.

In the same way, let your light shine before others, so that they may see your good works and give glory to your Father in heaven (Matthew 5:16).

Continuing to move in the direction where God was leading us, we decided to take Mitchell's passion for competitive baseball and create a tournament in his honor. Brad, our board of directors, and I got busy making this a reality. We prayed over this event, that God would open the doors so we could secure all the ballfields, and have plenty of umpires, volunteers, vendors, and teams that would show up for our *1st Annual Grand Slam 4 Mitchell Baseball Tournament.*

We were hoping that at least thirty teams would sign up for the first tournament. Oh, no, God had a much bigger plan. Sixty teams signed up. We all worked from sunup to sundown for this three-day tournament. We continue to hold the Grand Slam 4 Mitchell tournament every year in September, since this is childhood cancer awareness month and 68 percent of the children, we help have some form of cancer.

As each team checked in, we gave them their box of balls and gold ribbons—representing childhood cancer awareness—to wear on their shirts. One of our cancer children who loves baseball came out during our opening ceremonies. It was beautiful to witness the coaches and ball players take a knee as we talked about the significance of what they were playing for. All these children from ages seven up to fourteen watched and listened intently. They began to understand how grateful they should be to play a sport they love when some children are fighting for their tomorrow. Brad said in his speech, "One day when some of you lucky athletes make it to the big leagues, know that when you give your time to go to the children's hospitals and sign autographs on your jerseys and baseballs, you will make another child's wish come true. Just to let them feel a part of you, somehow, is how you can make a difference."

Several coaches and parents thanked us afterward for helping these young athletes to recognize this early on. We learned through each tournament, but the most important thing was to keep stepping out in faith and to be fully devoted to God in our walk. To watch what God does with the tournament next and see whose hearts he touches in the process is priceless.

How about you? When do you feel vibrantly alive? What do you feel drawn to? Asking these questions with an open heart and gentle curiosity will let you begin to discover your purpose. Take time to deeply contemplate these questions. Pay attention to everything that comes to mind and write it down as you listen for answers. Images of people and situations may begin to fill your awareness, and then you might notice feelings and impulses surfacing.

Ask: Am I beginning to feel excited? Energized? Is my heart full of gladness once I complete this task?

Maybe you feel a deep sense of calm and peace as you discern whether you need to take an important step in your life. Look to these feelings as a prompt from the Holy Spirit to follow the call of your heart. Invite the Holy Spirit in; he equips and empowers us to do far more than we could ever do on our own. Do not be intimidated by challenging circumstances or tough times. The third person of the Godhead lives inside you!

Many times, Brad and I have been pushed to the edge. The only way to step off the edge is by faith. Fear is what stops us. Have we been afraid to step outside our comfort zone, to go into uncharted territory? Yes, we have. How do we cope with that? We pray and ask the Holy Spirit, our Helper and Counselor, to strengthen us as we go step-by-step, minute-by-minute. And He goes with us.

If we are to speak to a crowd of people, we ask the Holy Spirit to fill us not with our words but with what God wants us to say to people in that moment. The Lord knows exactly who needs to hear what we have to say and as we obey him, the hope we bring begins to impact others for the better.

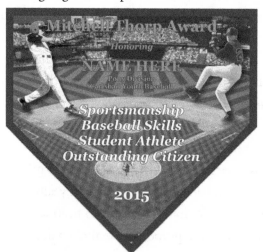

Mitchell Thorp Award given out to nominated players since 2010.

Matthew throwing out the first pitch.

Speaking to the players before the tournament.

Three-day tournament begins with sixty teams.

Grand Slam 4 Mitchell rings and medals.

Happy division winners received rings and medals for first and second places.

Chapter 26

Service Is Love in Action

Two years after we started the nonprofit organization, Brad had another God-inspired vision, which struck him when he noticed so many students volunteering at our events. We both recognized that kids like helping kids.

"Let's start a Youth Leadership Council program," Brad said one day in June 2012. "What do you think?"

"That is an amazing idea," I told him. "It could be another program under the foundation. We can train future servant-leaders. I think more than ever before, there is a need for more leadership training to inspire young people to dream, participate, and persevere."

Wow! I thought. *We lost our child but now have gained so many other children to teach that there is a higher purpose in serving the greater good.*

We wanted a servant leadership program to develop in our young members a true and everlasting love of servant leadership—which would empower them to fulfill a lifetime of service for the benefit of humankind.

The phrase *servant leadership* was coined by Robert K. Greenleaf in an essay he first published in 1970. Yet it is an old concept. Two thousand years ago, servant leadership was central to the philosophy of Jesus, who exemplified the fully committed and effective servant-leader. Mahatma Gandhi, Dr.

Martin Luther King Jr., Mother Teresa, and Nelson Mandela are more recent examples of leaders who have exemplified this philosophy. Now we could add the Mitchell Thorp Foundation to this list. Greenleaf said, "The servant-leader is servant first."[11] By that he meant, the desire to serve, the "servant's heart," is a fundamental characteristic of a servant-leader. It is not about being servile; it is about helping others. It is about identifying and meeting others' needs.

Brad and I took this new vision before our board, and they all agreed that this was a terrific idea. We began to seek out a youth leadership director, who could run the program and facilitate our curriculum with me. We hired Kelly Schwab, who ran it for two years, then passed the baton to Tom Watson.[12] Tom helped us bring more structure to the program. We recognized that we needed to come up with the Youth Leadership Council's mission, vision, and core values that best represented the foundation.

"Let's bring this task up to our students at our next meeting and see what suggestions they have," Tom said. "I will get one of the students to write it on the white board. We can come up with something."

"Great idea, Tom!" I said. "This will teach the students how to structure a mission, vision, and value statement so they will know what we stand for."

The day of the meeting came and as Tom explained their assignment, the students grew excited and came up with some brilliant ideas. With a little refinement from their input, we landed on a statement that we still use today:

Mission

The Mitchell Thorp Foundation (MTF) Youth Leadership Council supports the Mission of MTF by planning and executing service projects and events, which raise funds and increase awareness of MTF in the communities that we serve.

The Youth Leadership Council supports the values of MTF by empowering youth to develop leadership skills within a service-oriented environment.

Vision

Our vision for the Youth Leadership Council program is twofold:

* To increase the depth and breadth of services that MTF can provide, through the service and outreach of our youth.
* To develop in our young members a true and everlasting love of servant leadership, a love that will empower them to fulfill a lifetime of service for the benefit of mankind.

Core Values, "In the Spirit of Mitchell"

Giving: We will strive to give hope and faith to the families we support by understanding their struggles and needs and aligning them to the resources we can offer.

Integrity: We will demonstrate integrity by honoring our commitments, communicating honestly, and never compromising our ethics.

Leadership: We will demonstrate service-oriented leadership and will seek to promote the development of leaders within our organization and constituent community.

Collaboration: We will collaborate with individuals and groups that believe in our mission to enhance the services we can provide.

Youth: We believe that youth represent our future and seek to empower them and to recognize their service and accomplishments.

Culture: We believe in sharing faith and hope, when appropriate, within our team and the families we support. We value and welcome those of all beliefs and backgrounds to join our cause or to ask for our support. We believe in the importance of having fun as we work together in pursuit of our mission.

With a strong foundation, we began to recruit students from the eighth through twelfth grades. The Youth Leadership Council offers young people the chance to take initiative and make a difference. It teaches them how to mobilize others to want to make extraordinary things happen in their schools and community. We teach the practices different leaders use to transform values into actions, visions into realities, obstacles into breakthroughs and innovations, separateness into solidarity, and risks into rewards. It teaches the students how to turn challenging situations into remarkable outcomes.

We started the first few years with twenty-five students and now enroll as many as fifty to seventy students each year. Our new Youth Leadership director, Kenny Wood, came to us with years of training and development from The Ken Blanchard Company.

We knew the program would grow to a whole new level. Over the years we witnessed this growth as the program has become popular and an exclusive council to be part of. Participants say they like being part of something bigger than themselves. Plus, they experience the joy of giving back and helping families whose children are suffering from life-threatening illnesses, diseases, and disorders. They like to see how they are making a difference in their community.

Students have been impacted in a big way. Brad and I were overwhelmed to hear what some of the students said at their senior send-off celebration:

> My name is Bennett Hochner, and I'm a senior at Sage Creek High School. In the fall, I will attend University Southern California (USC). One of my favorite memories from being in the Youth Leadership Council (YLC) was volunteering at the Mitchell Thorp Foundation 5K race. I felt super important that day when they had me wear snazzy, technologically advanced headsets to assist with traffic and parking. Plus getting to work alongside a motorcycle police officer made me feel even more important. The event was both fun and heartening as I saw so many members of the community come together to make a difference for such a worthy cause. It touched my heart knowing that I was playing a part in making that difference.
>
> During my two years in YLC, I've learned not only a myriad of valuable leadership skills, but I will take away something much deeper—that anyone, regardless of age or title or occupation or wealth, is capable of making a difference in the lives of others, especially those who may need assistance of some type.
>
> Beyond teaching about leadership, the YLC also teaches empathy, compassion, and camaraderie. I've used the lessons learned from YLC in many aspects of my life. Especially over the past year, having open communication, working collaboratively with others, exhibiting patience, and understanding, and definitely showing genuine concern for others have been key.

In the future, I will continue to hold these lessons close, whether it's in college, at a job, or wherever life takes me. I just want to say thank you to Brad, Beth, Kenny, and the foundation for offering such a great opportunity to me and the other members of the council to learn so much about leadership, about helping others and about life. Thank you!

Student Jack Gogal wrote:

I have been in the Youth Leadership Council for four years. One of my fondest memories was at the 5K run. I recall waking up before dawn to prepare the balloon arch. When I arrived, only a dozen people were in an empty parking lot. No decorations, no food trucks, no bands, no people. Within an hour, that empty parking lot transformed into a crowded and excited celebration. Watching that transformation stuck with me. I can't pinpoint exactly when that empty parking lot turned into the 5K run. But I can say exactly where we started: inflating one small balloon and tying it to an archway with many more to go. From there, we each broke into tasks and worked on our small parts, and when all was said and done, we had ourselves a big event.

Youth Leadership Council has inspired me to pursue the ideals of servant leadership. Servant leadership emphasizes the importance of leading to serve others. We are encouraged to maintain an approachable attitude, listen well, and collaborate with others. Anyone stands to benefit from these strategies from the corporate CEO to students. Learning these strategies throughout high school has helped tremendously to build my self-confidence, particularly in public speaking and taking initiative. It has inspired me to pursue leadership not only in the Mitchell Thorp community, but also in my personal life. It's encouraged me to step up and form school clubs and extracurricular projects in the benefit of others. Although I will be away studying architecture at UC Berkeley next year, I hope to continue pursuing what the Leadership Council has taught me and am looking forward to the future.

It was important to the foundation and the YLC program to give students hands-on experiences through all our fundraising events—teaching them how to implement a big vision and to see how each step and task is implemented into a successful outcome. We even let the students come up with their own fundraisers. They learn how to structure it, create different tasks, and finally implement it from beginning to end. One year the students decided as a whole what their fundraiser would be. After several suggestions on the white board, the students voted on a pancake breakfast.

"Yeah!" They all cheered.

The funds raised from their event allowed them, in their next meeting, to tally what they had raised. Then they voted on what child and family they wanted those funds to go toward. One year they raised enough money to do a bedroom makeover for one of the children. Another year they raised enough to buy an iPad for a child with cancer. The next time they put the money toward new clothes and a wig for a child with cancer.

Kids like having fun. We tell the students our philosophy, which is "If you don't have fun while executing servant leadership projects, then it's not worth doing." The projects give them hands-on experience and new life skills that they may never have been exposed to before and will be with them for years to come.

We engage the students with the foundation as much as possible—whether we take them to city council when we receive awards or to the hospitals to deliver toys, or to help deliver a converted wheelchair van for a child and family. Students often said they liked our organization because they could see where their efforts were going and could participate in the process.

Christmastime is especially fun and heartwarming for the students because of our Adopt a Family program. The students are assigned to bring gifts for a family, which includes the affected child and siblings. We bring in lots of Christmas goodies, food, hot chocolate, and decorated cookies to keep the students going while they wrap gifts.

Forming the YLC program has given Brad and me and the foundation another beautiful extension of our love-in-action commitment to the youth in our community. It's a privilege to pour into and educate these students on what makes an impactful servant-leader. We've found it rewarding to see them blossom into confident, well-rounded human beings.

Service is love in action and a wonderful way to share our divine gifts with others. Opportunities to serve are endless! They may manifest themselves in small ways but have a large effect. Any act of kindness is a form of service. It might be volunteering to help feed the poor, but it also could be mowing the neighbor's lawn, letting someone go in front of you in the grocery line, preparing a meal for a family with a sick child, or carpooling children to school when their parents can't. Service ranges from full-time caregiving to something as simple as listening. Anything we do to make life a little easier for another is sharing our servant hearts.

When we begin to serve and help others, we start to find our true selves. Service is a spiritual practice, something Jesus demonstrated. Before he was crucified, he had a final meal with his disciples. We commemorate this day as the Thursday before Easter, which we call Maundy Thursday. *Maundy* loosely translates to "commandment." Jesus told his disciples—and us: "A new command I give you: Love one another. As I have loved you, so you must love one another" (John 13:34). Before he gave this commandment, he washed his disciple's feet. He told them in John 13:15, "I have set you an example that you should do as I have done for you."

Later one of his disciples, Peter, wrote: "Each of you should use whatever gift you have received to serve others, as faithful stewards of God's grace in its various forms" (1 Peter 4:10).

I take these words to heart, knowing, as Mahatma Gandhi shared, "The best way to find yourself is to lose yourself in the service of others." I follow Jesus' example of service, as well as his commandments; I serve others, finding Christ's presence in everything I do.

Christmas holiday party Tom Watson, director.

YLC training with Kenny Wood, director.

Wrapping gift project for children and families.

Toys ready for delivery.

Brad and me, with Jack Gogal and Kenny Wood

Shea Simmons and Shea Gahr,
longest in the program, for six years.

Chapter 27

Another Godly Encounter

On January 29, 2014, Brad was upstairs working in his office while I was downstairs in mine. We were both busy planning the next big 5K Warrior Spirit Run/Walk and Family Festival event. The foundation had grown so much over the years that we had now graduated from a walkathon to a full-blown run/walk, with a family festival, a kids' fun zone area, live bands, and many health and wellness vendors for participants to check out. This had become one of our largest events of the year and the community always looked forward to it.

With both of us busy as could be, we would get exhausted pulling off these events year after year. We prayed often for God's strength to get us through and to help everything fall into place.

This particular day, I was feeling stressed and at my energy limit. "Lord, is all our effort paying off?" I prayed aloud. "Are we still making a difference?"

Within moments of that prayer, Brad texted me.

You got to come up here. You won't believe this.

I ran upstairs to his office. "What's up?"

His face was jubilant as he pointed toward the center of the floor.

I saw a shining cross of light beaming through the window and onto the center of the floor.

We both looked at each other in amazement.

I was stunned. I had just prayed, and God had answered right away. I knew he was telling me, *Yes, the effort is worth it. Keep going. I am with you.*

"I was just talking to God downstairs about whether our efforts are still making a difference," I told Brad. "This is another blessing to let us know that yes, it *is* all worth it."

Brad's jaw dropped open.

We had lived in our home for twenty-four years, and as long as we had been there, we had never witnessed this phenomenon before.

We sat in his office and cried.

The cross stayed illuminated in his office until the sun went down that day. Brad got up and looked at his window blinds to see if they were causing this image. He flipped them and moved them, but the illuminated cross didn't change at all.

I ran to get my phone to take some pictures, as I knew no one would believe us!

When the cross of light appeared, my curiosity got the best of me, so I began to research what it meant when a cross appeared in a house. And what did the cross of light signify?

I learned that people take crosses as a sign of divine promise, and many believe they signify the return of Christ. The phenomenon of crosses of light appearing in windowpanes is not limited to any one place, nor is it an entirely new occurrence. There are signs of crosses that have appeared in the windows of churches all over the world. Though skeptics say it's just a bending of light in the frosted glass windows, no one can deny that the crosses are there. In our case it was not a reflection of a cross in the windowpane; it was beaming onto our carpeted floor!

What is this cross of light? It is the gateway between darkness and light, between this world and the world of the soul. As soon as the perishable personality is willing to be attached to this cross, the immortal soul within us will resurrect in the light of the heavenly realm. The cross also signifies acceptance of death or suffering and sacrifice.

Well, I can see this in our lives as we have become light in this dark world, and we understand the pain of death, suffering, and sacrifice, I thought.

Encounters like this were divine appointments with God—a specific time in our lives when God "showed up." It was marked by his presence, his power, and his personal touch.

An encounter with God looks different for everyone. Each person is uniquely made in God's image. He will communicate specifically to us so it will resonate within our souls. An encounter is an event or an experience that involves a supernatural manifestation of his presence in our lives. It is out of the ordinary and is often marked by some kind of physical sense of God's presence. Some may see visions, some may hear a word they know was specifically meant for them to hear, and others may feel his peace, joy, love, or strength. It's biblical to experience God in a way we can feel. When Jesus' disciples returned from outreach, Luke 10:21 describes Jesus as being "full of joy through the Holy Spirit." The Psalms are also full of accounts of people bringing their emotions to God and receiving hope and peace from him.

The cross of light did not return until a few years later—this time in Matthew's room. Now in college, he was set to come home for a visit.

Before Brad and I left to pick him up at the airport, I was praying for his safe return. Then I walked to his room to make sure everything was in order. As I entered his room, I saw a beautiful, illuminated cross on his floor. I smiled ear to ear and thanked the Lord for this sign.

I could feel deep in my spirit that the presence of God and Mitchell was in the atmosphere.

"Mitchell," I said, "your brother is coming home so I know you and God are here, and I am so glad you are. Mom feels your presence. Thank you, God, for showing up. Keep showing us all your beautiful signs and wonders so we can share them with others."

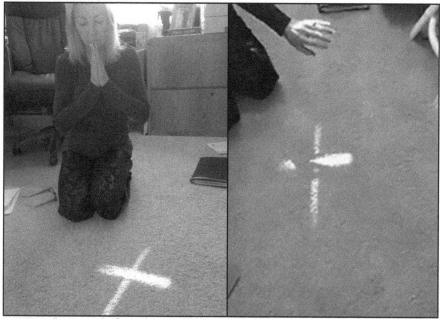

Cross illuminates the floor of Brad's office.

Beth runs her hand through the cross.

Checking the window to see how
and why this was happening.

The cross in Matthew's bedroom.

Chapter 28

Warrior Spirit

We woke up at 5:00 a.m. on February 6, 2016, to a glorious day. Knowing the forecast was sunny made both Brad and I feel at ease for our big event. Our adrenaline kicked into high gear as we realized all we still had to do before everyone arrived at the event. Brad, the volunteers, and I needed to hang banners, blow up balloons, help the deejay set up, help the band hook up speakers, construct the finish line arch, set up registration, put safety cones in place, help vendors find their assigned spaces . . . so much went on behind the scenes!

As the event start drew closer, people began checking in and getting their T-shirts, bibs, and timing chips. We felt the excitement in the atmosphere. More than a thousand walkers, runners, and spectators came out for the sixth annual Warrior Spirit Run/Walk and Family Festival. We named the event Warrior Spirit, because Mitchell was our warrior son, the strongest young man we ever encountered, but also because each child we help is a warrior, fighting every day for his or her tomorrow.

Three television stations and the newspaper covered the event. One of the reporters even told the audience about her battle with Lyme's disease growing up and how the medical bills nearly bankrupted her parents. She was honored to be part of such a worthy cause and encouraged the audience to donate.

Opening Ceremonies were about to begin. This year, for the first time, the Navy Leap Frogs skydive team jumped into the baseball field, with the last skydiver trailing a 1,500-square-foot American flag while the DJ played Lee Greenwood's "I'm proud to Be an American," followed by Alaina Blair, a high school student, who sang the National Anthem. We then acknowledged the mayor, city council members, firefighters, San Diego Friar mascot from the San Diego Padres baseball team, vendors, entertainment, and volunteers who made this event happen. It truly took a village.

My husband and I were humbled every time we saw so many people come and care for others they didn't even know—now that was community spirit! After all the dignitaries spoke, we called to the stage the fifteen families we were helping so they could tell how the foundation had helped them and thank those who came to walk or run for their child. As each family and child spoke, I looked into the crowd and saw some people wiping away tears. The crowd applauded. They were truly motivated to run and walk for these families and, with each step they took, to be thankful for their own heath.

God works in mysterious ways by connecting us. He knew exactly who we were to help, at the right time and the right place. That was our daily prayer to him—to bring to us the children and families who desperately needed our help.

Brad and I knew we had been chosen for this calling to help other children and families navigate the medical system and help them through our many programs. When I looked at each family, I was thankful that God allowed each one to come, as we never know from year to year who would be healthy enough to be there. But we were grateful for them all—for people like Renee and her son Ethan.

A Divine appointment put me in the bank where Renee worked. She had given birth to her son Ethan a year before and had just gone back to work. I was in the bank for foundation business and sat with her. She asked about the foundation.

"Our mission is to support families whose children suffer from life-threatening illnesses, diseases, and disorders by providing financial, emotional, and resource support to their desperate situation." I paused and sensed that there was something more to her question. "Why do you ask?"

She told me that she was a mother of five, and her youngest son, Ethan, had health challenges since he was born. He was diagnosed with hypoplastic left heart syndrome (HLHS) and esophageal atresia/tracheoesophageal fistula (TEF-EA). That meant he had a deformed heart and spine, as well as an esophagus that wasn't connected to his stomach. He'd had his first surgery, which attached his stomach to his esophagus, at six hours old. At one month old, he'd had his first open-heart surgery.

"My family has struggled under the burden of medical bills from all of this, even with my work insurance," she told me. "I'm grateful to be able to come back to my job, but Ethan is not out of the woods. He will need more surgeries. Ethan nearly died twice." Her voice quivered and she wiped away a tear. "But I am optimistic he will survive.

"I feel your pain as a mother," I told her. "We do our best to care for our children. I know you are overwhelmed." I pulled a business card out of my purse and handed it to her. "When you and your husband are ready, or if you feel you will need help, reach out, and I will send you an application for assistance."

She thanked me, and we went our separate ways. A year later, they were now one of our benefactors from this year's event.

As she stood on the stage with her family, she smiled. "We never expected to end up in such a difficult situation but having this amazing foundation and the Thorps come into our lives was destiny. They were our life savers when we were drowning in medical debt from all of Ethan's care."

Next on the stage was Connor's family, with Connor in his stroller. Connor started having seizures at three months old and was diagnosed at eight months old with West syndrome, the worst form of epilepsy. His parents, Kelley and Randy Dalby, began trying different integrative treatments, therapies, and medications to see if it would help. They even had Connor's gene mapping done, which was an emerging procedure when Mitchell passed and was very expensive. His parents hoped to use his genetic mapping for evidence that a disease transmitted from parent to child is linked to one or more genes and provides clues about which chromosome contains the gene and precisely where the gene lies on that chromosome. Genome sequencing and analysis now costs around $1,400.

Brad and I first met Connor when he was two years old. We offered to help the family through the foundation's medical and home assistance program and suggested that they form a team page on the foundation's website (we have our own crowdfunding platform) for Connor, as his care would go on for a lifetime, and the family had insurmountable medical and therapy bills.

Our foundation helped and followed this family for five years. We'd even connected his mom with someone in a pharmaceutical company. The company agreed to begin a collaboration with the goal of using Connor's gene mapping to develop new disease-modifying antisense oligonucleotide drugs to treat SCN2A disorders.

Using Connor's gene mapping sequencing, the researchers identified and revealed that SCN2A is a critical gene in neuronal function.

The mom found another child with the same disorder, and the two families joined to form their own nonprofit that focuses on discovering disease-modifying treatments for all those suffering from SCN2A mutations. Mutations in SCN2A are the most common cause of neurodevelopmental disease, epilepsy, and autism, and there are numerous associated health issues.

As I listened to this family talk on that day, I smiled thanked the Lord as he helped orchestrate all of it.

"We want to thank the Mitchell Thorp Foundation for all they have done for our family from the beginning when we were so lost on what to do," Connor's mom said. "We will be forever grateful to them for connecting us to Ionis Pharmaceuticals. Without them, we would not have had the hope or drive to continue this fight for Connor. They showed us how to never give up."

The next family on stage included a beautiful fifteen-year-old girl named Rebecca. We came to know this family six months before, when a friend told the mother, Michelle, to contact us for help. She was a single mom raising three children and trying to make ends meet. She had to cut her work hours in half to be with her daughter during doctor appointments and treatments.

Rebecca attended Matthew's high school, so he, Brad, and I went together for our initial hospital visit to meet them and to introduce ourselves and the foundation.

We chatted with the mom in private since she did not want her daughter to hear about all the financial struggles. We asked her about her most urgent and current needs and how the foundation could help them through our medical and home assistance program. I explained to the mom that the foundation could help, but her daughter's needs were far greater than what we could supply, so we urged her to start a team page for Rebecca to have the community and her school friends support her. "These extra funds will help carry you even further in most cases for this next year, since this journey for you all will be long," I told her. "As you know, most cancer treatments are eighteen months."

The relief on her face was priceless. "Yes, let's do this," she said.

We entered her daughter's hospital room and were surrounded by balloons, flowers, and get-well wishes from her schoolmates. She was loved by so many. We introduced ourselves and showered her with gifts and prayers. Then we told her about the Warrior Spirit run coming up.

Her face filled with excitement since she now had something else to look forward to besides chemo treatments. She was so full of light, much like Mitchell. A freshman at Carlsbad High School, she'd made the cheerleader team and was quite popular. She also loved competing in the local beauty pageants and had won several. Rebecca's twin brother played on the high school football team, and she had a younger sister.

We knew Rebecca would have a tough road ahead, as she'd been diagnosed with acute lymphoblastic leukemia (ALL). We received a call one month before the event. Rebecca's mom sounded desperate. She needed someone to help carry Rebecca down the stairs from her upstairs apartment into the car. Rebecca had taken a turn for the worse and needed to get to the hospital.

Brad immediately drove over and helped out.

Rebecca was admitted to the ICU. She battled this disease with grace and dignity but was disappointed when she learned she couldn't attend the event since her blood counts were down. Her mom and siblings thanked all her supporters on her behalf. Her mom took photos and video of the event to share with Rebecca.

Even though she physically was not there, I knew when she saw all her friends and family show up for her, she would feel all their love and support. Her supporters even made signs: "Keep fighting the fight!" and "Rebecca, you are a warrior princess."

Finally, beautiful fourteen-year-old Sophia spoke. Like Rebecca, Sophia was diagnosed with ALL. The local children's hospital had reached out to see if the foundation could help her family. And when we met them, we instantly connected.

As we got to know Sophia, we began to ask about her likes, her dreams, etc. She lit up when she talked about her horse and how much she enjoyed riding.

I smiled. "We have that in common! I'm a horse lover, too. I rode competitively as a hunter/jumper for years. What else do you like?"

"I like participating in beauty pageants," she said. "I've won several local pageants."

"Oh, my goodness, we also have that in common!" I told her. "I competed when I was young and went on to the Miss Illinois pageant. You know, Sophia, you have many dreams and aspirations, and you will get better from this. You will turn the page on this chapter in your life. You need to believe in your heart that you will get better; you will beat this disease." Even though I was unsure of their faith, I asked boldly, "Can we pray for you all?"

"Yes, of course," she and her mom replied.

Brad and I laid hands on her and began to pray and speak life into Sophia. Once it was over, I could tell the peace of the Lord was in that room and over them both.

I left them with a small book of biblical inspirational messages to help build their faith. "Read this daily," I said. "This will encourage you and build your faith. You will need to have faith to walk this journey. Sophia, believe that you will get well; that this season will soon pass, and in no time, you will move on to college."

Sophia looked at me with hope in her eyes.

"Trust me," I said.

As Sophia's treatment continued, her mom kept us updated. She had begun to lose her hair and was throwing up constantly from the harsh chemotherapy treatment. But she was such a warrior girl and sweet in spirit. While in treatment Sophia was brave enough to run for Southern California Miss Teen Mountain and took home the crown. She did a beautiful job representing her city and bringing a voice to childhood cancer.

Now here she stood, thanking her supporters at our event. Plenty of her friends showed up. Many of her princesses came to walk with her. Sophia presented like a professional, thanking everyone who came out to support her and her family and thanking the foundation for financial help. "I especially want to thank them for making me believe in myself and that I will beat this disease," she said.

The crowd cheered. I was so glad God allowed us to be part of her journey . . . part of all their journeys.

We could see God's fingerprints all over the foundation . . . how the ripple effect phenomenon had touched so many lives and how faithful God was to show up.

After the event, the people were happy to be part of something bigger than themselves. They knew that they made a difference in these children's lives too. One lady came to the stage and told me, "Thank you for putting this community event on, and thank you for pulling God into this public event."

Brad and I have always been bold in our faith and have been ambassadors of Christ, to spread his love to all those who do not know him. Our driving mission not only changes the life of a child, it also transforms others in the process. Glory be to God!

Reporter interviewing Brad and me.

San Diego Friar mascot with participants.

Navy Leap Frogs skydive to open the event.

The blowhorn starts the run/walk event.

Posing with Ethan, now three years old

Dalby family speaking to the crowd

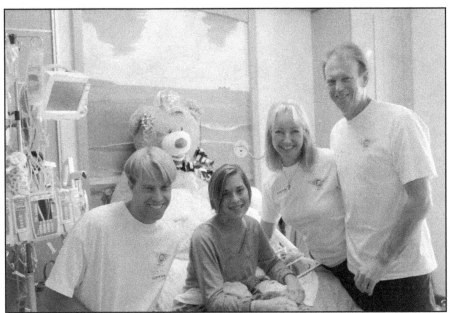

Meeting Rebecca for the first time

Meeting Sophia for the first time

Sophia speaking at the event

Part 7

Grand Visions and Persevering

Chapter 29

Pillars of Hope Vision

A new vision had been brewing in my spirit for some time. I woke up on January 5, 2014, and knew it was time to move forward. "What do you think about doing another type of event besides the 5k run/walk?" I told Brad. "I have this vision to honor and bring together doctors, researchers, therapists, and integrative practitioners and to recognize their work in helping the children we serve."

He looked at me in bewilderment.

"I think it's important to bring together both Western and integrative medicine, since these two disciplines can work together to help heal the body. I think it's time for them to embrace each and not be afraid of each other. Both professions deserve to be recognized for their work." I was becoming excited and talked more quickly. "Plus, I'd like to stir up my fashion background. We could sponsor a more formal event, but something that gives an energy of fun. It can have a prestigious feel since we could honor people with a Pillars of Hope award."

Brad started to chuckle. "Can I speak now?"

I laughed. "Yes, of course! What do you think?"

"I think this must be another God-inspired vision, and if you see it, I will see it too." After all this time together, he had learned not to question the visions God plants in our hearts.

"Yes!" I cheered and ran into his arms, squeezing him. My mind raced with excitement as I thought about the principles to win this award. As I brainstormed, I landed on just the right criteria. The "Pillar of Hope" award would honor the top doctors, educators of health, clinical researchers, therapists, or practitioners who were pillars of strength in the community. The honorees would continue to go above and beyond in caring for their patients. They would help educate the public on the most advanced medical treatments, help research, and discover new cures, and lead others to healthy lifestyles.

These were important values to me because when Mitchell was still alive, we saw hundreds of different doctors, looking for answers in both Western and integrative medicine. We wanted a doctor like the main character on the television show back then, *House*. Even though he was eccentric, he was brilliant and always pushed the envelope to solve difficult medical cases. He always thought outside the box in treating his patients and was not afraid to go the extra mile. Those were the medical people I wanted our foundation to recognize.

We worked hard on the event, putting in long hours and getting the word out. We chose to hold it at the Cielo Village in Rancho Santa Fe, California. This beautiful outdoor setting was landscaped in a Tuscan Italian theme, with white twinkle lights that lit up at night and a beautiful fountain that added to its charm. As I walked the grounds with Brad and our event planner, I began to see my vision come to life. I pictured where the runway would be, the staging area for the musician, and how the vendors would surround the perimeter.

"It's perfect!" I exclaimed.

And on September 6, 2014—nine months after my initial conversation with Brad, the Mitchell Thorp Foundation held its inaugural Pillars of Hope event. We had a terrific response. When attendees checked in, they were escorted to the red-carpet area where each person was photographed. Then, as each person stepped through the beautifully flowered archway, their eyes dazzled, as though they had been transported to a Tuscan Village. The evening featured elegant food, a hosted bar, live music, silent and live auction items, vendors, and the Pillars of Hope awards, followed by a New York-style fashion show.

During the evening, Brad and I told the audience about the foundation and how their contributions would help more children on the waiting list.

"When we started the Mitchell Thorp Foundation," Brad began, "it was about carrying on Mitchell's strength and courage, which he demonstrated during his five-year painful journey. We wanted to pay it forward, since the community came out for us during our struggles and held a walkathon to raise funds. We knew more families and children must be suffering and needing a helping hand too.

"Each year more than a quarter of a million children in the United States are diagnosed with life-threatening illnesses—with cancer being the number one diagnosis and affecting 1 in 285 children before the age of twenty. This affects roughly 1,200 children each year here in San Diego County alone. Families face financial burdens that are overwhelming and can be devastating.

"Mitchell forever changed our lives, and Beth and I are both so proud to be known as Mitchell's parents." He ended by thanking them for coming and encouraging them to enjoy the evening. Then he introduced me.

I took a deep breath, looked into the crowd, and smiled. "On a personal note, tonight I'm sharing with you about my God-given vision I had for this event, and here it is coming to life. If some of you are not aware about exactly how we serve children and families, I'm here to tell you where your dollars go in helping us carry out our mission. We kept it non-disease specific because no matter the diagnosis, it affects the family the same. Since our founding, we have grown from having one program to four.

"We have affiliations with Rady's Children's Hospital, Kaiser Hospital, Balboa Hospital, California Children Services, Children's Hospital Orange County, Children's Hospital Los Angeles, City of Hope Los Angeles, Lucille Packard Children's Hospital Stanford, and many other hospitals across the globe where we have helped parents send children for treatment and care. To care for our children and families, we support them through four programs.

"First is our Medical and Home Assistance program. Through this program, we provide financial support for medical treatments and equipment not covered by insurance. We also provide funding for air or other transportation, as well as gas cards for local transport and hotel stays. We help provide home improvements and basic living expenses. In addition, we connect patients and vendors through pro-bono legal counsel and advocacy services.

"Second is our Healing and Rehabilitation program. Through this program, we help with physical therapy and neuro motor integration services; integrative medicine and nutrition therapy services; educational sessions and retreats; counseling services; sibling support; and family and child adventure services—providing families with enriching camp experiences for siblings and children who are being treated.

"Third is our Wheelchair-Conversion Mobility Van program. Through this program, we help families purchase wheelchair-accessible vehicles, giving them the freedom to enjoy their time together. Time together is the most precious resource for these families. A handicap-accessible mobility van is a necessity, not a luxury, to transport disabled children safely.

"And fourth is our Youth Leadership program. MTF is all about helping kids. We believe the youth in our community need a place to volunteer and make a difference. The primary focus areas for this group of high school and middle school students are community service, fundraising, and the leadership development program."

Next, I shared my favorite part—our successes. "To date MTF has a 100-percent success rate in keeping families together and not having them end in divorce or separation. We're very proud of that when we consider that 78 percent of married couples caring for a terminally ill child end up divorcing or separating. We have helped families reduce their medical equipment costs by 50 percent. We have the highest Platinum Star rating with Guide Star for Charities and have received numerous awards for our work. But . . ."

I paused. "We still have so much work to do. The need is great. We have many children and families on our waiting list, hoping to receive assistance. Please consider donating and/or buying something here tonight to help us help them. These children and families are counting on us."

I turned to look at Brad, who stepped back up to the microphone. "The foundation would like to recognize this year's nominees to receive the prestigious Pillars of Hope award." As he mentioned each name, my heart filled with so much appreciation for the way the medical people truly cared about their work and their patients.

All these special honorees had helped the children our foundation had supported. The first nominee was Dr. Seth Pransky, M.D. from Rady's Children's Hospital. He was currently treating a child with Recurrent Respiratory Papillomatosis (RRP), a rare disease of the respiratory tract. The virus causes tumor-like lesions to grow on the larynx and, in some cases, the trachea and lungs. Currently there is no cure for RRP, only surgical removal of the tumors. If left untreated, the lesions may grow and cause suffocation and death. The family's medical bills had surpassed a million dollars, as these surgical procedures had to be performed every six to eight months. The hospital refused to continue treating the child because the family could no longer pay these enormous bills. Dr. Pransky intervened and took the child under his care as a test case, speaking to other doctors around the globe about this condition and how to treat it.

Our second nominee was Dr. Ken Drucker, M.D. from the Center of Advanced Medicine. He was a specialist who had opened his own practice to offer both Western and integrative medicine. He helped several of our children with different ailments and treated them holistically.

Ruth Westreich, president of The Westreich Foundation, was our third honoree. She was well known for her thought-provoking art, activism, and philanthropy to engage and unite people around the science and societal issues that erode and threaten human and planetary health. She and her foundation also provided an educational platform to inspire, connect, and support organizations and individuals working toward healthier people and the planet.

Our fourth honoree was Kim Schuette, a certified nutritionist and naturopath with Biodynamic Wellness, an organization dedicated to helping others through education and consultation. We could personally testify to her care and abilities, as she helped us with Mitchell's personalized nutritional formula so he could thrive, put on weight, and build his immune system on a cellular level.

After the award ceremony, the evening's emcee rallied the attendees for the live auction vacations going to the highest bidders. People laughed as the auctioneer kept the bidding war going before finally yelling, "Sold!" Next was the fashion show of runway models displaying fashions that attendees could buy. The entire evening was filled with fun and energy. We were exhausted at the end, but we knew people had enjoyed themselves, we'd raised some significant funds for our foundation, and we'd honored our nominees in the medical field.

When it came time to plan the following year's Pillars of Hope event, one of our board members, George Jackson, had an idea. "Instead of doing the Pillars of Hope with a fashion show, let's mix things up and do the event along with the San Diego Aviators world team tennis. I have a lot of connections here. I think it could be a fabulous event." George was a professional tennis player and played college tennis at University of Southern California. He knew a lot of people in this arena. And he really had the vision for it.

We all agreed, but wondered how we could pull it off.

This was where faith stepped in again, that profound knowing that comes before reality confirms it. Brad and I were not going to stop someone's God-given vision, so we started brainstorming the event. We knew we would still do the same things as before, but instead of the audience enjoying the fashion show, their VIP ticket would allow them to watch the tennis match.

"This is a tennis match like you have never seen," George said. "It is not your typical hush-hush match. It's interactive with a deejay and lots of fan engagement. We can get these professional tennis players to come to the Pillars of Hope event, along with their head coach John Lloyd, and talk about supporting MTF and Aviator tennis. Then they could take pictures and sign autographs with guests. We can even open this event to the whole family. The kids can play games with the tennis coaches, have food at the food trucks, and play games while the parents are enjoying the Pillars of Hope charity fundraiser. Then everyone reunites to watch the match. What do you all think?" George looked around the room expectantly.

"I love it," I said enthusiastically. "Let's do it!"

We did, and it was a wonderful success.

Each year we have continued to offer the Pillars of Hope event and have enjoyed each one. These special times have come to hold such significance to us, but I had no idea how much they meant to the medical community until one day I opened a letter and began to read what I knew was meant to encourage potential contributors:

> I was humbled to receive the Mitchell Thorp Foundation Pillar of Hope award in 2016. During this event I met countless families who have benefited from the foundation's efforts. We are extraordinarily grateful to have in our community this organization that focuses on the well-being of the *family unit* during the tumultuous course of childhood cancer therapy. I have witnessed firsthand the benefit of the foundation from my own brain tumor families whose lives were significantly changed because of the altruism shown.
>
> The Mitchell Thorp Foundation has gone far beyond a charitable organization. They have been paramount in establishing a Youth Leadership Council. Through community awareness and leadership, the foundation serves as an inspiration for seventh- through twelfth-grade students.
>
> Very few organizations see the "big picture" of charitable giving. Through their own life tragedy in losing Mitchell in 2008, the Thorps have embraced their sorrow and have turned it into the most beautiful way of honoring his legacy by helping those most vulnerable patients diagnosed with pediatric cancer and their families.
>
> I urge you to highly consider the Mitchell Thorp Foundation for any funding or donor-advised funds that would allow them to continue to help more children and families in San Diego, and beyond.

It was signed "John Crawford, MD MS," who was a professor of clinical neurosciences and pediatrics, interim director of child neurology at University of California San Diego, and director of pediatric neuro-oncology at University of California, San Diego, and Rady Children's Hospital.

My heart burst with joy and gratitude as I read this letter.

From the beginning, we always appointed God as the CEO of the foundation. His amazing grace helped align us with people who believed in our mission. If we have learned one thing over the years, it is that we serve a big, *big* God. He will often stretch us out of our comfort zones, but it is all worth it in the end.

In quiet times of prayer, as we consider each goal we set, we call on the unlimited mind of God for direction and confidence. We imagine good coming to the foundation as we envision and affirm success, not failure. We anticipate the satisfying feeling of a job well done. We use our energy and self-assurance to keep us on track. We believe in ourselves and in what God has established through us—and through Mitchell—to do his work. With our faith, the spirit of God within guides us step by step each day. As Genesis 24:40 says, "The LORD, before whom I have walked faithfully, will send his angel with you and make your journey a success."

We put our vision and faith into action. And regardless of whether our accomplishments lead to new opportunities and success, we are made stronger and wiser by our efforts and determination.

Pillars of Hope fashion show.

Pillars of Hope World Team tennis event.

Brad and me with honoree Dr. Scott McCarthy.

Brad and me with Sherryl and George Jackson.

Past honorees of the Pillars of Hope award.

Chapter 30

Persevering Through Trials

Early on May 25, 2011, Brad was preparing for a business trip, when he noticed a large lump on his neck. Worse, when he coughed, some blood came out.

"Honey," he said, as he gently shook me. "Something isn't right."

I slowly opened my eyes and blinked. When I looked at him, I saw the concern in his eyes.

"Look at this." He showed me the lump the size of a golf ball on the side of his neck and the blood on the tissue.

I jumped out of bed and dressed. "We need to get you to the emergency room. Call your boss and tell him you need to cancel the trip."

I sat in the waiting room while the nurse ushered him to take some tests. I couldn't help but think about all the times we'd sat in the hospital with Mitchell, waiting, wondering, hoping. "Lord, please take care of Brad," I prayed.

When Brad reappeared, he announced that we could go home since they wouldn't have the results for a day or two."

The next day, at my Bible study group, we prayed for Brad. Afterward, as I was walking to my car, my phone rang.

"Beth," Brad's voice sounded tight. "I have throat cancer."

My heart sank, and I shook my head in disbelief. *No!* This couldn't be happening. But it was. Our lives had just gotten shaken up all over again.

"My Bible study group just prayed for you. We'll get through this. Let's pray together that God's strength and courage will reign over you to battle this disease." I tried to sound strong, but as soon as I hung up, I looked to the heavens and cried out to the Lord. "Why? I cannot take another thing, God. I am not strong enough to go through this again."

I was still dealing with the grief from my son's passing, and my mother's passing six months later. We began to feel the heavy weight bear down on us again, and yet I didn't blame or become bitter at God. I remembered Job, who had been tested over and over. I knew that was how we needed to respond: "'The LORD gave, and the LORD has taken away; may the name of the LORD be praised.' In all this, Job did not sin by charging God with wrongdoing" (Job 1:21–22).

As I stood in the middle of the parking lot, God's voice spoke to my spirit: *I've got him.*

So short and simple. It startled me, and my only response was to thank him. I knew I could let go, and let God take care of my husband each step of the way. I would be there for him, and I would love him through it. We both knew this would not be an easy road to travel in the coming months, but God would walk with us, and we could trust that he had our good in mind.

God reminded me that this was Brad's journey, not mine, and for whatever reason he had to go through this. For six weeks, Brad endured forty-two rounds of radiation and chemotherapy. He began to look deathly frail. My six-feet-two-inch-tall, two-hundred-and-twenty-pound husband now weighed one-hundred-and-seventy pounds. He lost so much weight that the doctors told him they would put a G-tube in him if he lost any more. He was totally against that idea, and we did whatever we could to get soft foods and lots of protein milkshakes down him.

He was so deathly skinny that when I held him in my arms, I felt as if I were hugging bones. I closed my eyes as tears rolled down my cheeks. And I focused on speaking and praying life and healing into him—that he would beat this, that his immune system would stay strong, and that he would not die but live and declare the works of God, as it says in Psalm 118:17.

February rolled around and Brad was still healing from the cancer treatments. We had our annual 5k run/walk, and it rained. My volunteers kept an eye on him, and when he began to shiver, they rushed to get him a warmer coat. We both pushed through this event, and he showed up without ever complaining. Again, I was so amazed and grateful for him. Despite his condition and battling for his life, he selflessly helped others. Though attendance was down due to the rain, to our amazement, seven hundred people still participated—walking in the rain and kids running in the mud. We raised enough funds from the event to help the children and families that year.

As time marched on, and the treatment ended, he got worse before he turned the corner. We became excited watching his body begin to heal from all the radiation and chemotherapy. We both were glad to see him put on weight, even though he had problems swallowing his food, as he had no more saliva left and his throat was raw. Slowly but surely his body and throat began to heal.

Three years later, on January 13, 2015, a few months after our Pillars of Hope event, I awoke in the early morning to what felt like an electric shock and pins and needles running down the right side of my arm. I thought perhaps I'd slept on my arm too long. and it had fallen asleep.

As I was trying to wake my arm up, Brad woke up. "Are you okay?"

"It's my arm. I think it fell asleep. It's tingling really bad, like pins and needles are sticking me. I'm sure it will be fine."

The zapping sensation finally subsided a bit, and I was able to fall back to sleep. When I awoke a few hours later, my arm seemed fine, so I shrugged it off and didn't give it another thought.

Two days later the sensation happened again, waking me around 3:00 a.m. The electric shock was even stronger this time, which scared me. I shook Brad. "Something isn't right. It's happening again."

He immediately got up and grabbed his phone, shining the built-in flashlight in my eyes. "I just want to check to see if you're suffering a stroke or seizure."

His words scared me.

"I don't see anything unusual, but let's get you to the emergency room."

Matthew, who was home from college on Christmas break, was in his room sleeping. Brad was going to wake him, but I told him to let him sleep, that we could call him later from the hospital. Then we left at around 4:00 a.m.

We arrived at Scripps Hospital, and they tested me. Our good friend, Dr. Andrew Accardi, the head ER doctor, happened to be working. I hadn't been there long when I saw him walk by, and he caught a glimpse of me behind the drawn curtain. He threw it open. "What are you doing here? Don't we have a big event in a few weeks?"

Dr. Accardi also has a rock-n-roll band he plays in on the side. He always performs at our 5K Run/Walk. I smiled, knowing he had a wonderful sense of humor, but he was also very caring, and his joke put me more at ease.

I explained my symptoms. "I've got this," he said. "I'll order some tests right away, and let's see what we are dealing with. I don't want you to worry about a thing. You're in good hands." As he smiled and walked out of my room, I knew God had made sure Dr. Accardi was scheduled to work that day for me.

Dr. Accardi ordered several tests and a CT scan of my head. After I waited for a while for the results, he entered my room. His face revealed that something was seriously wrong.

"Beth, you have a tumor on the left hemisphere of your brain," he said. "It's five centimeters in diameter." He pushed the scan onto the reader and turned it on so I could see the images. "Here," he said and pointed at the large tumor.

I swallowed hard and gripped the side of the bed.

"It is called a meningioma tumor, a type of tumor that develops from the meninges, the membrane that surrounds the brain and spinal cord. Most meningiomas, about 90 percent, are benign. We will not know if yours is cancerous until we remove it."

Brad and I looked at each other. The concern and worry on Brad's face probably matched my own.

"In many cases, benign meningiomas grow slowly," he continued. "Depending on where it's located, a meningioma may reach a relatively large size before it causes symptoms. Your tumor has probably been there for years. Because it's grown so large, it is putting pressure on the brain, which caused you to have a seizure. We're going to need to take it out, so we've called Dr. Gosh, a neurosurgeon to come and talk with you."

I nodded, hoping that my tumor would be in that benign 90 percentile. We waited a bit longer until Dr. Sonjay Gosh came in, introduced himself, and looked at my scans. Then he assured me that he was the best surgeon for this in the area.

"I've removed many of these types of tumors," he said and explained the procedure, along with the risks and outcomes. "I'd like to schedule you for surgery four days from now on Tuesday, January 20." He paused. "If you do nothing to remove this, even if it is benign, you may have two years to live at best."

He talked with me as if he were ready to work on a car engine. It was all so systematic.

I knew he was a good surgeon, but I wanted to know his heart. "Doctor, are you a godly man?"

He looked at me and smiled. "Yes, in fact I am."

"Good, I just want to be sure who is working on my brain. I have many intercessors who will be praying over you when I come Tuesday for surgery, because in the end it comes down to me, you, and God in that operating room."

As he left, I wasn't sure what thoughts were spinning in his head, but I knew the Holy Spirit would work with him on that.

Dr. Accardi came back to see me, and since I knew him and trusted him, I wanted to hear his take on Dr. Gosh. "How well do you know this neurosurgeon?" I asked. "If you were me, would you pick him to operate on your brain?"

"Let me get back to you on that."

Having someone in my corner looking out for me was a blessing, and I felt truly grateful.

Within ten minutes, he returned. "Yes, he is one of the top surgeons in his field and specializes in these types of tumors. In fact, he is not always at this hospital, so today is your lucky day."

I knew luck had nothing to do with it.

"I happened to run into him and told him that you are a respected woman in the community, and I know you well and not to mess this up."

I felt relieved!

When we returned home, we explained to Matthew what was happening. I saw the worried look in his eyes. "I should stay here with you, Mom, and not go back to school," he said. He was scheduled to fly back to Texas on Monday, the day before my surgery.

I pulled him into my arms and hugged him.

"Mom will be okay," I told him. "I want you to go back. There is nothing you can do here, except pray that all goes well. And you can do that at school. I will be in the doctors' and God's hands, and Dad will keep you informed."

I did not want him to be here to watch his mother go through all this. He endured enough with his brother, Mitchell, and then with his dad.

"Let's pray," I said, so we all sat together, held hands, and prayed over me, the operation, and the doctors. And we asked God for there to be no signs of cancer or any complications.

I was grateful for those four days of waiting. They allowed me to be with Matthew and to process my feelings. I let my emotions wash over me in waves, knowing the only way to get to the other side was to walk bravely through. I cried, and I let it all out of me—the fear, the unknown, the questions. Would I ever be the same? Was my time up? I let myself feel every feeling and think every thought until I arrived at total surrender again. I reminded myself that a bad medical report wasn't bigger or more powerful than God, so I needed to tap into God's creative power for healing.

I am spirit clothed in human skin—living, moving, and having my being within God. I am one with the presence of God. Growths and tumors have no right to my body. They are a thing of the past, for, as Colossians 1:13–14 tells me, I am delivered from the authority of darkness.

Sometimes the simplest phrase can provide the most benefit, especially when we feel tense or scared. These words remind me that I am not alone, that whatever I am facing can be met, achieved, or overcome, because Brad and I are overcomers. We draw from the God's wisdom and protection. We rest in the assurance that God and I are one, which gives me a warm feeling of lightness and peace. As Philippians 4:7 promises, "The peace of God, which transcends all understanding, will guard your hearts and your minds in Christ Jesus." And 2 Thessalonian 3:16 says, "May the Lord of peace himself give you peace at all times and in every way. The Lord be with all of you."

As I spoke healing and life-affirming words, I unclenched my fists and breathed deeply. Then I took a nice, long soak in the tub. Still, I couldn't help but wonder, *How will life look different for me? What can I learn from all this? Is God calling me home?*

These were questions I couldn't answer, so I repeatedly moved my awareness from the spinning in my head to the source of my being.

I knew God loved me and everything was always in his timing and his perfect will. I did not know why bad things happened to good people and or why things kept happening to us. I wondered if God was pushing us toward something much bigger, since the enemy kept trying to take us out.

I remembered a verse in Luke, "It is your Father's good pleasure to give you the kingdom" (12:32, MEV). I realized that my faith sets me free from all worrisome thoughts. When I look at my life, I find evidence of God's love and see that he has not left my side. He has surrounded me with people who care about me. I have opportunities to express my highest self. Divine order is ever-present in my life. I may move through a range of emotions as I encounter situations that challenge me, but no matter what is happening around me, I can respond from a peaceful place within and remain anchored in spiritual principle. I am free from fear because I trust the presence of God within me. In God, there is nothing to fear. In God, there is only love.

Having those four extra days—without seizures!—was a miracle in itself, as it allowed us to call family, friends, and our church and request their prayers. Knowing that I had prayer support gave me peace. Romans 8:26–27 says,

"The Spirit helps us in our weakness. We do not know what we ought to pray for, but the Spirit himself intercedes for us with wordless groans. And he who searches our hearts knows the mind of the Spirit, because the Spirit intercedes for God's people in accordance with the will of God."

I surrendered, asking that God's will be done.

Tuesday, January 20 came, and I was to arrive at the hospital very early to get prepped for surgery. When I awoke that morning, I had such a peace and joy in my spirit that I found myself smiling! It felt as though my feet were not touching the ground—it was surreal. The peace of God filled my mind, my heart, and my life. I knew it could only be because of the power of prayer.

Brad, Pastor Jason, and my best friend, Terri, came to the hospital and were with me when the doctor and the physician's assistant came in.

"How did you sleep?" Dr. Gosh asked.

I smiled. "The more important question is, How did *you* sleep? You're the one who's going to work on me."

He laughed and held out his arms and hands straight toward me. "See? My hands are not shaking at all. They are calm and still."

"Praise God! That's a good sign," I said.

"How about if we pray together?" he asked.

Amazed and delighted, I agreed. We all joined hands as Terri and Pastor Jason prayed.

After the prayer, the doctor and his assistant left to scrub up. Pastor Jason and Terri hugged me and then left so Brad and I could be together. We kissed and hugged.

"If I do not wake up," I whispered, "know that Mitchell and God want me home. But if I do wake up, I will know that God has more work for me to do."

He kissed me again. "I love you. And I'll be waiting for you right here when you wake up."

When the nurse came to get me, Brad went to the waiting room to sit and pray with Terri and another dear friend, Vicki, one of our board members. I felt grateful that he wouldn't have to wait alone.

They put me under pretty quickly, so I didn't know what happened or how long it took. The surgery took longer than anyone expected, which put our prayer team on alert, and they continued to intercede for me. God answered, and seven hours later, Dr. Gosh told Brad that everything had gone well.

I woke up slowly in the intensive care unit. I felt like a truck had hit me. My head was bandaged, and I could hardly move.

When the physician's assistant came to check in on me, I asked in a groggy whisper, "How did it all go in the operating room?"

He leaned close to my ear. "It all went smoothly and great," he whispered back. "The prayers helped." He took out his iPhone and Facetimed Dr. Gosh.

"Hello, Beth," Dr. Gosh said. "You did really well in surgery."

I blinked and tried to nod, but the bandages were too stiff.

"Smile for me, Beth," he said.

That was the last thing I wanted to do.

"We had to cut a muscle to get to the tumor, and that muscle affects your ability to smile," he explained. "I repaired it, but I want to make sure it is responding. Can you try to smile?"

Slowly I managed a smile and was rewarded with the doctor smiling back at me.

"Very good, Beth!"

The way he said it made me think of a voice I kept hearing in my mind during the operation. A sweet voice kept telling me, "Come on, baby girl! You can do it, baby girl!" It was as though someone in the heavens was cheering me on to hang in there.

On the fourth day in ICU, I still could not move and just wanted to sleep. That afternoon, the nurse told me they were moving me out of ICU so I could start physical therapy.

By day five, I began to feel more alert. *Well, I'm still here so that must mean God has a lot more for me to do.*

That sounded good, but I wasn't sure how I could do much of anything. The whole right side of my body was paralyzed. Every time I tried to lift my arm and leg, they wouldn't cooperate. I wept as I pleaded, "Lord, please do not leave me like this."

On the seventh day, my team announced that I was a perfect candidate for brain recovery therapy. That meant that all the specialized therapists—speech, occupational, cognitive, and physical—would come in one by one to help me.

Since I was at high risk for falling, I had to wear a belt around my waist so nurses could grab on to me as they transferred me from the bed to the wheelchair. That was a trying time as each day passed with my having to relearn how to walk, feed myself, pick things up, and on and on. Because my right side was paralyzed, I had to do everything left-handed, which was awkward, since I'm right-handed. At least it did not affect my speech!

One day Brad joked, "You seem to be talking faster than normal!"

Perhaps I was, as the circuits in my brain were all discombobulated and having to find new pathways.

Visitors came and went, and my room looked like a florist shop. The nurses commented on how wonderful my room smelled. "You are loved by many people," one nurse said.

"Yes, I am. I am a blessed woman."

My naturopath/chiropractor came one day to check up on me. He provided some treatment and told me that he would bring in a foam twin mattress pad to place on top of the uncomfortable hospital bed. It felt like heaven when he brought it the next day. Ah, to feel the foam mattress beneath my bones!

"Thank you, thank you," I told him. "How can I ever repay you for this kind gesture?"

He paused and grimaced. "Well, there is one important thing . . . though I hate to bring this up to you right now."

"What is it?"

"It's my son," he confessed, then poured out his heart about his son who had threatened to commit suicide. "I have tried everything. I know your faith is strong and you have an anointing presence all around you. I can feel it. If I bring him to you, can you talk to him and pray over him?"

"Absolutely! You bring him by the hospital, and I will talk and pray for him."

When he left, I looked to the heavens. "God, by your grace, you have saved my life. Now I can save another."

It felt good to take the focus off my own challenges to breathe life and hope and encouragement in someone. I still could not walk or feel my right side, but I could speak and use my left arm, so I was good to go as far as God was concerned.

The following day, my naturopath/chiropractor entered my room with his son, Patrick. We chatted for a few moments until he felt comfortable. The nurses came and went, and we closed the curtain on my side of the room for privacy.

I patted the side of my bed. "Come, sit by me so we can talk."

He obeyed. As I asked questions, he told me how he felt so depressed that his life didn't have meaning. "I'm not sure about God, his purpose in life, or anything anymore."

I let him get it all off his chest, while I listened and silently asked the Lord for discernment. Then I asked Brad to join me in praying for him. "We command Satan, in the name of Jesus, to get his hands off this young man, because he has no authority here."

After we finished praying, Patrick gave a weak smile and thanked me. As he and his dad left, I silently prayed that the Holy Spirit would continue to work in him.

Now my days were filled with therapy appointments. While one therapist was working with me, she told me, "You need to embrace your new normal."

There is nothing normal about how my body feels!

"I know you are used to multitasking and doing many things a day, but you must embrace that you can do one thing a day right now. Then, gradually, you will build up to two or three things, then rest. This is a process for brain trauma patients."

It was surreal to accept what she was telling me. My brain still thought I could do all the things I had done before, but my physical body needed to heal and catch up. My brain and sensory system were heightened. I was much more sensitive now to loud noises, and I tired faster as I did a task.

I always ask myself when faced with a trial, "Lord, what is the purpose of all we have to go through? What are we to learn from here?"

What came to my spirit was that we understood before what parents were dealing with when living with a medically fragile child, but now both Brad and I could relate to what the children were going through and feeling and having a difficult time expressing to their parents. *We both now have our own personal testimonies as we go to the hospitals to talk to children and families,* I realized. *We are both walking, talking miracles who have come out the other side, beating cancer and a brain tumor.*

One day while I was lying in bed recovering, I listened to a podcast that Pastor Greg Laurie gave. He is an author and senior pastor of Harvest Christian Fellowship. He talked about the principles of being a world changer—how to let our light shine to impact our world. His principles encouraged me, as I listened and checked off a mental list:

(1) World changers have an active not a passive faith. We must use our faith, or we lose it. We build our spiritual muscles by staying in his Word and seeking God daily.

Yes, I can check that off my list. I've been reading God's Word daily for years.

(2) World changers do things with their faith. Faith without works is dead.

Yes, check! We have been stepping out in faith everyday through the foundation, bringing our ministry and hope to children and families for years.

(3) World changers' faith will grow stronger through testing. Our faith will be tested when adversity strikes. A faith that has not been tested is not trusted.

Well, that is certainly true for Brad and me!

A quality of endurance will come from testing. *Yes, we have endured and have come out of the fire to the other side. We could not possibly do what we do if we were not tested in so many areas to speak the truth to others.*

(4) World changers know where to go to build their faith. We go to God's Word in the Bible to plug in and recharge. We read and meditate on it and sing worship to him often.

Yes, check. We do this every day—it's how we start our day. It's part of our daily routine.

(5) World changers know that faith makes the difference between things happening and not happening. We have to put faith into action. We can stop the works of God by unbelief.

Yes, check, we have those both covered. We put our faith into action. Wherever God plants us, we suit up and show up, expecting God to reveal his plan.

(6) World changers are indestructible until God is done with them. We can stop worrying about when we will die; that is in the hands of God. We all will live as long as God wants us to.

Yes, check! I have worried in the past about this, but now I live freely, not worrying about it anymore. God knows how long he needs Brad and me to stay here doing his work, so we don't need to think about it.

(7) World changers are never alone. They know the Lord will never leave them or forsake them, even when they are suffering and being persecuted.

Yes, we have this one checked off, too. God has been walking with us through our whole journey and is still carrying us through to the end. I'm excited about where God will take us next.

(8) World changers are often not appreciated; they are often persecuted. Christians are the most persecuted today. So, we must hold our ground!

Yes, when we step out in faith, we will be questioned by unbelievers who do not believe as we do. Our job is not to judge but to be God's witness and to love one another regardless of beliefs.

(9) World changers affect the atmosphere. Am I a thermostat or a thermometer? Am I changing the world or is the world changing me? I laughed when I heard this principle. I liked to think that when I walked in a room, my presence was known, because Brad and I like to be the light that shines in the darkness.

Yes, check! We both move in this as we change the energy of the hospital rooms and homes or wherever we visit. Holy Spirit, continue to bring a godly atmosphere of love, hope, joy, and peace wherever we go.

(10) World changers have a reward waiting that will make it all worth it. Hebrews 11:40 tells us that "God had planned something better for us so that only together with us would they be made perfect." He gives us the promise

of the resurrection. One day our questions will be answered. One day God will restore.[13]

I closed my eyes as I listened to this last principle. *Yes, Brad and I know that we will see Mitchell and all our loved ones again. This is what we long for.*

Greg Laurie's message was exactly what I needed to hear to keep me pressing forward in my recovery.

In the coming days, I began to feel restless, especially because our big 5k run/walk was less than three weeks away. I told the doctors that I needed to be there, even if I had to be wheeled in a wheelchair. But I really wanted to walk! Talk about the power of the Spirit to keep me going. My adrenaline was in high gear. I had a big goal to reach for.

While in therapy, I worked on walking—boy, was that a struggle. Slowly but surely, I began to walk a little farther each day. My therapist spotted me so I would not fall. And after work, Brad walked the hospital halls with me.

The next big hurdle was to walk up and down a staircase. It looked to me as if I were staring at a mountain. I felt unsure and nervous, even though the therapist shadowed me and kept encouraging me. Then for the patients who were progressing, the next big challenge was to get us on a bus to try walking on the beach, to get us used to uneven surfaces. Though it was hard, I pushed through with my therapist, determined to get stronger every day.

I still could not lift my right arm or clasp anything. Instead of getting depressed, wondering if I would ever be able to function normally again, I became tough. I would not let the enemy take me out this way. The enemy wouldn't be roaring unless he knew God had great things in store for our lives.

"Keep working me hard," I told my therapists. "I want to get back to as normal as possible." *And I'm going to walk at our run/walk event. I will not be in a wheelchair,* I silently added, determined to keep that promise to myself.

Brad during his treatment—he lost fifty pounds.

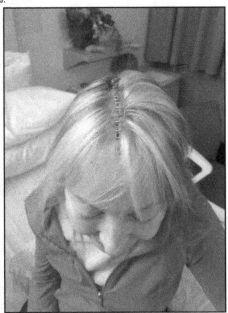

Me after my surgery with a head full of staples.

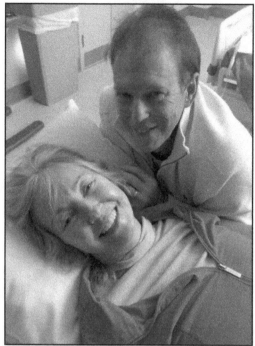

Still smiling despite my paralysis!

Brad helping me walk in the hospital.

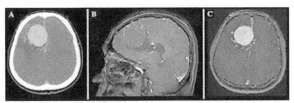

CT scan of a five-centimeter tumor in my brain.

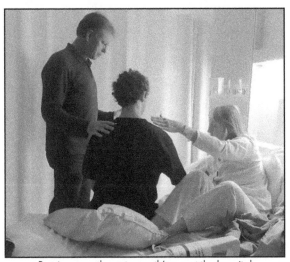

Praying over the naturopath's son at the hospital

Chapter 31

Overcomers

After two weeks in the hospital, I received the okay from the doctors to go home. I'd been pushing them to release me so I could get to our big event, which was now only four days away.

"Here are your papers to sign," the nurse said. "You are scheduled with the therapists next week to start all your therapy. Be sure you are there!" They'd made it clear that they'd release me but that I would need to come in for outpatient therapy—five days a week, six hours a day, for six months.

"Of course! I said I'll be there, so I'll be there." I smiled to relieve her anxiety. I was far from being 100 percent better, but knowing I could go home and return as an outpatient for therapy was such a relief. We had so many people counting on us, and I wanted to be there for the children and the families we were helping.

As I walked into our house, with Brad's assistance, I felt a sense of peace, relaxation, and protection surround me. I sighed contentedly. *This must be the same feeling, only stronger, when we are all called to our eternal home in heaven.*

I was ready to focus on the event—and we still had so much left to do. I did as much as I could, but I continued to wear out easily. And I couldn't run errands because I still was not allowed to drive. That meant I had to depend on others for everything, much like Mitchell and all the children we help felt.

That first night home, as I lay in bed, I thought about all we had endured. *Anyone walking in our shoes would have surely run away screaming into the night and given up*, I thought. *But we know we are overcomers.* As overcomers we have resolute confidence that Christ will live through us to express his life and light in us and out to this broken and dark world.

What Brad and I had gone through was hard, but our health challenges could not compare to what we endured with Mitchell.

I turned my attention to the event. My bliss was awaiting us in four days, when we could be with the children, families, and the community.

I was glad to be alive. Only God's grace allowed me to still be here. I was grateful. "God, I know you hear me, and I thank you for sparing my life. I know you have more work for me to do. I am so thankful that you and I are one, and I need you more than ever right now. I need your strength as I am weak. I need you to heal my body each day and to stand by me as I face the challenges that lay ahead."

I awoke bright and early the day of the event, ready and excited to face the day. My sister Linda was in town to help shadow me at the event, especially because I insisted, I would not use a wheelchair. Many people in my immediate circles knew what had happened and were looking forward to seeing me, and I was looking forward to seeing them.

I dressed in my running gear and wore earplugs to dull the loud noises. Fortunately, my Mitchell Thorp Foundation baseball cap covered all the staples in my head. I knew the hardest part of the morning would be getting through the opening ceremony and walking up the stairs to the stage to address the crowd.

Brad took my arm and helped me navigate it. I held onto the microphone pole to keep me from wobbling or falling—important, since my balance was still not all there yet.

Brad welcomed everyone, and acknowledged all the volunteers, vendors, and sponsors who helped and came out to this year's event.

"I'm so happy and proud of my wife, Beth." He turned and looked at me. "For those who do not know what we had to endure these past few weeks, to be here standing in front of you all is just amazing. Beth just got released from the hospital four days ago, fighting for her own life as they removed a very large brain tumor. When she woke up after the surgery her right side was paralyzed. She was unable to walk, lift her right arm, or even pick up a fork to feed herself. To have her standing here with us all today is a miracle."

The crowd cheered, and I waved and placed my hand over my heart. Brad brought the microphone to me so I could say a few words.

"By the grace of God, I am so glad to be standing here today with all of you," I said. "This was my drive and push to be with you, but today is not about me—it is about the children and families we are here to support. Thank you all so much for believing in our mission and knowing how much your support means to these children and families. I want to thank Dr. Andrew Accardi and the Dr. Dr. band who are here to entertain us today. Dr. Accardi was my ER doctor in the hospital. We should all feel comfortable knowing that if anything should happen, we have doctors in the house."

The crowd laughed and cheered.

After that, we invited several families to say a few words about the foundation.

Kara spoke first. "I want to express the incredible difference the Mitchell Thorp Foundation has made for our son and family. Our son Levi was diagnosed with a brain tumor, too, which required a major surgery and two-month hospital stay. It left him with left-sided weakness, vision impairment, and a rare hormonal disorder that will require lifelong treatment. We were fortunate to have family and community rally around us for our immediate essentials, but as time went on and Levi's needs grew, we began drowning in medical debt. Not only did our costs dramatically increase with the specialty rehabilitative therapies Levi needed, but also our income decreased as I could no longer work, due to caring for him. We felt under-equipped to find the level of financial support we needed. This is where Mitchell Thorp Foundation came in and carried us.

"I cannot describe the weight that was lifted to have the immediate financial needs met during this time. It allowed me to focus 100 percent on the healing of my son and the reinvention of our lives with this new direction. The work that the Mitchell Thorp Foundation is doing is miracle work. They step into families' lives when they are up against the impossible, navigating the life-threatening illnesses of a child or navigating the death of a child. We need more foundations who serve in this way. Please consider supporting them so they can provide help to more families like us."

Another mom and dad stepped forward, and the mom took the microphone. "We are so blessed to have been introduced to Brad and Beth and the Mitchell Thorp Foundation. Without them our daughter would not have been able to receive the surgery she so desperately needed to have. When Amelia was born, we were shocked that she had multiple craniofacial abnormalities. We later learned that she is also deaf. Her symptoms included a cleft lip and palate, she was missing part of the right and most of the left eyelid, she had a small VSD—hole in her heart—and was missing her auditory and balance nerve in both ears. The missing nerve bundle also includes the nerve that controls facial expression. The nature of her hearing loss does not make her a candidate for cochlear implants. She is a perfect candidate for an auditory brainstem implant, or ABI. The ABI is the only device clinically proven to restore a partial hearing ability to people without auditory nerves. Unfortunately, these implants are not yet approved by the FDA for children under twelve years old. We did extensive research and have talked to a doctor in Italy who is the leading expert in ABIs. He has been effectively implanting children with this device and has achieved great success.

"You all may wonder why we don't wait for FDA approval here in the United States. This approval process has been pending for years with no end in sight. The window of auditory learning and later speech development is relatively small, and it has to happen at a very young age to be successful. So, after all the tests, examinations, consultations with the experts, and lots of agonizing and prayer, our family has decided to take Amelia to Italy for a brainstem implant.

"We have to tell you all—as the Thorps wiped tears from their eyes when we told our story, we estimated a cost of $100,000 to cover the operation and the four-to-six-week stay in Italy, and how it is quite beyond our reach—they did not flinch a bit. They asked, 'How big is your network of family and friends, as this will take a big campaign to raise this kind of money. The foundation can help contribute and kickstart Amelia's team page, but this will take a village, and, in this case, it may take a country.'

"Beth shared her story about how the community helped raise $70,000 toward Mitchell's medical care. My husband and I began to find hope. She told us to have faith, not to waver, and believe that this would happen. We had never met anyone who talked like this before. Their faith is so strong it made us believe. We are here today as a witness and to thank all our supporters who came out for Amelia. We have currently raised $65,000 toward our goal."

As I write our story, you can be happy to know that Amelia's surgery was a success. Two doctors out of Los Angeles even flew out to observe this procedure and to learn how to treat her when she returned to the United States. Many other doctors from around the world observed the procedure as well. Amelia is the first child in the United States to have this procedure done, and the FDA now allows auditory brainstem implants to be performed on children twelve and under here in the United States. God knew to align them with us to make this happen.

Our next family stood up and the father chose to speak. "Our precious child Olive was born with many complications. She has hypoxic ischemic encephalopathy, cerebral palsy, global development delay, spasticity, clonus, GERD, and she is G-tube fed. As you can imagine she requires a lot of care. But this has not stopped her. She has a fighter's spirit and lights up the lives of everyone she meets. She has benefited tremendously from the health insurance I receive as a member of the armed forces. As she grows, however, she is requiring equipment that will train her to walk, which is not typically authorized fully by the insurance, because walking is not 'medically necessary.' We have been blessed to be part of the foundation now for two years. They helped us with her equipment so she can learn what it is to walk. We have been fundraising again this year for a vehicle so we can transport her safely. We do not know where we would be without the foundation's love and support. Thank you to the community who came out for Olive today. We are happy to report that we have met our goal to finally get the vehicle with a wheelchair lift."

As with the others, the crowd cheered.

I handed the microphone to the last family at the event. The mom spoke about their journey with their seven-year-old daughter, Jocelyn, who was diagnosed with leukemia.

"We did not know what to expect when we first met the Thorps in the hospital," she said. "I was so distressed, but they were loving and reassuring. We are thankful for the support, because I had to leave my job to be by my daughter's side, and my husband and I were not sure how we would make ends meet. We are amazed at the support and the love we feel out here today, and we want to thank our supporters for coming out for Jocelyn. We hope to be able to pay it forward one day."

After the event, I was exhausted, but filled with joy. God had used our experiences for his glory and to help so many children and their families. It made the next six months of challenging therapy worth it. I kept my eyes on the good we were doing, which helped me persevere to get back what was stolen. I prayed faith-filled prayers, speaking victory in the face of defeat. I stood my ground that the enemy would not have the last word over my life—God would. I declared that I would surely not die but live and declare the works of the Lord. The works like little Jocelyn. A year after the event, Jocelyn did a lemonade fundraiser to raise money to help charities that supported her. Her family asked us to come to their home. We were stunned when they presented the foundation with a check of $900—dollars she had raised from her lemonade stand to help another child and family.

When the roars of the enemy arise, I know it's time to notice that the enemy means to intimidate us and tempt me to give up. And that's when I dig my heels in deep because I *will* persevere in trials. He will not stop my dreams and visions.

Has my and Brad's recovery been hard? Yes. Were there times when we felt like giving up? Yes. But we didn't. We refused to—because we know God has called us to do good works and that he will see them through to completion.

I'm still working toward full recovery. I worked especially hard to master my right side. My face would grimace as I'd tell my brain to lift my right arm. At first it refused to respond, no matter how hard I tried. But as I persisted, slowly but surely, I began to lift it. Then with no feeling in my hand and fingers, I slowly began to work on clasping my fingers together into a fist.

The numbness and tingling down my right side took the longest to heal, since all those nerve endings were finding new pathways. But after four months, I was able to walk without someone shadowing me. I still have a long road ahead, but I know I'm not alone, and total healing will come. After all, that's what being an overcomer is all about. And if these children can overcome such tremendous obstacles, I can too.

Opening ceremony. I was there—though I had to hold onto the mic stand.

Dr. Andrew Accardi, lead guitarist.

Kara, Levi's mom, speaking to the crowd.

Amelia with the San Diego Friar.

Levi, so happy he won a medal.

Olive in her new walker.

Jocelyn's mom speaking to the crowd.

Pastor Jason praying over all the families.

Start of the run/walk event.

Jocelyn paying it forward at her lemonade stand.

Chapter 32

Loving Others in Action and in Truth

While I was at the office one day in October 2019, we received a phone call from one of the hospital social workers about a nineteen-year-old woman named Samantha. She had relapsed for the third time with osteosarcoma. Her oncologist recommended that she and her mom reach out to our foundation for assistance. Her doctor had recently received the Pillars of Hope award at our last event, so he was very familiar with, and impressed by, how the foundation helped children and families in crisis.

Brad and I agreed to meet with them. We prayed in the car before the hospital visit to let the Holy Spirit lead and guide us in what to say and how best to be there for this young lady and her family. We only knew this girl was battling for her life, and her mom was scared beyond words. Her leg had been amputated from the knee down to stop the spread of cancer, and now cancer had spread to her lungs. She was scheduled to have surgery on both lungs.

The social worker walked us into the room. With a bright smile, I introduced us as two angels who were there to provide aid for her and her family. Brad explained how the foundation works and that we were there to help her get over this hurdle. We showered Samantha with some comfort gifts—a warm blanket, organic lavender lotion, lavender Epson salts, an Amazon gift card, and a biblical devotional book to read to help build her faith. We then turned to her mom and gave her $1,000 in gift cards to help with groceries, gas, and other expenses.

Samantha's mom began to cry. She was a single parent raising two girls on her hairdresser income, which now had decreased by more than 50 percent while she was staying at her daughter's bedside. Even though she never brought up their financial burdens, we knew things must be tough for them.

We engaged in some small talk with Samantha and asked her about her interests, hobbies, and dreams. I could pick up that she was discouraged and frightened and felt all the emotions a person would feel in this situation. We let her and her mom tell us what was on their hearts.

As we had with so many other families, when they were finished, I said, "I'm not sure where you both are in your faith walk, but the foundation will be by your side to shore you up, and we will be here to personally pray over you and pour life into you both. Are you both open to the power of prayer?"

"Yes," Samantha said and looked at her mom for approval. Her mom nodded.

"Okay then, Brad and I will gently lay a hand on you, Samantha. And, Mom, we will hold your hand as we circle Samantha's hospital bed." We bowed our heads. "Father, Son, and Holy Spirit, we ask that you come and fill this room. We know that you see everything that has happened in the past until now. We ask that you pour out your healing to Samantha's body, that every cell, every organ in her body, will function in the perfect way that God created it to function. We forbid any malfunction in her body, in Jesus' name. And Father, we make a demand on Samantha's bones to produce perfect marrow. We make a demand on the marrow to produce pure blood that will ward off sickness and disease. We pray, Lord, that as each day goes by, you will strengthen her immune system so she can fight off any virus, cancer, tumors, and diseases. Anything that God has not planted is dissolved and rooted out of her body. We pray that you give wisdom to the doctors who are caring for her. We thank you, in Jesus' name. Amen."

They both remained silent, but a peace washed over their faces.

"We just shifted the atmosphere," I said, looking at Samantha. "And now you need to walk in your healing."

We then began laughing as the spirit of joy fell upon us. We talked afterwards, learning more about Samantha's dreams and visions.

"I desperately want to go back and finish school, since I had to drop out of college because of my medical condition."

"You will soon turn the page of this chapter of your life, and you will move into your destiny to go back to college," I told her.

"I started a small business making children's hospital gowns to be more appealing and functional for the port to be administered through," she said.

"Wow, that is terrific idea!" I said, and then had an idea. "What do you think about us collaborating with you? The Mitchell Thorp Foundation would like to purchase some of your hospital gowns to put in our comfort kits to hand out to children when we visit them in the hospitals. Plus, you can display them as a vendor at our 5k run/walk event that we put on each year. What do you think? The next one is coming up in four months."

She smiled and looked genuinely happy. "As soon as I can get out of here, we can make it happen for the next 5k run/walk."

We shared with her and her mom about our own personal journeys—Brad's throat cancer, my brain tumor surgery, and all the months of recovery. "So, we know our situation is not exactly like yours, but we know the battle you are facing. We also know that you are a warrior woman, and you will shine a bright light to others as you display your perseverance, your resilience, and your bravery to the world when you beat this."

Sometimes we all need someone to believe in us and to coach us to keep fighting the good fight and to never quit trying. We just need that mental push that tells us it is possible and that it's going to happen. We had Samantha immediately get involved in naming her team and writing a short message on what help they needed. I saw the hope in her eyes that she had something positive to look forward to and that she was doing something meaningful.

She began to see the scene in her mind and focused on visualizing it: walking up to the stage with all her friends and family surrounding her with love and support, sharing her story with others, and getting her friends to help push out her team page to raise more funds to help them. It was important for her to see herself not as defeated by what happened to her but as a warrior woman—to rise above it and get back out in the world.

"I want you to know this," Brad told her. "You will not be alone. All our other families and children the foundation is helping will be there, too, so you won't feel like you're the only one. We will put your family up in a hotel the day before so the drive to the park won't be long. We want you to relax and enjoy the day with your friends and family and the surrounding community. We want you to experience the love they have for you and the other children."

We kept tabs on Samantha throughout the months. A week before the event, her mom called. "I'm not sure if Samantha is going to be able to make it. They have her scheduled for treatment."

"Okay, no worries, we understand," I said. "But I speak through faith. Let's wait and see what happens. Take it day by day. And even if Samantha cannot be there, perhaps you and her sister can come represent her."

As soon as we hung up, I began to pray. "Lord, you know the situation better than I do. If it is your will to have Samantha join us at the event, then it will be done. If it is not your will, then we know it was not in her best interest."

The day before the event, Samantha called. "I'm coming with my mom and my sister!"

"That is amazing news! I know it isn't easy, and I know you feel tired, but you will have a resurgence of energy coming from this special day." I hung up the phone and looked to the heavens. "Thank you, Lord, for your faithfulness and your provision in making this all align for her."

Samantha didn't just show up! She brought her girlfriends to help her set up a pop-up tent to sell her gowns and hair scrunches for her team page. Such resilience! This strength comes only from the one source, our Lord Jesus Christ. How do I know? Because the Lord told us himself, through the prophet Isaiah: "Do not fear, for I am with you; do not be dismayed, for I am your God. I will strengthen you and help you; I will uphold you with my righteous right hand" (Isaiah 41:10).

We just have to believe. Brad and I were modeling the way for them—and for all our children and families we encounter—to grow their faith. It takes daily practice; we all need to boost our faith. It's like taking our daily vitamins or exercising. We read God's Word, listen to biblical podcasts, sing in our car as we worship him. As we practice our faith, we begin to see and understand how it carries us through all of life's circumstances and empowers us to think and dream big. The power of faith helps us transcend fear, doubts, or limitations and moves us into action. We may not see material outcomes or healings to our prayers right away, but we need to remain mindful that divine order is unfolding, and that answers and opportunities will come to us at the perfect time.

That's love in action.

Love transforms the world—it connects us, inspires us, and sustains us. As Brad and I concentrate on the love within us, we feel a fulfillment that inspires us to generously share God's love with others. Love is the energizing force behind all prayer, service, and kindness. We place our whole hearts into our prayers, into the help we offer, and into our kind words and deeds. Love has the power to go forth to do mighty work. With assurance, confidence, and grace, we are inspired by God to be his love's perfect instrument. As Colossians 3:14 says, "Above all, clothe yourselves with love, which binds everything together in perfect harmony" (NLT). And 1 John 4:12 says, if we love one another, God lives in us, and his love is made complete in us."

According to John Keyser of Common Sense Leadership, we can define love in action this way:

> Love in action is being humble, forthright, encouraging, helping others learn, grow, and succeed, giving them timely and helpful feedback, and helping them feel good about themselves.
>
> Love in action is being a servant-leader, leading as a shepherd, being alongside our people, leading through our conversations.[14]

The Bible explains it this way: "Let us not love with words or speech but with actions and in truth" (1 John 3:18).

As time marched on, we continued to follow Samantha's progress. She now has turned the corner and is back in college. I spoke to her mom who said that though Samantha is dealing with side effects from the chemotherapy, her spirits are good, and she is keeping very busy. "She is even president of one of her clubs at school," she told me.

"Of course she is," I replied. "She is our warrior woman!"

Soon after her mom and I spoke, we received an email from Samantha:

Dear Beth & Brad,

I know it's been a bit since the Warrior Spirit 5k event, but I just want to say thank you for everything. We had such an amazing time at the walk and are in continued awe of the impact your foundation has—not only on us warriors, but also the community.

I'm finally finished with chemo now! It has been a long road, and I feel so blessed that God placed you in my life to be a part of it. I still have quite the road ahead with appointments and trying to heal some of the side effects left over from chemo. I just wanted to give you a little update since it's been a bit!

As for the gowns, I will send you an email soon with more information! Also, I am attaching our rent statement for this month below. I am so grateful for your help. I see how much of a difference it makes, since it allows my mom to focus on getting me help instead of stressing about missing work. I cannot express my gratitude in words but thank you so much.

With love,

Samantha

The greatest commandment is to "love the Lord your God with all your heart and with all your soul and with all your mind and with all your strength." And the second one is this: "Love your neighbor as yourself" (Mark 12:30–31). That's putting faith and love into action.

After her operation showing such courage.

Giving a welcoming hug upon her arrival.

Chapter 33

A Legacy of Giving

When we began our journey, our legacy was not endowed or inherited, nor did we receive lots of money from a predecessor. Our legacy was built from the ground up, brought on from human tragedy to triumphantly building it day by day. It was an awakening in Brad's and my life that we did not want to do anything else in this world unless it had eternal significance. So we started helping one child and family at a time, which eventually grew to helping countless others. When we built Mitchell's legacy through the foundation, it was not about how much money or wealth we could amass, or how many awards or accomplishments we would receive. In the end, it came down to the impact we had on the hearts of the people we interacted with every day. That was the kind of legacy we wanted—and we have continually pursued.

One day I ran across an article, "What Is a Great Legacy?" by Rhys Jack, in which he talked about "those small acts of kindness done well, and without expectation of reward or recognition, that find a special place in people's hearts and that are the most important. That's a legacy."[15]

The article told a story about a wealthy businessman who awoke one morning to find the shock of his life—a local newspaper had prematurely printed his obituary, saying the merchant of death was dead. He realized that all the wealth he had acquired developing explosives for war meant nothing unless he could do something with it to help others. You would say this was his life's *ah-ha* moment. So, he gave most of his wealth to establishing a series of prizes "for the greatest benefit of mankind." The man's name was Alfred Nobel the creator of the Nobel Prize.

That is the kind of legacy Brad and I desire to leave—one that promotes the greatest benefit on humankind. We think about the benefit when we consider families like Blake and Shelly Matthews.

In May 2018, the Matthews' then two-year-old daughter, Charlie, was diagnosed with brain cancer. To make matters worse, the diagnosis came just two months after Shelly Matthews gave birth to their second child. Imagine the joy of giving birth to your second born only to face the brutal reality that your two-year-old daughter has brain cancer. The roller coaster of emotions was very real, and the overwhelming medical costs nearly wiped out this young couple just beginning their lives as parents.

As soon as we heard about their situation from her cousin who reached out to our foundation, we immediately scheduled a time to visit them. Families have no idea what to expect when we walk into their lives. They literally become part of the MTF family. The foundation came to their aid like so many families before them, helping with the unexpected medical costs and co-payments as Charlie underwent chemotherapy and stem-cell transplant procedures. We always come bearing gifts at that first visit to make sure the child has something new to play with and to bring some comfort. This time Brad and I walked in with two large bags and one wrapped gift for Charlie.

As we walked in, we spotted Shelly holding baby Nolan while Charlie and her grandma were playing with some toys. When she learned the presents were for her, she became so excited to open her gifts that she could hardly contain herself. Her eyes lit up as she pulled out of the big bag a large Minnie Mouse just about the same size as she was. She squealed. "Mommy, Mommy, can I open the next gift?"

Shelly laughed and told her she could.

Charlie tore open the gifts to find an Etch A Sketch and a new Minnie Mouse robe.

Brad and I loved seeing the joy on that little girl's face.

As the months passed and Charlie underwent intense treatment, we were by the family's side and celebrated their successes and hardships with them.

Several months later, in May 2019, while we were celebrating the foundation's tenth anniversary, we received a call from Steve Atkinson, television anchor for ABC 10 News, to let us know we were being honored with the ABC Channel 10 News and Lead San Diego Leadership award, which recognizes individuals and organizations dedicated to improving lives. We were surprised and thrilled. They also wanted to do a news feature on our winning the award and requested to interview and showcase a child and family the foundation had helped. And I knew just the family—the Matthews.

Channel 10 News planned for their anchor Steve Atkinson to present the award to us at Blake and Shelly Matthews's home. I got permission from Blake and Shelly, who were excited and eager to help out. "After all you have done for us, this is the least we can do," Shelly told me.

Two weeks later, the camera crew and anchor met us at the Matthews's home. Steve Atkinson interviewed Shelly and Blake as the camera crew filmed them. He asked questions about Charlie, her diagnosis, and then followed with details about how the foundation has helped.

"We are huge supporters for Mitchell Thorp Foundation," Shelly shared, explaining that Charlie underwent brain surgery followed by nine months of high-dose chemotherapy and three bone marrow transplants. "Charlie has such a rare tumor; we had to send out to eight different doctors for opinions, to three different countries and five states. Her tumor is still undiagnosed."

Shelly explained that they'd spent their life savings on medical bills and second opinion costs. "If it were not for the Thorps and the foundation, we would have lost our home. They helped us cover our mortgage, raise money through a fundraiser run, and cover medical bills. They visited us at her bedside several times and brought so many gifts for her and her brother for Christmas.

"They are more than just a name and a foundation. They truly care. They are angels to us. Charlie is thriving now, and I thank them every day! This is an incredible foundation and amazing people who run it. They have lived the pain and horror themselves with their son and have turned it into a bright light. They are role models to us, and we hope to pay it forward someday soon!"

After the interview, the crew filmed Charlie and Nolan playing on their new swing set. Charlie, with her vibrant personality, was not camera shy and played up to them.

"That's a wrap," the camera crew finally said.

We felt honored and humbled by the entire event. And it all came about because of the tragedy of losing our son. Mitchell's legacy has touched the hearts of so many children and families that the ripple effect continues to expand to touch others. We continually feel humbled as we think about the overwhelming responses we get from the families. Here are just a few:

Thank you so much for your wonderful gift! The Mitchell Thorp Foundation truly cares for all families in time of need. As your mission statement says, you provided financial and emotional support when we most needed it. We can't thank you enough for this wonderful act of kindness and generosity. We hope that our daughter develops the same qualities Mitchell Thorp had. We want her to be kind and gentle spirited and full of faith, just like he was. May God continue to bless your family and your foundation! With great gratitude.

We knew from the moment we met that you knew what we were going through and that you were going to be there for us. If it were not for the Mitchell Thorp Foundation, we wouldn't have had the support we needed, emotionally and financially. Thank you!

We're so grateful to the Mitchell Thorp Foundation. Our youngest daughter has a terminal lung disease. With the foundation's help, we can bring her home for the rest of her days. We cannot thank you all enough!

Thank you so very, very much for this help you are giving us. It means more than you might realize. I believe in God, but I had allowed myself to lose hope for my child. You popped into our lives at the perfect moment. You reminded me so beautifully that even in the direst circumstances, I can resolve to being hopeful by practicing gratitude and to trusting God to inspire me to find good in the midst of all situations.

We are thankful, grateful, and blessed by you and your family. May God continue to give you peace and love during the holiday season, with the most beautiful memories of Mitchell. Thank you for giving us hope and being a pillar of light and faith during our son's trials.

I want to sincerely thank you from the bottom of our hearts. You and your husband are incredible people. You are doing so much for others you don't even know, helping families and getting them through difficult times. Thank you, thank you, thank you! You guys are awesome!

Thank you so much for all the love and support you have blessed our family with. You helped us through the fundraising so we could purchase a wheelchair accessible van for our son. This has been so helpful in transporting him safely. Words cannot express the gratitude we feel. To see the joy on our children's faces is priceless. We also want you to know how much the prayers, love, and support have meant to us over the years.

As director of neuro-oncology at Rady Children's Hospital since 2009, I can personally attest to the tireless dedication of the foundation for the well-being of families whose children have been diagnosed with cancer. They exemplify each and every aspect of their mission statement.

We can all begin to leave a legacy by starting to teach our children and grandchildren to live generously and give back. Even starting as small as giving a quarter to Jocelyn's lemonade stand—which raised $900 to help another child and family like hers—makes a difference. This is one strategy to over-come one of the greatest challenges facing communities today: lack of involve-ment. Getting more people volunteering for different causes allows you and me to help someone else in need. And in return, we are richly blessed.

When willing and giving hearts come together, miracles do happen. Through the years, we have witnessed the distress of a lot of people who've had a hard time and were on the brink of bankruptcy and despair. We know, since we were one of them. We've also been on the receiving end, witnessing the greatest gift to mankind—love and support.

A great legacy is not so much about how much wealth and physical assets a person acquires. It is nice if this happens, but we must understand the weight of responsibility of giving it away to the benefit of mankind and to those who will carry the work their family has established into the future. As we all know, when we die, we can't take it with us.

The foundation has made its mission and legacy to support families like the Matthews family by providing financial and emotional resources through our programs. Over the last decade, the foundation has given more than $2 million back into the community to help families whose children are fighting for their tomorrows.

We are continuing Mitchell's legacy to help many other children over the next decades. Today and forever, Mitchell's spirit lives on through the foun-dation and these children. Mitchell's story is part of a bigger picture: There is a supernatural phenomenon at work in and through him and the Mitchell Thorp Foundation. The ripple effect draws people together in love and service to one another; it is "love in action" showing how one life can flow over into so many others, like ripples from a pebble cast into the still waters.

Blake and Shelly Matthew with Nolan (left) and Charlie.

Giving Charlie her Minnie Mouse doll.

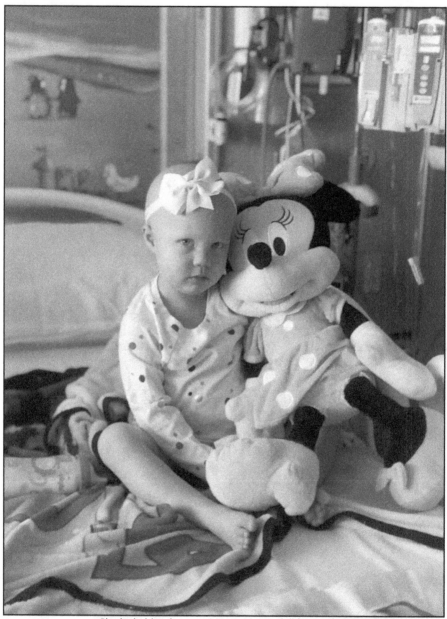

Charlie holding her new Minnie Mouse doll for comfort.

Connect *philanthropy*

A Legacy of Giving

Mitchell Thorp Foundation supports families during a time of crisis

Channel 10News anchor Steve Atkinson, Brad and Beth Thorp, and the Matthews family

Over the last decade, the foundation has given back more than $1 million, which has made an impact on 880 children and their families. MTF helps through its extensive programs: Medical & Home Assistance; Healing & Rehabilitation; Wheelchair Conversion Vans; and its Youth Leadership Council Program. The foundation pays the vendors directly, ensuring that the dollars are going as intended to support each child.

CELEBRATING ITS TENTH anniversary this year, the Mitchell Thorp Foundation was recently honored with the 10News Leadership Award, which recognizes individuals and organizations dedicated to improving lives in San Diego. Channel 10News anchor Steve Atkinson presented the award to co-founders Beth and Brad Thorp at the home of Blake and Shelly Matthews, whose three-year-old daughter, Charlie, was diagnosed with brain cancer last October, just six days after the birth of their second child. The Mitchell Thorp Foundation came to the Matthews family's aid, helping them with medical costs as Charlie underwent chemotherapy and stem cell transplant procedures. Shelly had to leave her job to stay by her daughter's side during medical treatments. "Having the assistance from the foundation helped keep our heads above water when we were drowning in medical bills and debt," says Shelly.

Every year, more than 2,000 children in San Diego County are diagnosed with serious, life-threatening conditions. The Mitchell Thorp Foundation has made it its mission to support families by providing financial and emotional resources. Each child and family MTF provides assistance to averages $1,500-$2,500 a month.

The Thorps, unfortunately, know firsthand what it means to have received tremendous community support. Their son Mitchell was diagnosed with a critical illness at age 13. Mitchell courageously fought for five years, but ultimately lost his battle with an undiagnosed illness. Nearly bankrupt with all the medical bills during that time, the Thorps received incredible community support via a walkathon, which helped them pay off their more than $100,000 medical bill. "This truly changed us to see goodhearted people wanting to help us, some we never even knew," says Beth. "We were never the same, forever changed, humbled and grateful for such generosity. We felt compelled to pay it forward." Today, Mitchell's spirit lives on through the foundation as the Thorps support the families who are clinging to hope and survival.

On July 21, the Pillars of Hope Grand Slam Party, benefiting the Mitchell Thorp Foundation, returns to the Omni La Costa Resort & Spa for its fifth year in partnership with World TeamTennis and the San Diego Aviators. The event will include food stations with wine pairings, a cash bar, live music, silent and live auctions, and more. Tickets also include VIP seats to watch the San Diego Aviators professional tennis match, plus DJ music, fun games, and autographs from players. *760.603.8853, mitchellthorp.org* MIA PARK

Ranch & Coast magazine ran this article on us. Reprinted by permission.

Chapter 34

Break Free

Through the years, my family has grown in insight and understanding—sometimes slowly, rapidly at other times. It took time for us to see what God can do with the power of one life. That one life was Mitchell who had so much heart and so much love and joy that radiated out of him like rays of sunshine. We often called him our sunshine boy. His journey impacted so many people; some in ways we may never even know. Through him, God brought us closer as we moved from pain and anguish to restoration and healing.

We have discovered along this life journey that we are always changing and always growing into our potential as spiritual beings, though sometimes it can feel as if we are not making much progress. Our spiritual development is a journey of discovery. As we serve a great big God, we are breaking free from the illusion of limitations. And even though we may not have been aware of our growth as it was happening, our development has been ongoing.

We may never understand why certain things happen the way they do and why, or how, God moves in each of our lives, but what we do know is God can turn tragedies into his glory and draw his people closer to him.

Looking back now, we see things more clearly from God's perspective rather than from our own. We see God's fingerprints woven throughout our

317

lives and the countless number of children and families we have touched and ministered to along the way.

Imagine for a moment that you are a butterfly emerging from its chrysalis and spreading its colorful wings for the very first time and taking flight. You greet this experience with enthusiasm and feel reborn. You are utterly transformed—you are ANEW—*a new* creation. The world feels exciting and new. You can have joy and peace again as you move through the pain of loss to healing and restoration. That's what happened for us.

The year 2020 came and we met it with great anticipation of what the Lord would unfold. Living in a state of expectancy keeps us excited to see how God shows up every day and who he brings into our lives. He is faithful and always surprises us. The year started out with a surprise honor—a proclamation from the County of San Diego, California, presented by supervisor Jim Desmond, honoring the Mitchell Thorp Foundation and the twelfth annual Warrior Spirit Run/Walk. It was a special day as we went downtown to the city council to accept the plaque, have photos taken, and say a few words.

Brad and I are always humbled and honored when the foundation is recognized. It inspires us to know that our work truly makes a difference.

On the day of the run/walk, February 1, more people attended than we'd ever had before. Over all these years we have gained the reputation of being the most inspirational run/walk and family festival in the region. It was the most spectacular day as everything fell into place perfectly—and we were *literally* the last event of that year, because the COVID-19 pandemic hit right after, shutting everything down.

It was a scary, chaotic, and confusing time for everyone, but Brad and I refused to worry, instead putting our trust in God, knowing he is omnipotent, limitless in his power and authority over this world. And we were reminded again that he would instruct us and teach us in the way we should go.

We must let go of what does not serve us, and what we have no control over, and instead put our trust in God. He sees and hears our cries, and has done so since the beginning of time. He wants his people to break free from oppression, anxiety, and fear. Those three qualities are not of God; they are evil in nature. God is our rock on which we stand. And he is all those things for you, too.

Turn to him if you feel anxious or worried, and he will comfort you. Express gratitude in your prayers and your private thoughts, even in the hard times. He reads your thoughts and wants to help you. Displace worrying thoughts with trusting and thankful thoughts. This combination of praise and trust drives away anxiety and powers of darkness. This act of faith can help you break free from negative thinking. As the Bible says, "Give thanks in all circumstances; for this is God's will for you in Christ Jesus" (1 Thessalonians 5:18).

If anything positive came out of this COVID-19 season, it gave people time to reflect on what is important in life. Brad and I used the shutdown productively, knowing that we did not want to waste any time. We launched our new website, made our 5k run/walk virtual, and I began to write our story. Even during all the chaos in the world, the Lord's favor poured out on the foundation, and we were showered with another blessing. Much to our surprise, we won Non-Profit of the Year 2020 from the Carlsbad Chamber of Commerce Business Achievement and Distinction awards. The award was titled A Bridge to the Future. We love to see what surprises the Lord has in store, and we are excited to walk this bridge into our future.

If there is anything we have learned through our long journey, through our darkest of times and into our brightest, it is that we have been called to be light in the dark. When the world seems dark and heavy, we can let our light shine even brighter. And that light is Jesus. As John 1:4–7 explains, "In him [Jesus] was life, and that life was the light of all mankind. The light shines in the darkness, and the darkness has not overcome it. There was a man sent from God whose name was John. He came as a witness to testify concerning that light, so that through him all might believe."

Back then God chose John the Baptist. Now he chooses you and me.

Taking on this monumental journey of writing this book, I would not let fear stop me. When you are deeply rooted in Christ, there is no fear. It did not stop my creativity as the Lord now spoke to my spirit and said, *Daughter, it's time to write our story.* And when the Lord speaks, I listen and move.

This book has been brewing in my spirit for a long time and has played over and over in my mind like a movie. So many people have told us over the years to tell our story, but I was not ready until now. Everything is in his timing.

I hope throughout these pages, your heart has been opened and touched by reading all the rich promises God has for you, too. My hope is that our story will bring you peace, love, joy, and perseverance to fight the good fight of faith in your life every day. Having faith is so important to God that the word *faith* appears 336 times in the King James Version of the Bible. Other Bible versions have varying counts: 458 times in the New International Version, 389 in the New King James Version, 378 in the New American Standard Bible, and 521 in the Good News Bible, just to name a few. Showing up that many times means that this principal holds significance. So ask yourself: *How strong is my faith?*

Since the beginning of time, people have wanted to understand the mysteries of life. We learn and grow from the discoveries of those who have come before us, and we hope that those who come after us will benefit from what we have learned. Throughout generations, many people have contributed to the understanding of the power of thought, prayer, devotion, and service.

We are a link in that chain, using our spiritual practices to improve ourselves and to help create a better, kinder world to leave for the next generation. We stand upon the shoulders of those who came before us and the shoulders of our almighty God to further his kingdom on earth as it is in heaven.

If you are feeling pain from past hurts, overwhelmed, or stuck in your life, you can break free. It doesn't matter what the difficulty is, you can find freedom in forgiveness. We did. Holding on to anger, fear, and resentment is like carrying a bunch of bricks everywhere you go. Each brick adds its own weight, and if you are not willing to release some of the load, the burden can become unbearably heavy. Forgiving not only lets you create a strong foundation of healing and growth, but it offers strength that you can build upon. It's simple to get started.

Pray this simple prayer:

Lord, I know I'm a sinner, and I ask for your forgiveness. I believe you died on the cross for my sins and rose from the dead. I turn from my sins and invite you to come into my life. Show yourself real to me. I release the power I have given the past over my present. I let go of the hold of unforgiveness and break free from the pain that I allowed others to have over my life. I release judgment, knowing it serves only to weigh me down. I breathe deeply now, thanking you for giving me the breath of life. I release my pain and lay it all down, one heavy brick at a time. I revel in the freedom of forgiveness. I need to break free. I want to trust and follow you as my Lord and Savior. I pray this in Jesus' name, amen.

With God we experience freedom. Romans 10:13 says that "everyone who calls on the name of the Lord will be saved." And Ephesians 4:31–32 tells us to "get rid of all bitterness, rage, and anger, brawling and slander, along with every form of malice. Be kind and compassionate to one another, forgiving each other, just as in Christ, God forgave you." That's about breaking free.

Today, my friend, celebrate your innate freedom to think, feel, and be anything you choose. Open yourself to the experience of your boundless nature and connect with the freedom that is your birthright. No matter your circumstances or your past, you can create and experience freedom. Limitations in your health, career, or relationships may leave you feeling powerless or stuck, but as you turn to God's wisdom, you can know that your impediments are only temporary.

Every obstacle that you encounter in this life provides you with an opportunity to attune your mind, heart, and being to your awareness of God. And know that the gospel is truth, "Then you will know the truth, and the truth will set you free" (John 8:32).

I wanted to sum up what the Lord kept showing me in the Bible as I sat to write this book's ending, and it is this: The year of the Lord's favor is upon us. It shows how the Lord has been with us every step of the way. Even if at times it didn't seem that way, he has been faithful. Our family has shared our pain and suffering and his goodness to all who need help. We are, and will forever be, his faithful servants to lead others to know God's love, grace, and mercy. The Lord has planted us on this earth to display his splendor through us.

Mitchell's life has no ending, as his spirit lives on in this life and in his eternal life. And because of his life, we will continue this ripple effect phenomenon by demonstrating love in action and in truth—by one life touching another for the better good of mankind.

> The Spirit of the Sovereign LORD is on me,
>   because the Lord has anointed me
>   to preach good news to the poor.
> He has sent me to bind up the brokenhearted,
>   to proclaim freedom for the captives
>   and release from darkness for the prisoners,
> to proclaim the year of the LORD 's favor
>   and the day of vengeance of our God,
> to comfort all who mourn,
>   and provide for those who grieve . . .
> To bestow on them a crown of beauty
>   instead of ashes,
> the oil of joy
>   instead of mourning,
> and a garment of praise
>   instead of a spirit of despair.
> They will be called oaks of righteousness,
>   a planting of the LORD
>   for the display of his splendor. (Isaiah 61:1–3)

Brad and me with Jim Desmond, receiving the proclamation.

The 2020 Nonprofit of the Year award.

Mitchell—the power of one life igniting change in others.

About the Author

Beth Thorp is cofounder and executive director of the Mitchell Thorp Foundation (MTF), a public 501(c)3 organization, with the mission to "support families whose children suffer from life-threatening illnesses, diseases, and disorders, by providing financial, emotional and resources to their desperate situation."

Her work in philanthropy has been recognized nationwide. Her awards include Non-Profit of the Year, Carlsbad Chamber of Commerce (2020); Distinguished Humanitarian award presented by Marquis Who's Who in America (2019); Leadership award presented by ABC-10 News and Lead San Diego (2019); Starfish Leadership award given to those who inspire, engage, and lead, presented by City of Carlsbad (2016); and Professional Woman of the Year from National Association of Professional Women (2011).

Beth has been featured on numerous media outlets, including ABC 10 News, KUSI TV, Fox 5 News, *Ranch & Coast* magazine, *San Diego Union Tribune, Carlsbad* magazine, San Diego, and Carlsbad Business journals, FM 90.0 talk radio, and *Union Tribune*'s "Community Spotlight" radio show.

A mother to amazing sons, Mitchell and Matthew, Beth enjoys long walks along the beach with her husband, Brad, and their two goldendoodles. She enjoys traveling, cooking, exercising, and spending time with family and friends. She and her husband live in Carlsbad, California.

For more about Beth or Mitchell Thorp Foundation, visit: www.mitchell-thorp.org.

Mitchell **Thorp**
FOUNDATION

We hope that you have enjoyed our story, that it touched your heart, and that it is beginning to transform you into *ANEW Creation*. With every book purchase, 100 percent of proceeds go toward our programs to bring hope and relief to children and families in crisis.

Our Programs

Medical and Home Assistance
Healing and Rehabilitation
Wheelchair Conversion Vans
Youth Leadership Council

To learn more about Mitchell Thorp Foundation, go to:
www.mitchellthorp.org.

Thank you for making a difference in a child's life who is fighting for their tomorrow.

We would love to hear from you! Please share how this story has impacted your life. Whether you need to share your testimony or ask for prayer, please feel free to reach out to us.

Mitchell Thorp Foundation
6965 El Camino Real, Suite 105-433
Carlsbad, CA 92009

Notes

1 2 Corinthians 5:7

2 Philippians 4:13

3 Nehemiah 8:10

4 Matthew 7:24: "Everyone who hears these words of mine and puts them into practice is like a wise man who built his house on the rock."

5 Gigi Alford, "NBA's Mutombo Joins Fight in Carlsbad Teenager's Battle to Overcome Mysterious Illness, San Diego Union Tribune, May 21, 2006.

6 This is a popular story from an unknown author.

7 "Rainbow Colors: Meaning of Seven Colors," Toppr, accessed July 17, 2021, https://www.toppr.com/guides/chemistry/environmental-chemistry/rainbow-colors/.

8 Jemi Sudhakar, "The Challenger of the Storm: The Eagle," LinkedIn, August 21, 2017, https://www.linkedin.com/pulse/challenger-storm-eagle-ms-jemi-sudhakar-/.

9 Mark Virkler, Four Keys to Hearing God's Voice (Shippensburg, PA: Destiny Image, 2010).

10 Ibid.

11 Robert K. Greenleaf, "The Servant as Leader," Center for Servant Leadership, accessed June 29, 2021, https://www.greenleaf.org/what-is-servant-leadership/.

12 Tom Watson directed the program for four years. Today Kenny Wood is the director.

13 Greg Laurie, "How to Be a World Changer," accessed July 17, 2021, https://harvest.org/?s=how+to+be+a+World+changer.

14 John Keyser, "Love in Action," Common Sense Leadership, March 23, 2016, https://www.commonsenseleadership.com/love-in-action/.

15 Rhys Jack, "What Is a Great Legacy?," Success, May 15, 2018, https://www.success.com/what-is-a-great-legacy/.

A free ebook edition is available with the purchase of this book.

To claim your free ebook edition:

1. Visit MorganJamesBOGO.com
2. Sign your name CLEARLY in the space
3. Complete the form and submit a photo of the entire copyright page
4. You or your friend can download the ebook to your preferred device

Morgan James
BOGO™

A **FREE** ebook edition is available for you or a friend with the purchase of this print book.

CLEARLY SIGN YOUR NAME ABOVE

Instructions to claim your free ebook edition:
1. Visit MorganJamesBOGO.com
2. Sign your name CLEARLY in the space above
3. Complete the form and submit a photo of this entire page
4. You or your friend can download the ebook to your preferred device

Print & Digital Together Forever.

Snap a photo

Free ebook

Read anywhere

CPSIA information can be obtained
at www.ICGtesting.com
Printed in the USA
JSHW030916050222
22601JS00001B/1